The Wit and Humour
of
Political Science

Lee Sigelman, Kenneth Newton,
Kenneth J. Meier, and Bernard Grofman

EDITORS

Copyright © 2010
American Political Science Association (APSA) and
European Consortium for Political Research (ECPR)
All rights reserved.

ISBN 978-1-9073011-0-0

Preface

Some years ago, Ken Newton began collecting funny and satirical articles on political science, with the intent of organizing a selection of them for a published volume. He put articles in a shoe box as he discovered them, and when retirement actually came along in 2008 he found that there was a considerable stack of material to be sifted and sorted. He wrote a book proposal and persuaded the editors of ECPR Press to publish it. When he met that most distinguished of political scientists, A Wuffle, at a meeting in Bologna, he asked permission to reprint some of Wuffle's finest work on post-rational theory, brushing your teeth, macaroni chain theory, and the like.

A few months later, Ken received the following email message from Lee Sigelman:

> For some years now I have had in mind a rainy-day project of organizing a selection of humourous articles on political science for a published volume. I have put them in a file as I came across them and now that it seems to rain every day, I have started the job. A few days ago I wrote to A Wuffle in California and asked him for permission to print some of his own fine contributions to the literature. He agreed, of course, and also told me that he had received an almost identical request from a political scientist in Britain, who is also preparing an edited volume. So I got your name and now I am writing to suggest it might be a good idea if we combined forces to produce a single book.

This is the true story of how Ken and Lee came together to start work on *The Wit and Humour of Political Science*, alongside Ken Meier and Bernie Grofman, who had already been conscripted by Lee for the American project. Ken and Lee had never met before, so the story only goes to show that while merely great minds may think alike, those with truly great minds think exactly alike.

Because the project was now transformed into a trans-Atlantic affair, it seemed obvious to try to make it a joint venture of the APSA and the ECPR. Once again the editors struck lucky and got the enthusiastic agreement of the two organizations to produce the book between them. For this we express our thanks to Clare Dekker and her staff, especially Mark Kench, in ECPR Central Services, and to Michael Brintnall and his staff at the APSA, especially Polly Karpowicz.

Dedication

For Lee Sigelman

1945–2009

Reprinted with permission of Creators Syndicate and the John L. Hart FLP. Copyright 2009.

Introduction

Although, as was long ago observed, "The trouble with political jokes is they usually get elected" (Lukes and Galnoor 1986), there is a rich vein of humour pertaining to politics. Political scientists, however, are not normally counted among its authors. As Ross Baker, himself a political scientist, has commented sarcastically, "Among the legendary thin volumes such as Ethics for Used-Car Dealers or *Love Sonnets for Bureaucrats*, one would invariably find a copy of *The Wit and Humour of Political Science*" (1979, 338). Even so, notwithstanding political science's reputation as a field of study only slightly less dismal than economics1, many political scientists—well, some, or at any rate, a few—do not fit the stereotype of grim, humourless curmudgeons.[2]

The humourous literature in political science, much of it clever, some of it even hilarious to a knowledgeable reader, is scattered in books as well as journals. Virtually all of it is invisible today, having made its appearance in diverse and sometimes rather obscure publications some two or three decades ago and vanishing since then. Moreover, it is often impossible, by title alone, to distinguish between political satire and political science, so there is no easy way to track this literature down. Our mission was to find these fugitive pieces and uncover among them those gems that could still speak to the present generation of political scientists so as to make the "wit and humour of political science" accessible to today's readers.

This volume collects what in our opinions are the wittiest and funniest pieces about political science and political scientists. We are confident that even a small investment of the reader's time will be sufficient to disprove Baker's slur on our discipline. Like all good humour, much of the work we have chosen for inclusion has a serious point. It helps scholars keep an open and skeptical mind, it picks out weak points in theory and methods, it points out how research may be going wrong, and it pricks the balloon of bombast, pretentiousness, and jargon. And, not only that, it's fun.

Most of the essays here have appeared in scholarly books and journals (e.g., the *American Political Science Review*, the *Journal of Theoretical Politics*, *European Political Science*, and, especially, *PS: Political Science & Politics*). The collection includes work by some of the world's most eminent political scientists—including, of course, the four editors of this volume—along with the distinguished American pioneer of post-rational theory, A Wuffle, and the influential German theoretician, Professor Dr. Dr. Dr. Dr. Otto I.Q. Besser-Wisser, who revolutionized political science with neo-postdistanciationalist politometrics. It also includes such classics as Rosa and Charlie Parkin's masterly neo-Marxist analysis of "Peter Rabbit and the Grundrisse" and Leszek Kolokowski's important treatise on "The General Theory of Not-gardening," as well as the work of such luminaries as Nelson Polsby, Heinz Eulau, James Scott, Arnold Rogow, William Keefe, and Robert Erikson. It covers virtually every aspect of political science, from writing a doctoral dissertation and getting a job to attending conferences and chairing departments to doing research—or at least pretending to—and getting that research published. Its contents make essential reading for all political scientists, even the most senior, but it may be enjoyed the most by younger scholars, especially those without tenure (or, worse yet, without a job), by other social scientists, and even—gasp—by readers unaffiliated with any academic discipline.

Notes

1. But even economists have an "economist jokes" web site.
2. Most academic communities have collections of jokes, satires, parodies, and humourous pieces about their work. Chemists, for example, have a Web site on dihydrogen monoxide, and longer satirical essays and pastiches appear in places like the *Journal of Irreproducible Results* (created by psychologists, but now covering all of the social sciences) and the *Annals of Improbable Research* (for the broader scientific community), while Wikipedia has its alter ego in the fact-free Uncyclopedia.

References

Baker, Ross. 1979. "Keefe Smiling!" PS 12: 338.

Lukes, Steven and Itzhak Galnoor. 1986. *No Laughing Matter: A Collection of Political Jokes*. London: Routledge Kegan & Paul.Wilson, Michael. 2005. "Alive and Thriving in the Midwest: Brawling in Cages." *New York Times* (July 28).

Comoediae Personae
(in reverse alphabetical order)

Editors

Lee Sigelman, deceased, was the Columbian School of Arts and Sciences Distinguished Professor of Political Science at George Washington University.

Kenneth Newton, a product of the bizarre fantasy life of Otto I.Q. Besser-Wisser and Dagobert D. Manteltasche, is Professor Emeritus at the University of Southampton and Visiting Professor at the Wissenschaftszentrum Berlin and the Hertie School of Governance, Berlin.

Kenneth J. Meier is the Charles H. Gregory Chair in Liberal Arts and Distinguished Professor of Political Science at Texas A&M University.

Bernard Grofman holds the Jack W. Peltason (Bren Foundation) Endowed Chair in the Department of Political Science at the University of California, Irvine.

Authors

Betty H. Zisk ("The Compleat Jargoner: How to Obfuscate the Obvious Without Half Trying") is Professor of Political Science at Boston University.

Garry Young ("The Dakota Effect") is Associate Director of the George Washington Institute of Public Policy at George Washington University.

A Wuffle ("Reflections on Academia," "Uncle Wuffle's Reflections on Prediction," "The Political Economy of the Automobile—Four Approaches," "Should You Brush Your Teeth on November 6, 1984? A Rational Choice Perspective," "The 'Minimax Blame' Rule for Voter Choice: Help for the Undecided Voter on November 8, 1988," "Why Democrats Shouldn't Vote (with acknowledgements to R. Erikson)," "Vindicating Anthony Downs," "Voter Advice in the Presidential Election of 2008: A Guide for the Perplexed," "Death, Where Is Thy Sting? The Senate as a Ponce (de Leon) Scheme," and "*Monopoly* Is a Capitalist Plot: A Hegemonic View of Games as Instruments of Economic Indoctrination"), after languishing several decades as a mere Assistant to Professor, following the publication of paper #13, assumed the role of Associate to Professor of Political Science at the University of California, Irvine.

Pierre van den Berghe ("The Academic Pecking Order," "On Publishing," and "Conventions and Professional Standing") is Professor Emeritus of Sociology and

Anthropology at the University of Washington.

Dick Tator ("A World Glut of Significant Correlations") is widely known for his research on how geographical concentrations of political extremists affect the weather.

Patrick A. Stewart ("About the Title of Your Dissertation") is Associate Professor of Public Administration at Arkansas State University.

Joseph Stewart, Jr. ("Rotisserie Political Science") is Professor of Political Science at Clemson University.

J. David Singer ("Cumulativeness in the Social Sciences: Some Counter-prescriptions") is Professor Emeritus of Political Science at the University of Michigan.

James C. Scott ("Perfecting the Pecking Order") is the Sterling Professor Political Science at Yale University.

P.S. Ruckman, Jr. ("About the Title of Your Dissertation") is Associate Professor of Political Science at Rock Valley College.

Arnold A. Rogow ("A Short Note on U and Non-U in Political Science"), deceased, was Professor of Political Science at City College of New York.

Nelson W. Polsby ("On Conferences"), deceased, was the Heller Professor of Political Science and Director of the Institute of Governmental Studies at the University of California, Berkeley.

H.G.W.J.G.C. Patella ("The Political Economy of the Automobile—A Fifth Approach: Transient Physical Neo-postdistanciationalist Theory") held the lap record for the Kneesdon Go-Kart track in 1992.

M.F. Parris ("Phil's Barber Shop Calendar for 1973–1974: The Ontology of Chronological Modification—A Structural Crisis?") is a British radio and television presenter, political columnist, and travel writer.

Rosa Parkin and Charley Parkin ("Peter Rabbit and the *Grundrisse*") are the offspring of Frank Parkin, Professor Emeritus of Sociology at the University of Kent.

Jeremy D. Mayer ("Zog for Albania, Edward for Estonia, and Monarchs for All the Rest? The Royal Road to Prosperity, Democracy, and World Peace") is Associate Professor of Public Policy at George Mason University.

Dagobert D. Manteltasche ("Owls and Larks, Knotters and Simplifiers: The Origins of Modern Political Science," "A Desipient Prolegomenon to the Deconstruction of Silence: Neo-postdistanciationalist Approaches," and "The Schartz-Metterclume Method") is Med Bit Sokker Distinguished Professor, University of the Arctic Circle.

Gerry Mandering ("The House that Polly Sci Built") has recently completed a study of cat juggling in Nebraska.

Forrest Maltzman ("Leaving Office Feet First: Death in Congress") is Professor of Political Science at George Washington University.

Matthew A. Light ("Perfecting the Pecking Order") is Assistant Professor of Criminology at the University of Toronto.

James H. Lebovic ("The Academic Conference: An Irreverent Glossary of Terms") is Professor of Political Science and International Affairs at George Washington University.

Leszek Kolakowski ("The General Theory of Not-gardening"), deceased, was a Senior Research Fellow at All Souls College, Oxford.

William Koetzle ("Death, Where Is Thy Sting? The Senate as a Ponce (de Leon) Scheme") is Manager of Legislative, Regulatory, and Political Affairs for the Chevron Corporation.

William J. Keefe ("On the Disciplinary Pecking Order," "On Textbook Adoption," "On the Theory and Practice of Academic Administration," and "On Recruiting Graduate Students") is Professor Emeritus of Political Science at the University of Pittsburgh.

Ronald Herring ("A Young Person's Guide to Positivism") is Professor of Government at Cornell University.

Jac C. Heckelman ("A Rational Choice Model for the Dakota Effect") is Professor of Economics at Wake Forest University.

Mark M. Gray ("Vindicating Anthony Downs") is Research Associate Professor at the Center for Applied Research in the Apostolate, Georgetown University.

Marleen Boudreau Flory ("Semantics and Symbioses: How to Write an Article to Impress Your Peers"), deceased, was Professor of Classics at Gustavus Adolphus College.

R.S.J. Featherstonehaugh ("Urban Politics and Sex at Birth") is the author of *Teach Yourself Sword Swallowing*.

Heinz Eulau ("On the Political Science Pecking Order," "On Marketing a Textbook," "On the Curriculum Vitae," and "On Serving as a Panel Discussant"), deceased, was William Bennett Munro Professor Emeritus of Political Science at Stanford University.

Robert S. Erikson ("Why the Democrats Lose Presidential Elections: Toward a Theory of Optimal Loss (with apologies to A Wuffle)") is Professor of Political Science at Columbia University.

Christian Collet ("Why Democrats Shouldn't Vote (with acknowledgements to R. Erikson)") is Associate Professor of American Politics at Doshisha University.

Hiram Q. Clavicle, III ("The Political Economy of the Automobile—A Fifth Approach: Transient Physical Neo-postdistanciationalist Theory") is currently researching the question, "Are there intelligent forms of life on Earth?"

J.S.R. Cholmondeley ("Urban Politics and Sex at Birth") is the author of volumes 7 and 8 of *The History of Rice Pudding: 1739–1743*.

Thomas Brunell ("Death, Where Is Thy Sting? The Senate as a Ponce (de Leon) Scheme") is Associate Professor of Political Science at the University of Texas at Dallas.

Sarah Binder ("Leaving Office Feet First: Death in Congress") is Professor of Political Science and Senior Fellow in Governance Studies at the Brookings Institution.

Otto I.Q. Besser-Wisser ("The Schartz-Metterclume Method" and "The RoWoCo and Flea Theory: Truth Behind the Conspiracy"), deceased, was Director of the Central Institute for Questions and Answers, University of the Arctic Circle, from 1916 to 1996.

Anonymous ("Politics Conferences: A Short Guide to Participants") remains anonymous.

Contents*

Prologue 1

    A Wuffle. 1986. "Reflections on Academia." *PS: Political Science & Politics* 19: 57–61.

    Dagobert D. Manteltasche. 2002. "Owls and Larks, Knotters and Simplifiers: The Origins of Modern Political Science." *European Political Science* 2: 36–42.

The Practice of Political Science

The Academic Pecking Order 15

    Pierre van den Berghe. 1970. "The Academic Pecking Order." Excerpt from *Academic Gamesmanship: How to Make a Ph.D. Pay*, 7–21. London: Abelard-Schuman.

    Heinz Eulau. 1985. "On the Political Science Pecking Order." Excerpt from "Editor's Note." *Political Behavior* 7: 3–6.

    William J. Keefe. 1980. "On the Disciplinary Pecking Order." Excerpt from Alan Rosenthal (ed.). *Impurely Academic: The Letters, Memos and Other Humorous Pieces of William J. Keefe, Political Scientist*. New Brunswick, NJ: Transaction Books.

    Arnold A. Rogow. 1960. "A Short Note on U and Non-U in Political Science." *Western Political Quarterly* 13: 1064–1066.

    Kenneth J. Meier and Joseph Stewart, Jr. 1992. "Rotisserie Political Science." *PS: Political Science & Politics* 25: 565–568.

    James C. Scott and Matthew A. Light. 2001. "Perfecting the Pecking Order." Excerpt from "The Misuse of Numbers: Audits, Quantification, and the Obfuscation of Politics." Unpublished paper.

On Journal and Research Monograph Publishing 43

    Betty H. Zisk. 1970. "The Compleat Jargoner: How to Obfuscate the Obvious Without Half Trying." *Western Political Quarterly* 23: 55–56.

    P.S. Ruckman, Jr., and Patrick A. Stewart, Jr. n.d. "About the Title of Your Dissertation." Unpublished paper.

---

* Previously published work reprinted with permission where origins are known.

Marleen Boudreau Flory. 1983. "Semantics and Symbioses: How to Write an Article to Impress Your Peers." *Chronicle of Higher Education* (January 26): 72.

Pierre van den Berghe. 1970. "On Publishing." Excerpt from *Academic Gamesmanship: How to Make a Ph.D. Pay*, 87–102. London: Abelard-Schuman.

On Textbook Publishing 57

Heinz Eulau. 1986. "On Marketing a Textbook." Excerpt from "Editor's Note." *Political Behavior* 8: 203–205.

William J. Keefe. 1980. "On Textbook Adoption." Excerpt from Alan Rosenthal (ed.). 1980. *Impurely Academic: The Letters, Memos and Other Humorous Pieces of William J. Keefe, Political Scientist*. New Brunswick, NJ: Transaction Books.

Preparing a Curriculum Vitae 63

Heinz Eulau. 1989. "On the Curriculum Vitae." Excerpt from "Editor's Note: The Iron Law of the Academy." *Political Behavior* 11: 93–97.

Conference Going 67

Pierre van den Berghe. 1970. "Conventions and Professional Standing." Excerpt from *Academic Gamesmanship: How to Make a Ph.D. Pay*, 7–21. London: Abelard-Schuman.

Anonymous. n.d. "Politics Conferences: A Short Guide to Participants."

James H. Lebovic. 2006. "The Academic Conference: An Irreverent Glossary of Terms." *International Studies Perspectives* 7: ii–iii.

Nelson W. Polsby. 1979. "On Conferences." Excerpt from "A Yank at the Court of King Hugh." *PS: Political Science & Politics* 12: 24–25.

Heinz Eulau. 1988. "On Serving as a Panel Discussant." Excerpt from "Editor's Note." *Political Behavior* 10: 3–4.

Administrative Service 81

William J. Keefe, 1980. "On the Theory and Practice of Academic Administration." Excerpt from Alan Rosenthal (ed.). *Impurely Academic: The Letters, Memos and Other Humorous Pieces of William J. Keefe, Political Scientist*. New Brunswick, NJ: Transaction Books.

William J. Keefe. 1980. "On Recruiting Graduate Students." Excerpt from Alan Rosenthal (ed.). 1980. *Impurely Academic: The Letters, Memos and Other Humorous Pieces of William J. Keefe, Political Scientist*. New Brunswick, NJ: Transaction Books.

Political and Social Theory 87

Leszek Kolakowski. 1990. "The General Theory of Not-gardening." In Leszek Kolakowski, *Modernity on Endless Trial*. Chicago: University of Chicago Press.

Dagobert D. Manteltasche. 2003. "A Desipient Prolegomenon to the Deconstruction of Silence: Neo-postdistanciationalist Approaches." *WZB-Mitteilungen* 101: 64–66.

Rosa Parkin and Charley Parkin. 1974. "Peter Rabbit and the *Grundrisse*." *European Journal of Sociology* 15: 181–183.

Gerry Mandering. 1979. "The House that Polly Sci Built." Unpublished paper.

Research Methods 101

Lee Sigelman. 1977. "How to Succeed in Political Science by Being Very Trying: A Methodological Sampler." *PS: Political Science & Politics* 10: 302–304.

Ronald Herring. 1980. "A Young Person's Guide to Positivism." *PS: Political Science & Politics* 13: 292.

Dick Tator. 1981. "A World Glut of Significant Correlations." *Newsletter of the Political Studies Association of the UK*.

A Wuffle. 2009. "Uncle Wuffle's Reflections on Prediction." Unpublished paper.

J. David Singer. 1975. "Cumulativeness in the Social Sciences: Some Counterprescriptions." *PS: Political Science & Politics* 8: 19–21.

M.F. Parris. 1974. "Phil's Barber Shop Calendar for 1973–1974: The Ontology of Chronological Modification—A Structural Crisis?" *PS: Political Science & Politics* 7: 14.

R.S.J. Featherstonehaugh and J.S.R. Cholmondeley. 2008. "Urban Politics and Sex at Birth." *European Political Science* 7: 318-323.

Dagobert D. Manteltasche and Otto I.Q. Besser-Wisser). 2002. "The Schartz-Metterclume Method." *Journal of Theoretical Politics* 14: 129–134.

Public Policy Analysis 133

Kenneth J. Meier. 2004. "Get Your Tongue Out of My Mouth 'Cause I'm Kissin' You Goodbye: The Politics of Ideas." *Policy Studies Journal* 32: 225–233.

A Wuffle. 1993. "The Political Economy of the Automobile—Four Approaches." *Journal of Theoretical Politics* 5: 409–412.

Hiram Q. Clavicle, III, and H.G.W.J.G.C. Patella. 1995. "The Political Economy of the Automobile—A Fifth Approach: Transient Physical Neo-postdistanciationalist Theory." *Journal of Theoretical Politics* 7: 101–104.

Voting Behavior and Party Competition 151

A Wuffle. 1984. "Should You Brush Your Teeth on November 6, 1984? A Rational Choice Perspective." *PS: Political Science & Politics* 17: 577–581.

A Wuffle. 1988. "The 'Minimax Blame' Rule for Voter Choice: Help for the Undecided Voter on November 8, 1988." *PS: Political Science & Politics* 21: 639–640.

Robert S. Erikson. 1989. "Why the Democrats Lose Presidential Elections: Toward a Theory of Optimal Loss (with apologies to A Wuffle)." *PS: Political Science & Politics* 22: 30–35.

A Wuffle and Christian Collet. 1997. "Why Democrats Shouldn't Vote (with acknowledgements to R. Erikson)." *Journal of Theoretical Politics* 9: 137–140.

Lee Sigelman. 1988. "Are Democrats Stupid?" *Journal of Irreproducible Results* 33: 2–4.

Lee Sigelman. 1990. "Toward a Stupidity-Ugliness Theory of Democratic Electoral Debacles." *PS: Political Science & Politics* 23: 18–20.

Lee Sigelman. n.d. "The Hobbesian World of Democrats." Unpublished paper.

Mark M. Gray and A Wuffle. 2005. "Vindicating Anthony Downs." *PS: Political Science & Politics* 38: 737–740.

A Wuffle. 2008. "Voter Advice in the Presidential Election of 2008: A Guide for the Perplexed." Unpublished paper.

Legislatures 189

Forrest Maltzman, Lee Sigelman, and Sarah Binder. 1996. "Leaving Office Feet First: Death in Congress." *PS: Political Science & Politics* 29: 665–671.

A Wuffle, Thomas Brunell, and William Koetzle. 1997. "Death, Where Is Thy Sting? The Senate as a Ponce (de Leon) Scheme." *PS: Political Science & Politics* 30: 58–59.

Garry Young and Lee Sigelman. 2008. "The Dakota Effect." *PS: Political Science & Politics* 41: 349–353.

Jac C. Heckelman. 2008. "A Rational Choice Model for the Dakota Effect." *PS: Political Science & Politics* 41: 677–678.

Executives 219

Lee Sigelman. n.d. "Presidents, Extramarital Sex, and the Public: Testing a Rational Theory." Unpublished paper.

Lee Sigelman. 1982. "The Presidential Horoscope: Predicting Performance in the White House." *Presidential Studies Quarterly* 12: 434–438.

Jeremy D. Mayer and Lee Sigelman. 1998. "Zog for Albania, Edward for Estonia, and Monarchs for All the Rest? The Royal Road to Prosperity, Democracy, and World Peace." *PS: Political Science & Politics* 31: 771–774.

Conspiracy Theories 239

Otto I.Q. Besser-Wisser. 2007. "The RoWoCo and Flea Theory: Truth Behind the Conspiracy." *WZB-Mitteilungen* 115: 74–75.

A Wuffle. 1978. "*Monopoly* Is a Capitalist Plot: A Hegemonic View of Games as Instruments of Economic Indoctrination." *Simulation & Gaming* 9: 252–254.

Prologue

Reflections on Academia*
A Wuffle

On Research

A professor must have a theory as a dog must have fleas.[1]—H.L. Mencken

An academic is one who knows more and more about less and less.[2]—Source unknown

If I have seen less far than others, it is because I have stood on the shoulders of pygmies.—Isaac Fignewton (A Wuffle)

I stopped being a behaviorist when I realized that I couldn't take credit for my own ideas.—Anita Greene

In academia, as in country music, only your successes count, not your failures. It doesn't matter how many publishers or journals rejected the manuscript, it only matters that it be published. One good paper is remembered; a dozen mediocre ones forgotten. —Ami Glazer

The thing that keeps most empirical political scientists honest is that somewhere out there is an unknown graduate student with your name on it.
—John Ferejohn

Theory—like mist on eyeglasses—obscures vision. —Charlie Chan (quoted by Jon R. Bond)

The plural of anecdote is data. —Ray Wolfinger

Mowrey's Law: Funded research tends to drive out unfunded in the marketplace of ideas.[3]—David Mowrey

In academia, citation is the sincerest form of flattery.[4]—A Wuffle

Academic courtship consists of the exchange of reprints. —Helen Wildman

Lending a book is, for most academics, the highest form of friendship.
—Simon Brett

A researcher and his hypotheses are never parted—except by death.[5]—d'apres Thomas Kuhn (A Wuffle)

Scholars who rest on their laurels are perhaps confusing their laurels with another part of their anatomy.—Sue Anderson

No research paper is ever remembered for more than one idea.[6]—A Wuffle

It is better to be the second author of a first-rate paper than the first author of a second-rate one.[7]—A Wuffle

On Universities

There were 93,000 professors in the U.S. in 1936, compared to 867,000 coal miners. Now the figures are dramatically reversed. In 1978 there were more than 600,000 professors, while the number of miners had shrunk to less than 150,000. —Everett C. Ladd, Jr.

No wonder there's an energy crisis! —A Wuffle

There are two kinds of professors. Those who add prestige to their department and those whose prestige rests primarily (if not exclusively) on the fact they're in the department they're in. —William Schonfeld

The present reputation of any department is based on the past work of its past members. Thus, the reputation of some departments can best be attributed to racial memory. —Anon.

The aim of every recruitment effort should be to recruit people who are better than you are. If you can't do that then you shouldn't be hiring. —Joseph Tanenhaus

The worst mistake any job candidate can make is to assume that people have read the material that's been sent them.—Nelson Polsby

All academics without tenure are young: all academics with tenure are (at best) middle-aged. —A Wuffle, inspired by F.M. Cornford

Forty: The age at which academics are no longer allowed to be "promising." —Arthur Clun

University politics are vicious precisely because the stakes are so small. —Attributed to Henry Kissinger

On Teaching

Professor: One who talks in other people's sleep. —Anon.

Work: What scholars do when they're not teaching. —Anon

He who can does; he who can't teaches; he who can't teach teaches teachers; he who can't teach teachers administers teacher ed.—Immemorial Cant

Required Course: One that no student would take otherwise. —Anon

Scholars have students; only gurus have disciples. —A Wuffle

Most teachers teach facts, good teachers teach ideas, great teachers teach how to think. —Jonathan Pool

Peretz's Law: If you understand the material you teach, then you try to present it clearly and simply to your students; if you don't understand it completely, you try to make it complicated, lest you be challenged in such a way as to let your ignorance show. —Paul Peretz

Student-faculty cooperation: The implicit deal that most students make with their professors that if you don't bother me, then I won't bother you. —Anon.

All good education is elitist in that it says to a student, you are not adequate as you are. There are better people than you. And you will be taught how they think, how they write, how they talk and what they know. —Neil Postman

The problem of education is that students don't know enough to know that they don't know enough—and most don't want to learn. —A Wuffle

On the Social Sciences

Thou shalt not commit a Social Science. —W.H. Auden

God gave all the easy problems to the physicists.—James March

In the social sciences, waiting for Newton is like waiting for Godot.
—Lee Cronbach and Philip Converse

The validity of a science is its ability to predict.[8] —Harry L. Schwartzburg, RCA Engineer *(although I doubt he said it first)*

To avoid the problem of scientific validity, three strategies are commonly followed in the social sciences: (a) eschewing falsifiable statements; (b) denying the possibility of objective truth, and (c) writing in French or German. The combination of these three strategies has been shown to be virtually irresistible, even to strong minds. Statements which on the face of it are unintelligible gibberish can always be blamed on a bad translation. —A Wuffle

Field research is to anthropology what the blood of the martyrs is to the Church.
—C. G. Seligman, Professor of Anthropology

The age of chivalry is gone. That of sophisters, calculators and economists has succeeded—and the glory of Europe is extinguished forever.
—Edmund Burke, circa 1790

An economist is one who observes something that works in practice and wonders if it will work in theory. —As told to Bernard Nelson by Victor Fuchs

If you put all the economists in the country end to end, they'd still point in different directions. —Harry S. Truman

The Economist's Motto: To err is human, to be paid for it divine. —Victor Fuchs

The leading advocates of the need to subject everything to the competitive test of the market are tenured economists. —Sheen Kassouf, Professor of Economics, UCI

Most adolescents dislike having to learn history. As children, they were taught that it was desirable to let bygones be bygones. —Anon.

Those who do not know the past are condemned to repeat History 101. —Anon.

Do not worship at the shrine of that Bitch-Goddess QUANTIFICATION!
—Carl Bridenbaugh, Presidential Address, American Historical Association, 1962

Geography is such an innocent science that we can expect much insight from it.
—William Burne, Professor of Geography, circa 1966

I dropped out of American Studies after the first exam, when I found out that the correct answer to all four questions was "hegemony." —Emily Polsby

The end or purpose of every art and science is some good. That of the most authoritative, i.e., of political science, is the greatest and most eagerly desired good—justice, or, in other words, the common welfare.
—Aristotle, *Politics*, Book III

Pick one and only one answer (be prepared to justify your response):

Politics is to political science as
- a. rhyme: reason
- b. id: ego
- c. faith: charity
- d. trial: tribulation
- e. Abbott: Costello—A Wuffle

Political science is the only discipline in which regression is progress.[9] —A Wuffle

If you can understand an article in the *APSR*, then something must have gone wrong in the refereeing process.—A Wuffle

A sociologist is a scientist who blames crimes on everything and everyone except the person who commits it.—Laurence J. Peter

Sociology is the branch of science with the most methods and the least results.—Henri Poincare, circa 1909[10]

Economics is all about how people make decisions; sociology is all about why they don't have any real decisions to make. —James Duesenberry, Professor of Economics

It is necessary to study sociology in order to learn why the advice of economists is so consistently ignored.—Wilfred Pareto

It is necessary to study economics in order to learn why the advice of all other social scientists should be consistently ignored.[11]—Any randomly chosen economist (A Wuffle)

In Conclusion

The only great social scientist is a dead social scientist. —Anon.

Tenure is never having to say you're sorry.[12]—A Wuffle, May 1976

Notes

*Only the famous are famous enough to be quoted. Thus, anything quotable said by someone not famous will (a) be attributed to someone famous, (b) be forgotten, or (c) be attributed to anon. Also as Arthur Clun (1974, 12) was the first to point out (but for which he will not be remembered), most quotable quotes are attributed by graduate students to their senior professors. For example, "nine out of fourteen Yale graduate students attributed 'Politics ain't beanbag' to Robert A. Dahl. Nearly as reliable was the attribution of 'we have nothing to fear but fear itself' to Richard E. Neustadt among Harvard Ph.D.s in government." Similarly, "University of Chicago economics graduates correctly named Milton Friedman as the author of 'Prosperity is just around the corner.'"

1. Cf. Lucy: "I've just come up with the perfect theory. It's my theory that Beethoven would have written even better music if he had been married!"
   Linus: "What's so perfect about that theory?"
   Lucy: "It can't be proved one way or the other."—"Charlie Brown" (Charles Schultz)

2. Cf. An intellectual knows almost nothing about almost everything. An academic knows almost everything about almost nothing.

3. Resemblance to Gresham's Law may or may not be intentional.

4. Cf. The quote attributed to Mae West, "I don't care what they say about my morals as long as they spell my name right."

5. Cf. "The great tragedy of science is the slaying of a beautiful hypothesis by an ugly fact." —Thomas Huxley

6. I.e., no more than one idea is ever remembered from any research paper. Most papers, however, are simply not remembered. (Whether there were any ideas there to be remembered remains an open question.)

7. In general, allocation of authorship credit is not zero-sum. The exception is married couples—only one of whom (usually the husband) is ever given credit for co-authored work.

8. By that test, economics may have claim to science—it was Lord Keynes who said, "In the long run we are all dead"—perhaps the only consistently accurate prediction ever made by a macroeconomist. On the other hand, historians have shown some ability to predict the past (or at least to show its inevitability). (Cf. the Fagin-Wuffle Law: "Hindsight is the only exact science.") Political scientists have been predicting the disintegration of the U.S. party system for nearly two decades. If we wait long enough, they're sure to be right. The most famous prediction in anthropology is that of Levi-Strauss: "Cannibals who eat kin should boil them; cannibals who eat strangers should roast them." Unfortunately for structuralist theory, this prediction is false. Indeed, baking is the most common cooking method used by anthropopagi; moreover, "natives . . . have discovered a veritable smorgasbord of ways of preparing people" (Shankman 1961, 61, quoted by Harris 1979, 169).

9. Cf. Q: "Why didn't the political scientist climb the mountain?"
   A: "Because the statistical program to do so wasn't available in SPSS."

10. In fairness to Poincare, he wrote this at a time before modern political science had been invented.

11. Cf. "Politics is too important to be left to economists" (A Wuffle, July 29, 1981).

12. Publish or perish is not, however, meant to be taken literally. In April 1914, a University of South Carolina assistant professor who was denied tenure kidnapped the president of the university and unsuccessfully sought to convince him to reverse the tenure denial. When that strategy failed, the assistant professor committed suicide. Cf. Confucius Say: "He who has assistant professors for friends need not watch soap operas."

References

Clun, Arthur. 1974. "The Rule of Anticipated Reactions." *PS* 7: 12.

Harris, Marvin. 1979. *Cultural Materialism.* New York: Random House.

Shankman, Paul. 1961. "Le Roti et le Boulli: Levi Strauss' Theory of Cannibalism." *American Anthropologist* 71: 54–69.

Owls and Larks, Knotters and Simplifiers: The Origins of Modern Political Science

Dr. Dr. Dagobert D. Manteltasche

Theory

As Helmut Spargel (1984: 4,689) once observed, "The world is divided into two kinds of people: owls and larks." Larks believe in the principle of "early to bed and early to rise." For them this is both a pragmatic virtue (they feel at their best early in the day), and a moral injunction. Owls march to a different tune—but only at night. They rise and sleep late because they work best that way. The classic owl story is George Bernard Shaw's invitation to a breakfast meeting during his first visit to the United States. He inquired what time this would be, and on learning that it could be at any time between 7:00 and 8:30 a.m., politely declined the invitation explaining that he would have gone to bed by then.

Spargel's brilliant insight is of direct relevance to recent discussions of neo-postdistanciationalist theory (Clavicle and Patella 1995; Manteltasche and Besser-Wisser 2001), and to some of Wuffle's (1984; 1993) seminal work. Nevertheless, it is probably safe to say that Owl and Lark Theory has not yet been fully incorporated into political analysis. This article is a first step towards rectifying this puzzling omission.

As we all know, Owl and Lark Theory is challenged by Knotter and Simplifier Theory. As Chitinous and Gastropod observe, "The world is divided into two kinds of people: knotters and simplifiers." Knotters believe that the world is terribly complex and only very abstruse and complex theories can hope to explain even the smallest part of it—even better to express them in arcane language, and best of all in arcane symbols. The ultimate triumph for the knotter is to theorise about a problem you didn't even know was a problem in a language you can't understand. Simplifiers believe in plain talk about the real world. The classic example is the opening sentence of the Communist Manifesto: "The history of all hitherto existing society is the history of class conflict." Simplifiers dismiss Knotter Theory as "bullshit" or occasionally, though with reluctance because it complicates things, they refer to "the higher bullshit" or to a "high bullshit quotient."

Most seminar-room debate boils down to pitched battle between knotters and simplifiers. The simplifier says that A causes B, that black is black, white is white, and that two and two are four. The knotter comes in, sometimes with an Oxford stammer and long, thoughtful pauses, saying, "Well, yes . . . , I wouldn't exactly disagree with what you say about the Peruvian salt industry . . . though I do feel . . . that it is just slightly more . . . complex than you sometimes seem to imply . . .

there might be a case, perhaps . . . for adding something of a gloss . . . a footnote, if you catch my drift . . . perhaps it is just a small point, but not entirely without potential significance . . . I think it might be suggested . . . perhaps . . . that the Andalucian ant industry works on just . . . slightly different principles . . . It might just help to refine the analysis just a little bit if . . . etc. etc."

Is the world divided either into owls and larks, or knotters and simplifiers? Or is it divided into both owls and larks and knotters and simplifiers? Even more crucial: what is the relevance of this to modern theories of politics? The null hypothesis of this article is that there is no empirical relationship between the two dichotomies, or indeed, between them and anything of any interest whatsoever.

Methods

Field work was conducted in Western Europe and North America between 1965 and 2001 at academic dinner parties, and after-seminar drinking sessions, attended mainly by political scientists. Most dinner parties were held on a Friday or Saturday, but more informal drinking usually occurred during the working week. Tests show that there was no significant difference in the results according to day of the week or the formality of the event. Pilot testing was conducted between 1960 and 1965 when it was discovered that interview reliability and validity were maximised if questions were asked after a good dinner with liberal quantities of Mersault or a good Brunello, or both. For this reason the number of observations and tests of significance are given in bottles of Mersault or Brunello, or their functional equivalents when field work was done in Australia, California, and Spain.

After a couple of bottles few respondents found it difficult to classify themselves as owls or larks. Larks launched into an account of how, that very morning, they had completed their daily eight kilometre run, milked the cows, baked the bread, and put the finishing touches to their latest string quartet, all before breakfast. They do their best work in the morning, go to the cinema in the afternoon and by nine at night they are normally tucked up in bed and fast asleep ready for an early start the next day. Owls complained bitterly about the early morning habits of their spouses, their children, the milkman, and the people in the flat above. One owl described how he was wakened and brought a cup of tea at about 9:00 a.m. by a person or persons unknown, though in twenty years he had never gained sufficient consciousness at that early time to work out who it was (his wife confirmed this, and said it was she). Thirty minutes later the same person (still unknown) handed him a large piece of paper on which his name was clearly printed, to remind him who he was. On a good day he was ready to start work about six hours later, and after an early dinner at about 9:00 or 10:00 p.m. he sat down at his word processor, normally finishing at about 4:00 or 5:00 a.m. Although this respondent had won two Nobel prizes, the larks at the table obviously disapproved of such decadence.

An infallible method was devised for assigning respondents to the knotter or simplifier categories. Reactions to the statement "the world can be divided into two kinds of people: owls and larks," showed beyond all doubt that the world is divided into two kinds of people: knotters and simplifiers. If their reaction to the statement was "Well . . . I feel . . . that it just might be slightly more . . . complex than this . . . possibly . . . though I'm not sure . . . one should take into account . . . several factors . . . which may be inter-related in a complex fashion . . ." —they were classified as knotters. Such people often went into the details of diurnal cortisol levels, circadian chronotypes and hPer2 discoveries; they discussed migrating birds and jet-lag; they elaborated complex typologies and sub-types involving owls, larks, starlings, storks, swans, eagles, swallows, and owlarks; and one drew a "crucially important distinction between thrushes and starlings," but I am unable to follow the reasons for this.

Among the knotters who rejected what they called the "dichotomisational assumptive ontology of the problematic" was a group of post-modern discourse analysts (at least, I think they rejected it) who had wondered/wandered in from the street looking for drink. The significance of this will become clear later in this article.

The first conclusion of this research, therefore, is that the world is divided into both owls and larks, and knotters and simplifiers. Everyone without exception recognises the eternal truth of the owl-lark dichotomy, but they do so in a way that confirms the eternal truth of the knotter-simplifier dichotomy. Both Spargel, and Chitinous and Gastropod, are correct, therefore. The question that naturally follows is: how do the two categories relate to each other, if at all?

Research Results

The initial results of more than thirty-five years of field work are presented in Table 1, which shows clearly that the great majority of owls are simplifiers, and that the great majority of larks are knotters. If we reverse columns and rows an equally striking pattern appears. The great majority of simplifiers are owls, and the great majority of knotters are larks. These results are almost as robust as the best Brunellos consumed during the field work. We can safely conclude that not only is the world divided between the two types but that the two types are interrelated in a systematic manner. Whatever God may choose to do with the universe, it seems, he or she does not play dice with the mental patterns of political scientists.

Table 1	Percentages	
	Owls	Larks
Simplifiers	45.2	5.2
Knotters	4.8	44.8
Total for all four cells adds up to 100%. Based upon 1,363 bottles of Meusault and 1,768 bottles of Brunello. Significant at 12.5% proof.		

Table 2	Percentages	
	Simplifiers	Knotters
Owls	44.8	4.8
Larks	5.2	45.2
Total for all four cells adds up to 100%. Based upon 1,363 bottles of Meusault and 1,768 bottles of Brunello. Significant at 12.5% proof.		

What, I hear you ask, gentle reader, does all this have to do with political science? The answer is simple. Our sample of owl-simplifiers and lark-knotters was broken down according to specialist sub-areas of political science—classical theorists, comparativists, public policy, state and local government, public administration, methodology, IR, theory, voting studies, etc. Unfortunately this failed to produce anything of interest; specialists were randomly distributed between the owl-simplifier and the lark-knotter cells. But then, tipped off by the rejection of Owl and Lark Theory by the post-modern discourse analysts (mentioned above), the minority of deviant cases were examined—the owl-knotters and lark-simplifiers. Much to the author's surprise, post-modern discourse analysts are overwhelmingly of the deviant owl-knotter type, whereas rational choice theorists are deviants of the lark-simplifier type, as Table 3 shows.

Table 3	Percentages	
	Discourse Analysts	Rational-Choice Specialists
Simplifiers	95.4	4.4
Knotters	4.6	95.6
Based upon 75 bottles of Meusault and 87 bottles of Brunello. Significant at 10.5% proof.		

This distribution reveals that both discourse analysis and rational choice are, without a shadow of doubt, the products of mistaken identity. Discourse analysts appear to have incorrectly deconstructed the floating signifiers in the sedimented layers of their reflexively individualised modes of post-modern expressivist life-contingencies. By mis-deconstructing their self-historicity, they have transgressed the non-linearity of their own post-modern intellectual discontinuities, thereby mystifying the ontological identity of their own life-articulations. The best solution for them seems to be to de-reconstruct the essentialist meta-connectedness of their language formations, thereby realising the objective subjectivity of their own larkfulness. In re-problematising themselves this way, they could make it possible to engage in more plausible forms of non-referential knotting. In brief, if they were to objectively de-reconstruct themselves, they could subjectively re-deconstruct the essential knotterfulness of the deep-structures of their intellectual paradigm, and move smoothly into another specialism of political science, where they will live happily ever after.

Equally, it is evident that rational-choice theorists have not analysed their own life-game rationally. As larks, who mistakenly try to simplify, they are a classic case of edogenously induced disequilibria, in which an over-simplified game-theoretical apparatus has resulted in the sub-optimisation of preferences. As a consequence of incomplete information and exponentially mounting sums of discounted punishment pay-offs, median lark-simplifiers typically try to re-equilibrise with hypothetical forms of multi-polar modelling of new institutional rational choice and n-dimensional multi-stage chicken games. This only makes the problem worse because it generates an over-supply of unboundedly-rational equilibrium outcomes for each multi-dimensional setter model, and no parsimonious way of choosing between them. To correct this simple but sad mistake they need only do the rational thing by defecting to a more sensible lark-knotter game, at which point they will give up rational choice for other forms of political science, and live happily ever after.

Summary and Confusions

This article shows conclusively that the great majority of well-adjusted political scientists are either owl-simplifiers or lark-knotters. The deviant categories of owl-knotters and lark-simplifiers are populated almost entirely by post-modern discourse analysts and rational-choice theorists who have either discursively misconstructed themselves or irrationally analysed their own life-game choices.

An entirely different interpretation of these empirical results is suggested by neo-postdistanciationalist theory, which argues that discourse analysts are extreme owls who get up so late and stay up so late that they never meet ordinary people, and only talk to each other. There may well be some truth in this theory, but the difficulty of neo-postdistanciationalist theory is its failure to offer a convincing explanation for rational-choice theory. This, however, is not a problem for post-neodistanciationalist theory, which can explain rational-choice theory, but not post-modern discourse analysis. It claims that rational choice theory is the problem of people who have changed from larks to owls—a not uncommon change after puberty—but who have not yet adjusted to the appropriate simplifier mode. In other words, rational-choice should be seen as a passing and transitional phase among those who have moved from a lark to an owl life-style without managing to make the appropriate intellectual adjustments. Post-neodistancialists argue that the problem naturally resolves itself after a period of time, and recommend that it should be allowed to run its course until it naturally expires. They warn that exactly the same mistakes will be made all over again by the next cohort of young people changing from owls to larks but not managing the concomitant change from knotter to simplifier, although there is absolutely nothing one can do about this.

These are interesting and fruitful lines of inquiry but we need more research. In particular we need to build into the analysis another powerful explanatory variable, namely the division of the world into those who take baths and those who prefer showers. The author is applying to various research councils and foundations for 1,363 bottles of Mersault and 1,768 bottles of Brunello to continue with the second wave of the project.

References

Abramson, P.R. 1997. "Probing Well Beyond the Bounds of Conventional Wisdom." *American Journal of Political Science* 41: 675–682.

Clavicle, H. Q., III, and H.G.W.J.G.C. Patella. 1995. "The Political Economy of the Automobile: Transient Physical Neo-postdistanciationaIism." *Journal of Theoretical Politics* 7: 101–104.

Manteltasche, D. 1984. *The History of the Rice Pudding 1832–1838* (vol. 4.). Broadwoodwidger: Last Resort Press.

Manteltasche, D., and O.I.Q. Besser-Wisser. 2002. "The Schartz-Metterclume Method." *Journal of Theoretical Politics*, forthcoming.

Matthews, R.A.J. 1997. "The Science of Murphy's Law: Life's Little Annoyances Are Not as Random as They Seem: The Awful Truth Is That the Universe Is Against You." *Scientific American* 276: 88–91

Schrank-Schlussel, F. 1996. "The Social Functions of Incomprehensibility." *Tiler and Grouter Quarterly Review* 36: 1463–1510.

Spargel, Helmut. 1984. "Phantasmagorical Approaches to the Analysis of Neglected Trivia." *Eskimo Nell Annual Review* 21: 4689–4742.

Wuffle, A. 1984. "Should You Brush Your Teeth on Nov. 6 1984? A Rational Choice perspective." *PS* 17: 577–581.

Wuffle, A. 1993. "The Political Economy of the Automobile—Four Approaches." *Journal of Theoretical Politics* 5: 409–412.

Practice of Political Science: The Academic Pecking Order

The Academic Pecking Order
Pierre van den Berghe

The academic game cannot be played successfully without an adequate understanding of the status hierarchy or pecking order of the players.... There remain three basic commodities over which most men spend most of their lives fighting: power, wealth, and prestige. Academics fight over all three, but most of all over the last. Universities and colleges are, first and foremost, institutions in which positions are gained or improved by patting your colleagues' backs, or by deprecating their efforts, or by a judicious combination of both techniques.

This is not to say that professors are indifferent to power and wealth, but the scope for invidious distinctions on these two dimensions is not very great. The salary ratio of a full professor to a beginning assistant professor is only about two to one. How unsatisfying for a Nobel Prize winner in Physics to think of himself as only twice as good as the young Ph.D. from Kansas State who may never get anything worthwhile published. (By comparison, the head of a corporation can regard himself as twenty or thirty times as valuable as a junior executive or production engineer.)

Power also does not differentiate well enough among professors. The basic power of professors is to flunk students, and hence to affect adversely their life chances. This power is jealously guarded and shared equally by all teachers, from the most junior assistant professor to the most senile full professor.... The trouble with this power, however, is that, since it is equally shared by all professors, it cannot serve as a basis for making invidious distinctions among them.

Luckily, there remains prestige as a basis of differentiation among professors. Here the possibilities are limitless, and professors have developed a pecking order of such scope, complexity, and subtlety as to deserve admiration. Vanity, a trait ascribed to certain male birds of bright plumage and to females of the human species who display varying portions of their epidermis on the screen or stage, is likewise the dominant characteristic of college and university teachers.

... Every academic belongs to at least three discrete status systems: he is a member of the larger society, of his college or university, and of the group of people who share his specialty.

In the larger society, the professor is ascribed a solid place in the upper middle class, though his unkept lawn, unwashed car, black friends, or long-haired progeny may occasionally attract the ire of his neighbors. However, even withal his status is sufficiently secure that he can afford such harmless eccentricities.

In any case, most professors could not care less what their neighbors think of them, because their social life is almost exclusively confined to other academics. Whether professorial homes are grouped in a gilded ghetto as is the case in some small college towns, or physically dispersed over large metropolitan areas, professors constitute something close to an occupational caste with strict rules of commensality.... For most academic families, the supermarket and department store are the only significant links with the outside world.

... Professors belong to two large groups of colleagues: the staff of their college or university, and all fellow specialists in their discipline. Only the members of a given department at a given university share common membership in both of these larger groups. Thus the department is the academic habitat par excellence, the principal scene for the enactment of competition for prestige.... Universities and colleges, as even laymen know, are ordered in a hierarchy of prestige. The layman's hierarchy does not necessarily correspond to the academic person's evaluations. Thus, it may be socially prestigious to go to an "elite" liberal arts college tucked away in the hills of New Hampshire or Connecticut, but such places do not rank high in the preference of most academics, except for a few snobs and eccentrics who genuinely enjoy teaching. With a remarkable degree of consensus, professors rank institutions of higher learning into a number of pyramidal categories. At the top, there are ten or twelve great universities, with the twin giants of Harvard and Berkeley among them; then one finds a further fifteen or so distinguished institutions trembling on the edge of greatness but lacking the aura of the great ones. Following is roughly a score of highly respectable schools, which, however, begin to show certain weaknesses, especially in graduate training and facilities; then come some fifty to seventy-five colleges that do a decent job of educating undergraduates and to whose staff one can belong without having to apologize or explain where the school is located; a further 200 to 250 schools might still perhaps be described as on the right side of academic respectability, but one would rather not be there if one had a choice. Finally there is the great dismal mass of the 2000-odd institutions that are of "higher learning" only by the most charitable of definitions.[1]

... One's university affiliation pegs one at a certain level *vis-à-vis* colleagues on other campuses, but within one's institution many finer status distinctions are made. First, in a given college or university, the various departments are placed on a rough scale of intellectual distinction, and, interestingly, the order is much the same everywhere: medicine, mathematics, and the natural sciences are high status subjects, while education, agriculture, social work, and nursing rank low; the social sciences and humanities have intermediate status with yet finer distinctions between the specific fields, e.g., economics frequently ranks higher than sociology....

On the whole, however, ... a top prestige symbol in academia is how little one teaches. The higher one's rank and the more exalted one's reputation, the fewer defiling "contact hours" one has with students, and the more senior the students....

So much for the main factors making for prestige competition within the university. Let us now turn to the external prestige system—the prestige determined by the recognition of colleagues in your discipline. The overwhelming majority of them are attached to other institutions and are thinly spread all over the world. Each discipline thus constitutes a vast network of people isolated from each other except during the brief ritual of the annual convention when scholars converge on some large city's Hilton Hotel for three or four days of inebriated gossip, frantic job-hunting, and unashamed prestige-mongering. The national, indeed the international, nature of this prestige system, as well as the imputed expertness of the judgments passed makes the body of fellow specialists the ultimate measure of a scholar's worth. Unless your work is known and discussed by other experts in your field, you are a strictly local figure. It is immaterial that most criticisms be adverse, as they most typically are; the important thing is that you be spoken and written about, preferably by people you have never met.

These two academic prestige systems—the one rooted in the local university and the other based on national recognition in the professional association—are intricately interconnected. Thus, in order to gain the respect of your professional peers, you must be affiliated with a respectable institution. If you are located at Apache Creek Junior College[2], you have obviously fallen by the wayside, and no self-respecting school will condescend to pull you out of the hole. Conversely, tenure and promotion at the better universities depend in good part on publication and on some test of professional recognition outside the home campus.

The principal ground on which these two forces meet is, of course, the academic department. And, since the national system is paramount, day-to-day prestige competition between members of a department consists mostly in impressing upon others how much better known than your colleagues you are outside the home university. . . . By far the most effective way of establishing prestige is to be frequently away from the campus on long-distance trips. The top dogs in any department are the ones who are constantly attending international conferences, giving lectures at other universities, or consulting with government or industrial firms—in short, the professorial jet set. The jet-propelled professor does almost everything except that for which he draws his salary. His undergraduates have to be content with lecture notes hastily scribbled on the back of airline menus between the martini and the crab cocktail; the university that pays his way to give a prestigious public lecture will have to be satisfied with a few associations of ideas hastily thrown together between planes to the accompaniment of saccharine music at O'Hare airport. Some professors even keep a mental note of their annual air mileages. The truly big-league log at least 100,000 miles (about fifteen transcontinental round-trips). Meanwhile, the graduate teaching assistants get valuable experience, and the undergraduates get what is known in polite society as the short end of the stick but what in student culture goes by a more vivid (but alas, unprintable) simile. The airborne professor is no longer simply absent-minded, he is also absent-bodied, a fleeting shadow that can occasionally be sighted picking up his mail in the departmental mail room.

Short of being physically absent from campus, prestige competition calls for at least being inaccessible, ostensibly in order to engage in prestigious work, namely research or writing. The device of the secretary to answer the phone and screen visitors is of course widely used inside and outside of academia. But only a few of the more senior professors who are departmental chairmen or have large research grants have private secretaries. So professors have devised other ways of making themselves unavailable, especially to students. They can stay at home where they can keep a nice little tax-deductible study. More ingeniously, they can have unnamed office doors where only the initiated can find them. Or else they can get lost between their multiple offices. Thus a professor can belong to both an institute and a department and have an office in each; or he can abscond to the entrails of the library where he has a cozy cubicle and cannot even be reached by telephone.

Notes

1. This last category has been termed "academic Siberia," a designation unfair to Siberia, whose institutions of higher learning are undoubtedly of better quality. Perhaps one should speak of academic Alaska instead. The reader should excuse my refusal to name any schools (beyond the reference to Harvard and Berkeley), as doing so might adversely affect the sale of this book.
2. The name is meant to be fictitious, but such a place probably does exist, in which case I proffer my apologies in advance.

On the Political Science Pecking Order
Heinz Eulau

Now, among the many absurd things academics do (and do to each other), none is more absurd than the "rating" of individual scholars or whole departments on whatever it is that is being rated. We became innocently aware of this game that some colleagues play at the expense of other colleagues just twenty years ago when, to our surprise, we found ourselves in 17th place on a rank-ordered list of "immortals" or "great men" (there not being any women on the list) in political science who were said to have made their "most significant contributions" from 1945 on. This ranking, the good surveyors told us, put us in "political science's hall of fame." It sounded all very thrilling indeed, especially because we thought of ourselves, at that time as still today, as at best a minuscule speck on the stellar firmament.

What quickly sobered us was this: the documentation bore little resemblance to the hyperbolic vocabulary of the survey's authors. In the first place, we shared the 17th rank with three others at the very bottom of the list of twenty. Second, on scrutinizing the "data" more carefully, we noted that we had been named by a mere ten of our colleagues across the country, or 2.9% of the 350 respondents—nothing to write home about. Third, in the spirit of quantification to which we are addicted, we calculated a gap of almost 34% between the "vote" we had received and that given to the *capo di lista*—as it should be—the late, lovable V. O. Key, Jr. This really put us in our place. And finally, as if it had been necessary, the authors of the survey called our attention to "one of the most striking characteristics of this tabulation—the apparent lack of consensus as to the men (indeed!) who have made significant contributions to political science."

We have been told that a similar list has been composed more recently, and that we are not on it. As we are not on it, there is no need to read it. And as we have not read it, we can talk with authority about it. It is probably as absurd and nonsensical as the earlier list, on a par with those lists of the country's "ten best-dressed men" (or, in this case, also women) who serve as role models for all of us, or that mythical apparition, the "All-American College Football Team." So much for the influence of the "general culture" on the culture of our science.

. . . [W]e are sometimes amused by some of our colleagues' faith in the *Social Science Citation Index*. There, they tell us, you will really find a scholar's true market value, measurable by the number of times he/she is cited, or by the inches of displaced space. . . . Our own preferred test for judging the quality of an academic department relies on a less ambiguous criterion—the number of Mercedes-Benzes, BMWs, Volvos, or Peugeots imported and driven by a department's members. Our justification for the validity of this measure is as follows: as travel broadens one's perspective and stimulates thought, and as a scholar traveling in Europe can do so cheaper by buying a car and then bringing it home, and as such an imported car lends prestige to its owner, clearly the automotive test is both a reliable and valid measure of a department's greatness.

On the Disciplinary Pecking Order
William J. Keefe

MEMO TO: Faculty, Department of Political Science

FROM: WJK

RE: Hegemony and the Public Interest

It is with a heavy heart that I report to you the following findings taken from the summer issue of *PS*:

1972 APSA PANEL PARTICIPATION: CHAIRMEN, PAPER READERS, AND DISCUSSANTS

Michigan	28
Harvard	19
Chicago	16
MIT	16
Indiana	12
Wisconsin	12
Ohio State	11
Pittsburgh	11
Princeton	11
Texas	11

Interpreting the table:

1. Harvard, Chicago, and MIT have now drawn slightly ahead of us. (It is characteristic of aggressive, new graduate departments to place unusual emphasis on the participation of their faculties in professional meetings.)

2. Unless this trend is reversed, it is only a matter of time before other departments with rising expectations—e.g., Yale, Berkeley, Stanford, North Carolina, Columbia, Northwestern, UCLA, Minnesota—overtake us.

3. We are plainly in trouble, threatened on all sides by departments that will do anything to gain professional luster and thereby enter the ranks of that select group of prestige departments.

4. Remember that when your back is up against the wall, your shoulders against the wheel, your ears to the ground, your loins girded, and your eyes fixed firmly ahead, you are likely to feel somewhat uncomfortable. That, philosophically speaking, is the lesson to be learned from all of this.

5. This memo is in lieu of our regularly scheduled fall-winter department meeting.

A Short Note on U and Non-U in Political Science
Arnold A. Rogow

Helsinki, Finland, has many claims to distinction, not the least of which is the appearance there in 1954 of an article written by Professor Alan Ross of Birmingham University. Professor Ross's article, "Linguistic Class-Indicators in Present-Day English,"[1] argued the point that the British upper classes may be distinguished solely by their language. Professor Ross labeled such language U (upper class), and attached the label non-U to the terms and expressions extensively employed by lower elements in British society. Among examples listed by Professor Ross were non-U *cycle* for U *bike*, non-U *greens* for U *vegetable*, and non-U *wealthy* for U *rich*. In 1956 Nancy Mitford published in *Encounter* a commentary on Professor Ross's article which aroused considerable discussion here and abroad. Miss Mitford's effort served to popularize U and non-U classifications, and they continue to have a certain vogue in intellectual circles.

U and non-U distinctions may be utilized in a variety of language areas to designate usages which are, in Professor Ross's words, "correct, proper, legitimate, appropriate" from usages which are "incorrect, not proper, not legitimate." The vocabulary of political science[2] is particularly suited for such analysis. Certain terms, by common agreement, exemplify sophisticated, modern, knowledgeable usage. Other expressions fall in the category of crude, obsolete, and uninformed language. Moreover, U and non-U distinctions may be applied to individuals, institutions, publications, and orientations. Indeed, it is the premise of this short paper that political scientists can establish their status in the profession by locating themselves with reference to a variety of U and non-U designations. It is hoped that the following U and non-U distinctions will assist in such efforts.

An ear attuned to professional language can readily identify U and non-U terminology. Currently, *behavior* and *methodology* are entrenched in U vocabulary. *Symbol* is U; *word* is non-U. *Variable*, *role*, and *interaction* are U. So are *model*, especially *equilibrium model*, *matrix*, and *cell* (*cells in a matrix* is exceedingly U). *Empirical* is U, as in *empirically oriented*, whereas *value* is non-U, as in *value-oriented*. *Scale* and *scaling* are U. *System* is U; *government* is non-U. *Politics* is non-U unless preceded by *comparative* or *systematic*, whereupon it becomes very U.

Quantitative is U, against *qualitative* non-U. *Influence* is U; *power* is non-U. *Process* is as U as it can be. *Group* is non-U unless preceded by *reference*, *small*, or *interest*, in which case it is U. Only non-U persons refer to *pressure groups*. U articles feature *correlations*. *Mathematics* and *statistics* are U; *philosophy, history,* and *political journalism* are non-U (as in "He is essentially a *political journalist*."). *Sociology*, especially *political sociology*, is U. *Game theory* is ultra-U in U circles.

Academic institutions may be classified in U and non-U terms. At present, *M.I.T.* and *Northwestern* are very U. *Chicago* used to be U, then became non-U, and is now seeking to recapture U status. *Michigan State* has always been non-U, but is trying hard to be U. *Universities in the Deep South, state colleges, women's colleges,* and *denominational schools* are non-U. *Teachers' colleges* are infra-U among non-U institutions.

Bureaus of Applied Social Research and *Survey Research Centers* are U; *Governmental Research Bureaus* are non-U. The *RAND Corporation* is U, and so is the *Center for Advanced Study in the Behavioral Sciences*. The *Citizenship Clearing House* and *Pi Sigma Alpha* are non-U. The *Ford Foundation* is U; the *Eagleton Foundation* non-U. The *National Science Foundation*, which is U, has no use for political scientists no matter how U they are.

Among newspapers, *The New York Times* is U; all other newspapers are non-U. *The Reporter* is U, *The Nation* non-U. The *American Political Science Review* usually publishes articles by U people; U articles appear less frequently in the regional journals. The principal U journals are *Behavioral Science, World Politics, Journal of Conflict Resolution, Administrative Science,* and *PROD*.

U sociologists who are significant for U political scientists include *Paul F. Lazarsfeld* and *Talcott Parsons; Robert Lynd* and *C. Wright Mills* are non-U in sociology and political science. *Pareto, Michels,* and *Bentley* are U; *A. Lawrence Lowell, W.W. Willoughby,* and *Ogg and Ray* are non-U. *Max Weber* is as U as *Karl Marx* is non-U. Many political scientists acquire U status by moving to U universities; U political scientists, as a rule, do not sacrifice U rank by moving to non-U universities.

U and non-U distinctions are applicable within departments. U departments have *chairmen;* non-U departments have *heads. Research* is U, and designations which include the word *research* are U, such as *research grant, research professor, research assistant,* etc. *Teaching* and *teaching assistant* are non-U. Related terms are U *scholar,* and non-U *administrator* (as in "What we need are more *scholars* and fewer *administrators*."); U professors go on *leaves-of-absence;* non-U professors take *sabbaticals. Seminars* and *graduate students* are U; *lecture courses* and *undergraduates* are non-U. U personnel teach *advanced courses;* non-U personnel teach *introductory courses. Fellowships* are U; *internships* are non-U. Courses which meet at 10 A.M. are U courses; those which meet at 8 A.M. are non-U. The *MWF* class schedule is U. *TTS* is non-U, but *TT* is U and *T or T only* is very U. *Office* is U but *office hours* are non-U. *Study* is non-U unless it is located in the home (as in "I can't get any work done at school so I spend most of the time working at home in my *study*.") *Secretaries* are U, whereas *wives who are secretaries* are non-U.

Research orientations are susceptible to U and non-U classifications. In general, *research books and articles* are U, *textbooks* are non-U and *collections of readings* are the most non-U of all (as in "All he ever publishes are *'scissors-and-paste'* jobs."). *Small group research* is U; *large group research* is non-U. U research publications present *hypotheses*; non-U research publications report *findings*. Books which *examine the role of elites* are written by U political scientists. Books which are *critical of the role of elites* are written by non-U political scientists. On the other hand, books which are *critical of reform and radical movements* are U books; books which *propose reforms and radical changes* are non-U. *Free Press* books are U books; books published by *Henry Regnery* are non-U (and frequently anti-U). *Novels* are non-U, especially *novels by political scientists*.

Politicians favored by U individuals are *Stevenson, Humphrey,* and *Rockefeller*. Politicians who are non-U are *Kennedy, Symington,* and *Lyndon Johnson*. *Nixon* is non-U for both U and non-U political scientists. The only U labor leader is *Reuther*, although some U people have some non-U *affection* for *Harry Bridges*. The differing behaviors of U and non-U personalities are conspicuous at the annual meetings of the American Political Science Association. U individuals tend to associate with U individuals and meet privately in hotel rooms. They rarely appear at *panel* (U, as opposed to *roundtable* non-U) meetings unless they are scheduled to give papers. Political scientists who are non-U occupy most of the chairs at these

meetings, frequent publishers' cocktail parties, and are fond of celebrating their graduate student days at breakfast reunions. U people habitually attend APSA meetings in Washington and New York, but seldom attend meetings elsewhere.

Our short sketch of U and non-U usage cannot claim to be definitive. But it is hoped that this initial venture will encourage efforts to sharpen the designations and distinctions which have been presented. Such efforts certainly should contribute to the continuing effort to appraise the state of the discipline with special reference to its major focus and interests.

Notes

1. Non-U.
2. U.

References

Mitford, Nancy. 1956. In Nancy Mitford (ed.), *Noblesse Oblige: An Enquiry into the Identifiable Characteristics of the English Aristocracy*. London: H. Hamilton.

Ross, Alan. 1956. "Linguistic Class-Indicators in Present-Day English." In Nancy Mitford (ed.), *Noblesse Oblige: An Enquiry into the Identifiable Characteristics of the English Aristocracy*. London: H. Hamilton.

Rotisserie Political Science

Kenneth J. Meier and Joseph Stewart, Jr.

Rotisserie games have grown up around most major sports—football, baseball, basketball—why not political science? The basic principle behind rotisserie games is that armchair athletes can get vicarious thrills by selecting players who perform well in real games. Although the rules vary, the game usually begins with each game player drafting a given number of players (henceforth designated "athletes") who participate in that sport. Game players are awarded or lose points for the performance of their chosen athletes that week. For example, a running back in football gets points for touchdowns but loses points for fumbles. The game player selects a group of athletes from those he/she[1] has drafted; these athletes are designated to play that week. Game players then receive points for all the athletes they own who play that week. The player whose athletes amass the largest number of points is the winner. An entry fee is usually charged, and weekly and season winners are awarded cash prizes.

The most difficult part of rotisserie games is devising the point system for the athletes. Below is our point system for Rotisserie Political Science (RPS). Because political science does not have natural seasons similar to most other sports, we have arbitrarily declared that a political science season shall be of 12 months' duration beginning on January 1. Points are awarded only for activities during that calendar year, although, as detailed later, some awards may be given for multiyear performance. Otherwise, points cannot be carried over into another season.

The Point System

RPS points shall be awarded in four categories: (1) publication, (2) convention participation, (3) professional development, and (4) assisting in the professional development of others.

Publications

Points for publications are awarded in the year in which the manuscripts are accepted, not in the year in which the publication appears in print. For book authors, "accepted for publication" means when the author receives the page proofs.[2] Because the value of various outlets differs, points for publication will differ as follows:

Articles. The "coin of the realm" in most research-oriented political science departments is acceptance in a peer-reviewed journal.

Points	Activity
+15	Article accepted by the APSR
+10	Article accepted by AJPS, JoP, WPQ, or SSQ[3]
+5	Article accepted by a refereed journal not listed above
-2	Article accepted in which Greek letters outnumber English letters

An apparently necessary but not sufficient condition for getting an article accepted is the coveted "revise and resubmit." Because smart editors do not dispense revise and resubmits unless there is a greater than .5 probability of eventually publishing the work, these indicate quality work on the part of the recipient. Revise and resubmits receive the following points:

Points	Revise and Resubmit at
+6	APSR
+3	AJPS, JoP, WPQ, or SSQ
+1	Another refereed journal not listed
0	*Public Administration Review* (unless the person actually resubmits the manuscript, in which case: -7)

Because there is no free lunch and to prevent RPS players from drafting individuals who subscribe to the "blind hog" theory of publication[4] (you know who you are), there are also penalty points for rejected manuscripts

Points	Article Rejected at.
-4	*APSR*
-2	*AJPS, JoP, WPQ,* or *SSQ*
-1	Another refereed journal not listed
+2	*Presidential Studies Quarterly*

The penalty for rejection is doubled if the author (1) has previously had the manuscript rejected, (2) submits the manuscript to another journal without changes, and (3) has the editor send the manuscript to a referee who recommended rejection at the first journal.

Additional article publication points are awarded for the following:

Points	Activity
+3	Having a funny title
+1	Saying something funny in a footnote
-1	Making up the page numbers in a citation
-6	Citing yourself incorrectly, aka "The David Nice Rule"
+65	Sending a birthday card to your manuscript if it has been under review at a journal for a year, aka "The Kathy Kemp Rule"

Citations to an author's work also contribute points:

Points	Activity
+1	For every 10 citations to previously published work in the *Social Science Citation Index*
-1	For every citation to previously published work in the *Social Science Citation Index* if the citation is a self-citation

Book Publishing. The point system for books follows the general logic of article publication with the following points:

Points	Activity
+20	Book accepted by a major university press[5]
+10	Book accepted by a minor university press
+5	Book accepted by a commercial press
-2	Book accepted by a commercial press which goes out of business after accepting, but before publishing, your book
-8	Book published by a university press which then decides to quit publishing in political science (The University of Tennessee Press Rule)

The Tedium Rule of Book Publishing: The practical difference between a political science article and a political science book is that it is much harder to stay awake for an entire book. The tedium rule seeks to correct that problem. Books should be limited to no more than 250 pages including index, bibliography, etc. To enforce this rule, authors will be penalized one point for every 10 pages beyond 250 pages in their book. Thus, a 300-page book would earn a deduction of five points from whatever total is otherwise earned by the publication.

Additional book points:

Points	Activity
+6	The book wins an award
+2	The book is issued in hard cover
+2	The hard cover edition has a dust jacket
+1	For every $1 under $20 in the list price of the paperback edition
+5--5	The cover or dust jacket includes the author's picture. In such cases, the author's picture will be rated by Lee Sigelman (for females) or his infamous unnamed "middle-aged woman who has an inordinate fondness of looking at pictures of men" (for males) on the Sigelman Ugliness—"Yummie to Yecch" Scale.[6]
-3	The book is published without an index

Points can also be earned by having your book reviewed. The following points are awarded for reviews of your book even if the book was published in an earlier year.[7]

Points	Event
+1	For each review of the book that appears
-4	The reviewer misspells the author's name
+6	The book is panned in *Public Choice*

Reviewing Books. Reviewing books is perhaps more important than writing books. Were it not for book reviews, some journals would not be read at all. The following points are awarded for book reviews:

Points	Activity
+2	Reviewing a book
+1	Reviewing a book but saying only positive things about it
+4	Reviewing a book if the author responds in the next issue
+1	Relating humourous incidents about the author in the review

Convention Participation

Program Division. Publications, like athletes, often appear in tryout camps before they are called up to "The Show." To recognize the political scientists who are building a strong farm system, points are awarded for convention participation in three categories: (1) the program division—for those on the official program, (2) the audience division, and (3) the networking division. Program points are awarded for the following activities:

Points	Activity
+4	Presenting a paper
-1	If no one in the audience addresses a question to the paper giver
-2	Actually reading the paper to the panel/audience
-3	Presenting a paper without a dependent variable
-5	Presenting a paper and not knowing if there is a dependent variable

Just as books can be tedious, so too can paper presentations. The tedium rule for convention programs provides for a 1-point deduction for each minute over 15 that the presentation lasts. Presentations over 40 minutes in length also carry a one-year suspension from accruing any other program division points.

Other Conference Program points:

Points	Activity
+6	Winning the best paper award
-12	Winning the best paper award if the person was on the best paper award committee

Points	Activity
+3	As a discussant, discovering a non-trivial thread linking all of the panel's papers
-3	Failing to pre-register
-10	As a discussant, ignoring the papers presented and presenting the paper you wanted to present, the proposal for which was rejected before you were stuck being a discussant.
-15	Failing to show up at your own panel, aka "The David Brady Rule #1"

Attendance Division. Attendance at panels is dropping at the same time participation on the official program is rising. Obviously the incentives to attend panels on which one is not a participant are insufficient to induce people to sit through three papers and two discussants. To correct this problem, RPS offers points for attendance at program functions.

Points	Activity
+1	For each panel attended other than the one upon which one is a participant, with the following bonuses:
+2	Staying for the entire panel
+4	Appearing on time if the panel is held at 8:45 AM
+6	Staying for the entire panel even if one is in the wrong room
+1	Asking a question of one of the panel members
-2	Identifying yourself before asking a question (if you are that important, people will already know who you are)
-12	Taking more than two minutes to ask a question

The Non-Program Bonus Rule: Any person earning points in the attendance division who is not listed on the official program (other than those who are not listed because of a failure to pre-register) will have those points doubled.

Networking Division. Conventions are not just for presenting research or listening to papers. Conventions are major networking events that can further the careers of political scientists. All political scientists want to be one of that elite group of individuals in the discipline whose "reputation exceeds his/her vita." Networking points are awarded for the following:

Points	Activity
+2	Buy a convention paper (limit of four points total)
-3	Buy a copy of your own paper
-6	Steal a convention paper from the paper room
+10	Attend the *JoP* editorial board breakfast meeting, eat breakfast, and leave before the meeting starts if you are not on the editorial board, aka "The Tom Dye Rule"

Points	Activity
-1	Wear your nametag outside the convention hotel
+1	Interview a candidate for job (limit of three points)
+2	Interview a candidate for a funded job (limit of six points total)
+2	Scout out a free cocktail party (unlimited points)
+2	Discuss a scholarly book with an editor
+1	Attend the business meeting
+9	Say something funny at the business meeting
-3	Say something serious at the business meeting
-16	Fail to attend the business meeting if you [are] an association officer, aka "The David Brady Rule #2"
+1	Have your name appear in *PS* (other than on the preliminary program of the APSA)
+2	Have a regular photo appear in *PS*
+8	Have your obituary appear in *PS* if you are not dead
-10	Ask a journal editor if a decision has been made on your manuscript
-15	Underreport income to get lower APSA dues

Professional Development

Professional development is a category where milestones and millstones in a political scientist's career are recognized. Points are awarded for the following:

Points	Activity
+8	Receiving an endowed chair
+2	Getting a fancy title without any endowment
+6	Promotion to full professor[8]
+4	Receiving tenure
-2	Being named department chair
-12	Being denied tenure
-17	Being named a dean

Assisting the Professional Development of Others

Political scientists not only should try to further their own careers, but also to develop the skills of other political scientists. To recognize such altruism, coauthor points are awarded as follows:

Points	If your coauthor is:
+6	a graduate student
+9	a graduate student who is smarter than you are (you probably don't

	know who you are)
+3	an assistant professor
+1	an associate or full professor
-3	Paul Sabatier

Other altruistic activities merit points. These include:

Points	Activity
+3	Reviewing a person for tenure or promotion
+6	Reviewing a person for tenure or promotion with less than 30 days lead time
+1	Writing a letter of recommendation (one point per recommendee)
+4	Writing a letter of recommendation, but signing someone else's name (points are doubled if you use the actual stationery of the person whose name you sign)
+1	Reviewing a manuscript for a journal
-6	Suggesting in a manuscript review that the author cite your work
+9	When reviewing a manuscript, reanalyzing the author's data and getting better results

Game Options

Game players will have to make a wide variety of decisions. The initial distribution of athletes will occur by a draft in which all political scientists are available for an RPS team. Say you have the first draft choice. Should you take Lee Sigelman or Bernie Grofman? Trades will also be allowed. For example, another game player might offer you Susan MacManus in exchange for David Brady and Ron Weber.

Some will be upset because we have taken no notice of differences in fields. There are two ways to do this. First, a game could be defined so that participants must field a team of 10 that includes one political scientist each from specified fields: theory, international relations, comparative politics (area studies), comparative politics (cross-national studies), voting behavior, political institutions, and political methodology—with three other political scientists chosen from any field in an attempt to create an advocacy coalition (Sabatier 1988).[9]

Second, games could be designed so that all political scientists in the draft pool are from the same field. For example, there could be a game with only public administration specialists (for those who like low-scoring games). Specialized games could have specialized rules. For example, in the comparative politics (area studies division) game, a political scientist could get bonus points if her country is covered on the front page of the *New York Times* but lose points if the country ceases to exist.

How We Plan to Make Big Bucks on This Game

We have put more thought into ways that we, and you—the game players—can make big bucks on this game. One strategy would be to negotiate incentive clauses in your contracts. For example, you might negotiate a $1,000 bonus if you earn more than 300 points in RPS in a year.

The really big bucks will, as usual, be made in merchandising. First, we shall be introducing political scientist playing cards. In addition to making us money, these cards will provide data on individual players for use in drafting a team. One side will have the traditional snapshot of the political scientist, and the obverse will include at least five years' worth of RPS statistics. There should even be room for catchy tidbits such as "Chuck Bullock has led the University of Georgia in article points for five straight years."

The logical extension of player cards is to publish an RPS book. The book would present career statistics and permit the authors to reveal juicy items about political scientists. For example, "Tom Mann has successfully made the transition from German novelist to congressional specialist." "Ken Meier received a low pass on his public administration prelim exams in graduate school. This is a sad commentary on either Ken or public administration or both." "Jim Campbell was having a great year last year until he suffered a rotator cuff tear in his theory at the Midwest meetings. Jim is likely to miss all of next year."

To further promote the game and make money, we shall give awards, appropriately subsidized by major corporations, for game players who have notable years. The political scientist scoring the most RPS points will be awarded the Ft. Howard Paper and Pulp Recycling Co. Most Valuable Player Award. The Waste Management, Inc. Rookie of the Year Award will be awarded to the first-year RPS player with the highest score. We have tentatively lined up corporate sponsorship for several other awards: the Dow Chemical Award for the highest scoring player in the Peace Studies division; the Tammy Faye Bakker Award for the highest scoring player in the Religion and Politics division; the Duncan Yo-Yo Award for the player with the largest standard deviation in annual points amassed over a five-year period; and the Chrysler Corp. Comeback Player of the Year Award for the player achieving the largest positive change in team point totals from one season to the next. These awards will be conferred at a banquet where we will be charging each of you money to attend at the same time that a corporate sponsor will be paying all expenses.

Once the methodology for rating political scientists is accepted, a futures market can be created. For example, if you have a good team drafted for 1993 and have cash left over, you could buy a futures contract on, say, Robert Salisbury. Assume that Professor Salisbury has a futures price of 625 RPS points. If you think he will perform better than 625 in 1993, you would purchase a futures contract on Salisbury. If you think he will do worse, sell him short.

Space limitations prevent us from listing all of our ideas about how we can make big bucks from this game. If you think of any, drop us a note. We own the copyright on the game, but we are happy to license moneymaking extensions for a modest fee. We have no objection to others getting rich off the idea as long as we get a piece of the action.

Notes

1. It is a sexist myth that all rotisserie players are male. One of the authors knows the female accountant who won the 1984 Arthur Anderson rotisserie football league by selecting athletes who looked good from the rear. While this is unlikely to be a good decision rule for political scientists, it does point out that intuitive strategies are often as good as rational strategies in rotisserie games.

2. This rule is obviously targeted toward individuals whose major writing activity appears to be signing contracts to write books, but never quite getting around to writing the books.

3. If you do not know what these initials mean, you should not be playing the game.

4. This theory—often pronounced "blind hawg"—holds that even a blind hog finds an acorn "ever' now and then." Its adherents flood the desks of journal editors with manuscripts on the presumption that with enough attempts, by random chance, one will be accepted. To these people, a .01 level of significance takes on a whole new meaning. Practitioners of this theory seldom get anything published but use any success as evidence of the validity of the theory.

5. Major university presses are those associated with major universities. Major universities are designated by the Engstrom Rule, which holds: "The quality of a university is inversely related to the number of colors on the university's stationery." Major university presses, therefore, are those associated with universities that have only one color of ink on plain white stationery.

6. For a fuller explication and an application of this scale, see Sigelman (1990).

7. It is wishful thinking to expect your book to be reviewed in the same year it is published (or perhaps even the next one).

8. This title is commonly mispronounced. It should be pronounced as if it were spelled "fool professor."

9. Paul contends that we do not cite his work enough. Accordingly, we have resolved to add one gratuitous cite to Paul's work in everything we write. This is it.

References

Cronin, Thomas E. 1991. "On Celebrating College Teaching." *PS: Political Science & Politics* 24: 482–91.

Sabatier, Paul A. 1988. "An Advocacy Coalition Framework of Policy Change and the Role of Policy-Oriented Learning Therein." *Policy Sciences* 21: 129–68.

Sigelman, Lee. 1990. "Toward a Stupidity-Ugliness Theory of Democratic Election Debacles." *PS: Political Science & Politics* 23: 18–20.

Perfecting the Pecking Order
James C. Scott and Matthew A. Light

> Louisa had been overheard to begin a conversation with her brother one day, by saying, 'Tom, I wonder'—upon which Mr. Gradgrind, who was the person overhearing, stepped into the light and said, 'Louisa, never wonder.'
>
> Herein lay the spring of the mechanical art and mystery of educating the reason, without stooping to the cultivation of the sentiments and affections. Never wonder. By means of addition, subtraction, multiplication, and division, settle everything somehow, and never wonder. —Charles Dickens, *Hard Times*

The year is 2020. Richard Levin has just retired after a long and brilliant career as President of Yale and has declared this "2020 The Year of Perfect Vision." Every last building is rebuilt and shining, the students are even more precocious, accomplished and unionized than they are today, *US News and World Report and Consumer Report* (now merged) has ranked Yale University Number 1 across the board—up there with the very best hotels, luxury automobiles and lawnmowers. Well, . . . nearly across the board. It seems that the quality of the faculty, as reflected in the all-important rankings, has slipped. Yale's competitors are shaking their heads at the decline. Those who know how to read between the lines of apparently serene "Yale Corporation" pronouncements can detect a rising, but, of course, still decorous, panic.

One sign of concern can be read from the selection of President Levin's successor, Condoleezza Rice, the retired Secretary of State who most recently led a no-nonsense, business-like, streamlining of the Ford Foundation. President Rice was chosen for the promise she represented: the promise of leading a thoroughgoing restructuring of the faculty using the most advanced quality-management techniques: techniques perfected from the crude beginnings the Grandes Ecoles of Paris in the late nineteenth century, embodied in Robert MacNamara's revolution in the Department of Defense in the 1960s, Margaret Thatcher's managerial revolution in British social policy and higher education in the 1980s, further developed by the World Bank, and brought to near perfection, so far as higher education is concerned, by the Big Ten universities and making its way, belatedly, to the Ivy League.

We know, from confidential sources among the members of the Yale Corporation, how she captivated them in her "job interview." It was her comprehensive plan for massively improving the quality of the faculty—or, more accurately, for improving its standing in the national rankings—that convinced the Corporation that she was the answer to their prayers.

She excoriated Yale's antiquated practices of hiring, promoting and tenuring faculty. They were, she said, subjective, medieval, unsystematic, capricious and arbitrary. These customs, jealously guarded by the ageing—largely white male—Mandarins of the faculty, whose average age now hovered around 80, were, she claimed, responsible for Yale's loss of ground to the competition. They produced, on the one hand, a driven, insecure, junior faculty who had no way of knowing what the criteria of success and promotion were beyond the tastes and prejudices of the seniors in their department and, on the other hand, a self-satisfied, unproductive, oligarchy of gerontocrats heedless of the long-run interests of the institution.

Her plan, our sources tell us, was beguilingly simple. She proposed using the scientific techniques of quality evaluation employed elsewhere in the academy, but to implement them, for the first time, in a truly comprehensive and transparent fashion. The scheme hinged on the Citation Indices: The Arts and Humanities Citation Index, the Social Science Citation Index and the granddaddy of them all, the Science Citation Index. Sure, these counts of how often one's work was cited by others in the field were consulted from time to time in promotion reviews, but as President Rice, she proposed to make this form of objective evaluation systematic and comprehensive. The citation indices, she stressed, like the machine counting of votes, play no favorites; they are incapable of conscious or unconscious bias; they represent the only impersonal metric for judgments of academic distinction. They would henceforth be the sole criterion for promotion and tenure. If she succeeded in breaking tenure, it would also serve as a basis for automatically dismissing tenured faculty whose sloth and dimness prevented them from achieving annual citation norms (ACN for short).

In keeping with the neo-liberal emphasis on transparency, full public disclosure and objectivity, President Rice proposed a modern, high-tech, academic version of Robert Owens's factory scheme at New Lanark. The entire faculty is to be outfitted with digitalized beanies. As soon as they are designed—in Yale's distinctive blue and white—and can be manufactured under humane, non-sweatshop conditions, all faculty will be required to wear them on campus. The front of the beanie, across the forehead, will consist in a digital screen, rather like a taxi-meter, on which will be displayed the total citation count of that scholar in real time. As the fully automated citation recording centers register new citations, these citations, conveyed by satellite, will be posted automatically to the digital read-out on the beanie. Think of a miniature version of the constantly updated world population count once available in lights in Times Square. Let's call it Public Record of Digitally Underwritten Citation Totals (PRODUCT, for short). Rice conjures a vision of the thrill students would experience as they listened, rapt, to the lecture of a brilliant and renowned professor whose beanie, while she lectured, was constantly humming, the total citations piling up before their very eyes. Meanwhile, in a nearby classroom, students worry as they contemplate the blank readout on the beanie of the embarrassed professor before them. How will their transcript look when the cumulative citation total of all the professors from whom they have taken courses is compared with the cumulative total of their competitors for graduate or professional school? Have they studied with the best and brightest?

Students will no longer have to rely on the fallible hearsay evidence of their friends or the prejudices of a course critique. The numerical "quality grade" of their instructor will be there for all to see, and to judge. Junior faculty will no longer need to fear the caprice of their senior colleagues. A single, indisputable standard of achievement will, like a batting average, provide a measure of quality and an unambiguous target for ambition. For President Rice, the system solves the perennial problem of how to reform departments that languish in the backwaters of their disciplines and become bastions of narrow patronage. This publicly accountable, transparent, impersonal measure of professional standing shall henceforth be used, in place of promotion and hiring committees.

Think of the clarity! A blue-ribbon panel of distinguished faculty (chosen by the new criterion) will simply establish several citation plateaux: one for renewal, one for promotion to term associate, one for tenure and one for post-tenure performance. After that, the process will be entirely automated once the beanie technology is perfected. Imagine a much-quoted, pace-setting Political Science Professor, Harvey Writealot, lecturing to a packed hall. Suddenly, because an obscure scholar in Arizona has just quoted his last article in the *Journal of Recent Recondite Research (RRR)* and, by chance, that very quote is the one that puts him over the top, the beanie instantly responds by flashing the good news in blue and white and playing Boola-Boola. The students, realizing what has happened, rise to applaud their professor's elevation. He bows modestly, pleased and embarrassed by the fuss, and continues the lecture—but now with tenure. The console on the desk of President Rice's office in Woodbridge Hall tells her that Harvey has "made it" into the magic circle on his own merits and she, in turn, sends him a message of congratulations broadcast through the beanie by text and voice. A new, distinctive, "tenure-beanie" and certificate will follow shortly.

Members of the Corporation, understanding instantly how much time and disputation this automated system could save and how it could catapult Yale back into the faculty-ratings chase, set about refining and perfecting the technique. One suggested having a time-elapse system of citation depreciation; each year's citations will lose one-eighth of their value with each passing year. An eight-year-old citation evaporates in keeping with the pace of field development. Reluctantly, one member of the Corporation suggested that, for consistency, there be a minimal plateau for retention, even of previously tenured faculty. She acknowledged that the image of a bent professor's citation total degrading to the dismissal level in the middle of a seminar is a sad spectacle to contemplate; another suggested that the beanie, in this case, could simply be programmed to go completely blank, though one imagines the professor could read his fate in the averted gaze of his students.

Practice of Political Science: On Journal and Research Monograph Publishing

The Compleat Jargoner: How to Obfuscate the Obvious Without Half Trying

Betty H. Zisk

In the formative years of our Discipline, eminent scholars (e.g., Socrates) devoted themselves to the professional guidance of neophytes. The tradition was nurtured by men like Aquinas, Rousseau and the senior Mill. Considerable effort was made to inculcate in the young a sense of the appropriate skills and behavior necessary for professional acceptance. The advent of the Great Triumvirate (Rice, Bentley and Weber) signaled, however, the diversion of our resources into other channels. With little advance warning, the "spooks" were exorcised; the teacher-scholar replaced the inculcation of Orthodoxy with the quest for reliability.

A valiant few have tried, since that fateful era, to revitalize the pedagogical effort.[1] One seminal work in this tradition, Arnold Rogow's (1960) "A Short

Magic Words for Political Scientists

Rules— Choose any 3-digit number. (A table of random numbers may be utilized if needed.) Find the corresponding acceptable professional phrase by locating the relevant number in each column. You now need only a few verbs, gerundives and disclaimers, and your article is complete. Example: 123 = latent empirical parameters.

Column 1	Column 2	Column 3
0. valid	0. systematic	0. role(s)
1. latent	1. isomorphic	1. paradigm(s)
2. explicit	2. empirical	2. program(ming)
3. proximate	3. analytical	3. parameter(s)
4. parasymmetric	4. theoretically-significant	4. typology(ies)
5. comparative	5. dynamic	5. conceptualization
6. quasi-	6. longitudinal	6. assumption(s)
7. value-neutral	7. operational	7. orientation(s)
8. hypothesized	8. policy-oriented	8. variable(s)
9. tentative	9. functional	9. inter-relationship

NOTE: Scholars in potential riot areas may wish to substitute the following for one row of the above: 9-a. relevant, 9-a Black, 9-a confrontation.

Note on U and Non-U in Political Science," appeared in 1960. Rogow's study, however, did not attract the scholarly attention it deserved. The need—indeed, this major hiatus in our Discipline—might have gone forever unheeded, had it not been for the recent insights of Philip Broughton of the U.S. Public Health Service. Broughton's landmark study, "How to Win at Wordsmanship: The Systematic Buzz Phrase Projector" (Broughton 1968) is addressed primarily to government employees. The core concept is elegant: the key to successful exposition is the well-chosen complex phrase. The means (utilization of thirty carefully-researched "buzz words") are relatively easy to master. The applicability of this work to our Discipline is obvious: an analogous list of scholarly terms could assure the apprentice author of public and scholarly acclaim. It has been our modest task to compile such a list. We believe, however, that widespread replication of our work is necessary, and an exploration of the possibility of utilizing computers for generating additional words is now under way, if adequate funding can be obtained.[2]

The hypothesized dynamic orientation (857) of this tentative systematic typology (904) is obvious. Our purpose is to help the fledgling author to play a valid functional role (090) which takes into account all latent isomorphic variables (118). In addition, one explicit operational assumption (276) is the lack of a contradiction between this value-neutral empirical program (722) and a quasi–policy-oriented conceptualization (685).

Notes

1. A few have made the effort, however, through example rather than by injunction. See especially the contributions of Talcott Parsons and Herbert Marcuse.

2. We would welcome communications from other scholars. We have not been able to take into account the inter-regional variations in etymological salience, nor have we yet extended the effort to the rich cross-national context. With adequate foundation support, these next steps may be possible in the near future.

References

Broughton, Philip. 1968. "How to Win at Wordsmanship: The Systematic Buzz Phrase Projector." *Newsweek* (May 8): 104.

Rogow, Arnold. 1960. "A Short Note on U and Non-U in Political Science," *Western Political Quarterly* 13: 1064–66.

About the Title of Your Dissertation
P.S. Ruckman, Jr., and Patrick A. Stewart, Jr.

An association of scholar-wanna-be's from Illinois recently met to consider the "colon principle." The "principle" asserts dissertation authors aspiring to be taken seriously appear to be convinced that the title of their work must include the use of a colon (we note the radiating effect of the principle with respect to conference papers, especially those that are re-hashed versions of previous conference papers). Our repeated (three) searches of dissertation titles in *PS: Political Science* confirmed the veracity of the "principle" again and again.

We considered constructing a multivariate turbobit model of colon use (a mathematical modeling technique created by Mr. Stewart as a result of his understandable disgust with the all too familiar shortcomings of logit, probit, tobit and scobit), but a severe lack of variance rendered the project abruptly silly. Nonetheless, we have little doubt that such a model—had we bothered to construct it—would have explained a minimum of 103.7 percent of the variance in dissertation titles. In sum, we judge the colon norm as firmly entrenched as many other primary academic norms (e.g., citing one's own work—regardless of its relevance, ignoring the work of members of the profession who offend you—regardless of its relevance, holding a pen in your hand while your work is being "discussed" at a panel, nodding your head and pretending to write the comments of your discussant when she/he has said something patently ridiculous, using the word "interesting" as a panel chair or discussant).

We are, of course, bothered by the complete lack of published research on dissertation titles in general. The dissertation title is, after all, the only portion of the dissertation that is likely to be carefully read by readers of *PS: Political Science & Politics*, potential employers, friends and relatives at the graduation ceremony and second and third field committee members.

Rampant inattention with respect to the correlates of colon employment has, however, prompted us ponder a manner in which to assist the advanced graduate student. Even Uncle Wuffle fails to address this critical issue. In an effort to raise colon consciousness, we compiled a list of items which we feel constitute an impressive array of words, phrases or symbols that one does not want to follow the colon in one's dissertation title.

Myth? or Fiction?
Who Could Ever Know?
The Effect of the 1964 Civil Rights Act on 1958 School Desegregation Policy
How Attitudes Could Not Possibly Predict Behavior

An Analysis of Two Scatterplots

A Comparison of Trueman, Eastman, and Doll

Putting the "Histo" Back Into Histogram

The Misplaced Emphasis on Theory

Patterns of Emotional Responses to Rational Choice Theories

A New Cure for Outliers

A Factor Analysis of Chaos

A Skeptical View of the Idiots Who Do Critical Analysis

Coding Schmoding!

The Effects of Bribery on Inter-coder Reliability

The Overestimated Effects of Missing Data on Small N's

Does Political Efficacy Matter?

A Recursive Model of Congressional Communication with Constituents

How Political Culture Determines the Scope of Natural Disasters

What God Thinks about Homoskedasticity

Does the Extensive Utilization of Polysyllabic Phraseological Embellishment Ornamentation and Phonetic Adornment Exacerbate Attention Deficit Disorder and Have Empirical Consequence for the Validity of a Survey Instrument?

Theorists Who Run With the Methodologists, and the Community Colleges That Hire Them

A Dichotomous Model of U.S. Citizenship in Kansas

A Reevaluation of My Previous Thoughts

The Evil Consequences of Normative Analysis

How the Replicability Criterion Maintains the Bourgeoisie

A Focus Group Perspective on Groupthink

A Content Analysis of Deconstructionist Literature

Is Covariance Really All That Necessary?

How Co-authorship Affects R^2

An Unusual Zero-Order Bivariate Relationship

Divine Intervention as a Pulse or Step Function

Non-recursive, or Just Simple Two-Way Causation?

We recognize, of course, that this list—while exhausting—is not exhaustive. And we certainly encourage further research in this generally overlooked area of concern. More importantly, we hope that this piece will be cited and no one will particularly notice (or raise specific concerns about) the additional three lines which this publication will contribute to our vitas.

Semantics and Symbioses: How to Write an Article to Impress Your Peers

Marleen Boudreau Flory

Recent Ph.D.'s who have just begun to write articles for publication may be ignorant of secrets well known to experienced and established scholars. The following set of guidelines is meant to help these young ignoramuses, who may have the outdated notion that scholarly articles ought to have interesting theses, be clearly written, and present new ideas. Young scholars who foolishly persist in such thinking had better start filling out applications to law school.

The title

Try to hide the subject of your article from the reader. After all, you don't even know him; why should you help him? Use obscure language. Make the title as long as possible. Abstract nouns with qualifying adjectives are particularly suitable: "Semantic Differentiation and Symbolic Symbioses in the Tragedies of Shakespeare" (for an article about the conjunction "and").

Hyphens tend to impress: "Pre-pubescent and Post-adolescent Emotion-centralization"—and, of course, they have the virtue of confusing your reader further. References to chronology—or any use of numbers —give the impression of a rigorously scientific and accurate work to follow: "Fourteen and a Half Instances of 'but' in the Manuscripts of Shakespeare's So-called Early January Letters of January 1–2, 1594."

A title might also include the word "re-examination," or, for those interested in a slightly dry and witty note, "again": "A Re-examination of Conjunctive Copula in Some Lost Medieval Manuscripts of Euripides," or "Homer's Iliad, Book 14, Line 242, Again." Be careful of punctuation; a question mark here alters the tone altogether.

Such titles point out your scholarly acumen in recognizing the need to look again at long-established conclusions. This is a particularly productive approach to publication, as you can "re-examine" to your heart's content without needing to change any of the old conclusions. Articles of this sort should always end: "And so we see that Lord's theory is probably correct after all."

The footnotes

Footnotes are far more important than the text of the article. All your readers will read the footnotes, but only a few the article itself. Put the first footnote at the end of the first sentence (although more experienced and confident scholars will try to put it at the end of the title). Ideally, the first page should have only a single sentence printed on it, as the footnote should fill the rest of the page.

The first footnote is especially useful for fawning on the famous, most of whom you need not know. Thank everyone you have ever met or heard of who writes on your subject—prehistoric faucet spigots from the upper Nile delta.

You can praise those who could potentially help you in your career for "the inspiration of a monumental (or seminal or ground-breaking or epoch-making)" article or book on Nilotic spigots. Thank the old graduate school professor who gave you "the courage to pursue the complex subject of faucet spigots in the first place." Never forget to add: "But, of course, for all the many mistakes of judgment in this article I alone am responsible." Heaven help your career if a reviewer calls you "Bluffenwoofer's student" in an unfavorable review. But never thank your wife or husband, who survived three years of your moodiness in a basement apartment in New Haven, living on spaghetti and climbing over stacks of spigots. Spouses should be mentioned only in a foreign language in the dedication of a book and never by name: "A ma femme tres sympathique."

The first footnote should include a summary of all prior work on spigots. It is important to destroy the validity of other scholarly work in order to validate your own, and to represent yourself as having read every word ever published on the subject (when, of course, you have not).

The use of "important" and the abbreviation "e.g." solve both problems neatly. Simply write: "Important earlier works on faucet spigots include, e.g., Hans Wassermann's 'Der Faucet-Spigot Problem der Nilotische Delta.'" This is the best opportunity to destroy a scholar whose book has really said all that needs to be said on spigots; by focusing on a single detail: "Wassermann's dating of the first period of development from 1131 B.C. to 1050 B.C., when Ringklinger's work has shown the later date must be 1055 B.C., casts doubt on the credibility of his whole work" (which extends to 900 pages).

Subsequent footnotes are also the place for personal attacks on other scholars, because you need to back up your point of view in the text with facts and an argument, but not in the footnotes. There, you can say with impunity: "I pass over the absurd theorizing of Klingerhelften," or "No serious scholar accepts the rather peculiar ideas of Belle Aquario that spigots were smeared with raspberry juice and buried on the night of the full moon."

The savagery of the attack increases in proportion to the excellence of the work: "Perhaps Wassermann had better review basic chronology if he believes what he writes about the relative chronology of ovoid to 'beaked type' spigots." Show that the lack of rigor in scholarly publications on your subject has driven you to an emotional outburst: "And to think that the study of spigot chronology is supposed to encourage clear thinking!" Vocabulary matters here, and the scholar might well memorize the following important words and phrases: "thinly argued," "jejune," "palpably absurd," "embarrassingly unsubstantiated."

Don't allow your reader to follow the footnotes easily. Constantly crisscross references: "See footnote 19 above and also footnote 32 below." Refer to a very important book or article in the footnotes by the abbreviation *op. cit. supra.* But cannily omit the first reference.

A certain modesty is expected of young scholars, but use your apology for not having consulted esoteric material to make yourself look even more scholarly: "I regret my inability to consult 'Early Tibetan Faucet Spigots' in *Folk Chronicles of Early Tibet* (1743) in the Lo-Herpa monastery because of the death of my Sherpa guide in an avalanche."

Finally, justify your ignorance of subjects and fields other than your own by condemning all other scholarship as "trendy," or, if it is cross-disciplinary, "superficial": "Dunhoffer's Pulitzer Prize–winning book, *Faucets and Folklore*, is a slick and trendy overview. The pictures, however, are of some interest."

The article

If the title and the footnotes have the "right look," almost any text will do. Probably no one will read it, but here are some general hints just in case. It is central to success to make the article as difficult to read as possible as soon as possible. One tactic is to begin with a 30- to 40-line quotation in a foreign language. German script is excellent for this purpose if your editor will agree. Another is to have the first pages contain a dozen statistical tables. Yet another is to start the discussion with a subject totally unrelated to the apparent topic suggested by your title (insofar as the reader has been able to decipher it).

A study of the chronology of Nilotic spigots could begin, "Many Renaissance poets found in the starting and stopping of water a symbolic mod for the beginning and end of life." It takes some pages to get back to faucets from here, and the advantage is that your reader is not only puzzled but also dimly believes that your study has some broader significance. Most readers think articles are good in proportion to their inability to understand them.

The first paragraph should also make a grandiose claim, if possible: "A new look at Egyptian chronology and history has been long needed." It must be written in the impersonal passive voice, however, so that you cannot be held culpable for not doing what you propose.

Style is important. Remember that the real purpose of the style you choose is to help you protect yourself. Write everything you can in the passive voice: "When 15 Bronze Age spigots were excavated and subjected to chemical analysis, they unfortunately dissolved." Obviously, some fool in the laboratory mixed the chemicals incorrectly, but no one can blame you. Use style to elevate the mundane to the arcane. Many words ending in "tion" help here: "The centralization and quantification of spigot production and distribution will be examined."

One of the most successful ways of intimidating your reader is to invent new terminology. Such invention implies that no word currently exists to describe adequately your ideas on the subject, and may change you from a junior untenured professor to a "seminal thinker." So, in your discussion of spigot shapes, describe the two camps of opinion as the "comparatists" and the "ideo-spigoters." *Never* define your terms. If possible, translate them into German.

Keep before you at all times a mental picture of the board of trustees counting pages. And never forget two important truths about scholarship:

Its real purpose is to produce as much as possible on as little as possible.

It is not so important for you to be right as it is for others to be wrong.

On Publishing

Pierre van den Berghe

Publication of research, we are told, is the scholar's main contribution to science and society. With rare though notable exceptions, scholarly publication does not have any beneficial consequences for anybody except the author and his nuclear family, a handful of typographers and printers, and the shareholders of paper mills. These conditions explain both the low quality of the printed output, and the popularity of publication among authors, especially college professors. In fact, publishing has become a compulsion. The average academic author does not write because he has something to say, because he hopes to contribute to knowledge, or because he has fun doing it; rather, he writes and publishes in order to improve his vita. This document is frequently the only thing about him which his colleagues will ever read; it is the passport to academic success; and, beyond the routine acquisition of a Ph.D., published titles are the main ornament of a vita. Scholarly publication is thus an extremely elaborate and patient exercise in vita construction.

The gamesmanship of publication involves a set of difficult dilemmas which lurk in the subconscious of many players, but are seldom explicitly stated. Let us turn to some of these problems.

Quantity versus Quality

For most people, of course, this problem never arises, because quality is beyond their reach. But insofar as a real dilemma exists, the optimum strategy of Scholarly Status Maximization (SSM) is clear. Rush into print, at least in the early stages of your professional career. For one thing, you have no reputation to lose. For another, most people who are instrumental in hiring or promoting you will never read anything you wrote besides your vita. Consequently, quality of publication is almost completely irrelevant to career chances.

There are . . . partial exceptions to this strategy, however:

Publishing beyond a certain amount can be regarded as excessive. The best SSM strategy is to adjust for the average productivity of the department where the author hopes to stay. If his rate exceeds the departmental average by a substantial and painfully embarrassing margin, pressures against "rate-busting" are brought to bear against him. Arguments are then advanced that if you publish so much it cannot possibly be any good, and you may have to change jobs. The prudent untenured faculty member should thus endeavor to publish only slightly more than his competitors, or, should he be a rate-buster, he should conceal the fact and use his "excessive" publications only for purposes of negotiations with outside schools. This may require the production of a special toned-down vita for internal consumption.

The marginal utility of any given publication for SSM decreases as the size of your bibliography increases. E.g., while your first book, even if it does not sell, probably adds at least $50,000 to your life income, your fifth book will have only an imperceptible effect on your salary. It follows that once you have attained the status of full professor on the strength of a sizable bibliography, the marginal utility of further publications is minimal. In fact, if you attain national stature, it is probably best to stop publishing altogether, on the grounds that your reputation can only decline by further exposure to intellectual scrutiny.

Prestigeful versus Obscure Outlets

The neophyte would hardly consider this a dilemma. Does it not stand to reason that he should try to place his prose with the most prestigious journals or publishers? For the beginner, this strategy may commend itself. Your colleagues will rarely read your prose, but they will often weigh your bibliography in terms of the prestige of the journals where you publish. Beyond your first faltering steps as an assistant professor, however, the optimum strategy calls for publishing in obscure journals (POJ). At the risk of belaboring the obvious, the reasons for the POJ strategy are as follows:

a) Even college sophomores now read the leading journals, but only real scholars publish in and read the Proceedings of the Jamaican Society for the Advancement of Science. The more obscure the quotation, the more prestigious it is to quoter and quoted alike.

b) What happens, you may ask, if you do not get quoted? You still win. The odds are heavily in favor of somebody else writing the same article, or at least one on a closely related topic within five years. If he writes the same article and does not quote you, you write a rejoinder to the journal where he published his piece, and you kill two birds with one stone:

1) You expose him as a plagiarist and establish yourself as a superior scholar.

2) You add a title to your bibliography.

If the person who does not quote you merely writes in the same area but differs with you in his approach, you follow the same procedure and merely substitute for the charge of plagiarism one of poor scholarship or incompetence.

Articles versus Books

The number of books published in a given field is inversely related to the intellectual sophistication achieved in that field. Very few books are written in physics, mathematics, or chemistry; a great many in political science, sociology, education, and home economics. This fact should not deter a scholar to write books if he belongs to a discipline in which many books are written. In fact, SSM dictates a prolific and verbose output if such is the characteristic of the field.

Especially useful in this connection is the inflation of an article into a book. Once upon a time, scholars condensed their 500-page dissertation into one or two ten-page articles, usually with little if any loss in content. Now, the successful academic in the verbose fields blows up a ten-page article into a 500-page book.

Concentration versus Dispersion

The common-sensical thing, of course, would seem to be to spread one's publications in many different journals so as to reach a broader public. This might be termed the "hippopotamus technique" after the winning habit of these pachyderms to mark their territory when on land by quickly rotating their tails while defecating, and thereby spreading their telltale droppings. Early in one's career, this technique is not efficacious, due to the overabundance of scholarly hippopotamuses. Besides, publication dispersal may open one to charges of eclecticism, marginality to the discipline, and the like. By contrast, the "rhinoceros technique" —i.e., the rapid accumulation of a strategically located pile—is frequently more visible in early career stages. The hippopotamus technique, like POJ, is introduced later in one's professional existence.

To Plagiarize or Not to Plagiarize

The printed output of academics falls in four broad and overlapping categories:

a) Tediously footnoted rehash of the works of others. This probably accounts for 60 percent of the output. Such books and articles comprise a category which is accepted as both legitimate and competent, but it has the drawback of being excruciatingly boring.

b) Unwitting restatement of other works. This type of writing accounts perhaps for another 30 percent. It is regarded as poor scholarship if detected.

c) Outright plagiarism. This accounts perhaps for some 9 percent of the printed output. Plagiarism was once completely accepted. Bach, for example, shamelessly pirated Vivaldi, but then he was under tremendous publication pressure, having to produce something like a concert a week. Besides, he had many sons to feed, and it was some years before they started helping him out. Today plagiarism is frowned upon, but undetected plagiarism can be quite useful to the less imaginative professor who wishes to establish a claim to creativity.

d) Original ideas. These take at best 1 percent of the printed space, and may be disregarded here as an insignificant residual category to be mentioned only for the sake of completeness.

Let us summarize the main rules of the publishing game. Like chess, the game can be broken into the opening, middle, and end phases:

a) Assistant professors should publish, preferably in prestige journals.

b) Associate professors should continue to publish, but preferably in obscure journals.

c) Full professors would often do well to become deans and stop publishing altogether.

The pressure on professors to publish is often said to create anxiety, to stifle creativity, and to encourage the production of a vast amount of trivia or worse. Journals are like proliferating repositories of academic night soil, which, far from fertilizing the ivory tower, slowly drown it in a steadily rising tide. It looks as if the hippopotamuses and rhinoceroses are slowly suffocating in their own waste. Stifling conditions, however, are not so much created by the quantity and quality of the output as by the deadly seriousness with which most professors take their publishing. Viewed as a game, publication is at least as entertaining as chess and no more unproductive.

Practice of Political Science: Textbook Publishing

On Marketing a Textbook
Heinz Eulau

This textbook business is as competitive as any business in this era of deregulation. Just to call a text *American Government* will never do. Instead, you will have to choose among "elements of," or "principles of," or "foundations of," or "essentials of," or "introduction to," or "perspectives on," and so on. Moreover, these introductions, perspectives, elements, principles, or foundations are invariably "new." *American Government* may be alternatively "modern," or "contemporary," or "changing," or "basic." Some of the announcements even promise "understanding." If you don't trust all these nouns or adjectives, you can rely on subtitles. Modest authors use just two nouns, like "Institutions and Policies," or "Stability and Change," or "Theory and Practice," or "Policies and Politics," or "Conflict and Consent"; or they mix noun and adjective, like "New Directions" or "Changing Expectations." Less modest authors serve up three words, like "Origins, Institutions, and Policy," or "Ideas, Institutions, and Issues," or "Economics, Law, and Policies," or "People, Politics, and Policies," or various other versions of the same sort of thing. It clearly takes a good deal of imagination to come up with three words, and you must never use four. More venturesome authors will give you a title that doesn't tell you what the book is about, like "The Irony of Democracy," or "Democracy at Risk," or "Democracy Under Pressure," or "Unfinished Democracy," or the bestselling "Government by the People" as a synonym for the difficult word "democracy." But, then, these titles require subtitles to bring you back down to earth, say, "The Great Game of Politics," or "The Rules of the Game," or "The Ideal and the Reality," or "An Uncommon Introduction to American Politics," or simply "The American Political System," whether introductory, essential, fundamental, or what not.

Somewhere along the line, your choice of a text is facilitated by other adjectives that presumably tell you about what is called an author's "approach." Approaches are manifold, in alphabetical order: "alternative," or "behavioral," or "constitutional," or "dynamic," or "economic," or "institutional," or "pluralistic," or "processual," or "radical" and, most recently, "rational." Where the text has been adopted, publishers evidently think, will help you in your choice. There seem to be two strategies. Either you list just two or three prestigious universities whose repute is nationwide, like Harvard, Yale, or the University of California; or you list 99 colleges plus, from Alpha to Omega. There is, moreover, a direct and positive relationship between the reputation of the author and the reputation of the adopting institution. If you are famous, a few prestigious adoptions will suffice;

if your name is not a household word, list all the adoptions you legitimately can. For whatever reason, some publishers prefer a single author and other publishers prefer several authors. A single hot-shot author is likely to have "produced" not only a book but also many Ph.D.s who can be counted on to adopt the master's text. As to multiple authorship, three names appear to be the norm, but we note an ever-so-slight tilt toward four. Then there is the issue of illustrations—photographs or cartoons that even the most half-witted student must appreciate versus statistical tables or graphs that require something more than knowledge of the three R's. It's all a question of marketability.

On Textbook Adoption
William J. Keefe

Dear Austin:

As you know, I have adopted *The Governing of Men* for all the courses I have taught at the University of Pittsburgh over the past decade, including courses in political parties, the legislative process, and a course known simply as Basic Fundamentals. Your royalties from Pitt, thanks to me, run to the tens of thousands.

I employ two criteria in adopting a text. First, I turn to the index to see if my name is there; if it is, I note this on a 3 x 5 card. Second, I make an instantaneous judgment whether I like the author; if I do, I note this on the same 3 x 5 card. Often my second ranking is influenced by my first finding. But in any case, I then sum the numbers, counting 70 points for the first indicator of enduring book value and 30 points for the second. Any book that receives 70 enduring value points I adopt immediately. Use of this scientific method takes the guesswork out of adoptions, eliminating the need to read the books prior to adoption, in fact eliminating the need to read the books at all.

With this information at hand, you can therefore imagine my dismay when I learned from the *DEA News* that *The Governing of Men* comes in as . . . the most incomprehensible book ever written, if I understand the authors' central point. As soon as I saw that number, I got out a copy of your book and tried to read it. I can honestly say that I did not understand a single word in it. What in the world is that book about? Since most of my undergraduates have personal subscriptions to the *DEA News*, and will read this analysis, I am going to have lots of explaining to do when classes resume in the fall.

I asked Bert Carroll to read your book to see if he thought it was [incomprehensible]. Although he knew a few of the words, since he had gone to Harvard, he said it was too difficult and just gave up. Morry Ogul volunteered to read the preface and got part way through it; he says you write with the same easy, fluid style of Talcott Parsons but he has no idea at all of what you are saying. Chuck Jones said that he could not stand the strain of trying to read it but also said that if it is as incomprehensible as people say it is, and we now know it to be, he will serialize it in the *Review*, possibly in fact listing it on the cover.

I have not read the Wassermann text (which ranks as the most readable in this study), though I have had the Wassermann Test several times, the first when I was a senior in college. Incidentally, in each case the results were either uncertain or negative. But the point is that I plan to adopt Wassermann in place of Ranney.

I think you will agree with me that the profession is enormously indebted to the DEA News for this important exposé. That this information will absolutely destroy the sales of your book is simply one of the prices we must pay for scientific advances.

Cordially,

William J. Keefe

Practice of Political Science: Preparing a Curriculum Vitae

On the Curriculum Vitae
Heinz Eulau

"The Iron Law of the Academy": there is, I [have] discovered, an inverse relationship between the length of an academic's self-presentation in his or her academic *apologia pro vita sua* and genuine scholarly accomplishment, even after controlling for age or status and all that sort of thing. The law prescribes that the more undistinguished one's career, the more lines are needed to present it. I haven't formalized the law as yet, but the empirical evidence is overwhelming, at least at the aggregate level of associational directories, and some inconvenient outliers notwithstanding.

Practice of Political Science: Conference Going

Conventions and Professional Standing
Pierre van den Berghe

Apart from printed evidence of scholarly status, the annual convention or meeting of the professional association is the greatest prestige show in the academic world. Conventions mean many things to many people. Ostensibly, they are a forum for the exchange of ideas and the presentation of papers on the latest advances in the discipline. In fact, this is little more than a pretext to justify the university's paying your travel expenses. To graduate students, conventions are a slave market for academic employment. More senior academics have a chance to peddle their manuscripts to publishers' representatives. Old classmates exchange gossip over cocktails. Various committees transact business. Foundation and government agents are solicited for support. All these varied and useful functions are overshadowed, however, by the fact that the annual meetings are first and foremost rituals of prestige competition. Professors strut around on the soft carpets of hotel lobbies with the assiduousness of birds of paradise in their display dances, but without even the excuse of a tangible reward such as the favors of females.

Unknown young scholars attend conventions to court the favor of the nationally known ones, and the latter in order to receive the homage of the nonentities, to bask in the sunshine of their glory, and to defend their territory against challengers. Regular attendance at conventions can actually be a substitute for publishing as a method for achieving a reputation. If the people who matter have seen you often enough, your name will be bandied about and suggested for editorial boards, offices in your professional society, and the like. After a decade of diligent attendance and proper courting of the mighty, you may find yourself an established star of a magnitude quite disproportional to your scholarly accomplishment. You will then be one of these people about whose accomplishments colleagues are understandably hazy, but whose name will nevertheless appear on a great many committees and boards. You will in fact have become the recipient of an unearned academic reputation, but as relatively few people can tell the difference between that and the *bona fide* article, the sources of your recognition are of little consequence.

Meetings are excellent barometers of professional standing. You know that you are leaving the drab herd of mere teachers of undergraduates when the following things begin to happen with increasing frequency:

1) People whom you cannot remember having ever seen claim to have met you at such and such a place.

2) Important colleagues recognize you on sight without having to cast a furtive glance at the name tag on your lapel.

3) Colleagues who have never met you read your name tag and exclaim: "Oh! I have long wanted to meet you," or "I am using your book in my class," or "I have just read your article in such-and-such journal."

4) People whom you only know slightly approach you and say: "The grapevine has it that you are unhappy at X. Would you be interested in coming to Y?"

5) Graduate students deferentially approach you as the authority on the subject on which they are writing their thesis, and ask for advice or for clarification of a fine point in your thinking.

6) You accidentally overhear your name mentioned in colleagues' conversations.

7) Your name is formally cited by colleagues reading papers. (It doesn't matter whether their comments are positive or negative.)

8) Rumors and anecdotes circulate about you. (Their nature is unimportant.)

9) Publishers' agents ask you: "Won't you write a textbook for us?"

10) Your feuds with colleagues become notorious.

11) A slight expectant hush follows your appearance in a group.

12) People approach you with greater frequency than you approach others.

13) Your own former classmates become openly envious.

If these flattering things do not begin to occur between five and ten years after getting your Ph.D., they will probably never happen. You might as well stop attending professional meetings and withdraw to the security of your college, where you can at least cut something of a figure at the faculty club and make students laugh at your jokes.

Politics Conferences: A Short Guide to Participants

Anonymous

The Destroyer

The Destroyer comes in two strains. The first sees the conference as a meeting of gladiators; great minds clashing, in which only the blood of equals is spilled. A more virulent strain has a propensity to turn up (uninvited) at the conference graduate panel, purring with pleasure in humbling a 22-year-old graduate giving a paper for the first time. Merciless savagery of nervous conference novices is the hallmark of the Destroyer.

The Expense Account Merchant

Most commonly found amongst the Head-of-Department species, the Expense Account Merchant is easily recognised by peers (though not by university finance departments) for absurdly ostentatious conference expenditure.

Invariably in charge of departmental finance, the Expense Account Merchant spends amounts on taxis to airports equivalent to the research budgets of several Economic-and-Social-Research-Council projects. Such necessary transportation arrangements are financed relatively easily, usually via an outright ban on the use of the departmental photocopier by Ph.D. students.

Characterised by stays in expansive and expensive holes in other parts of town away from the madding conference crowd, Professor Expense Account attracts a small crowd of hero-worshippers and hangers-on, generally junior researchers in search of crumbs from the tables of the great and the good.

The Jobseeker

Arguably the saddest conference figure of all, the Jobseeker cuts a pathetic figure, ingratiating him/herself with some of the profession's finest, who just happen to have placed an advert in the previous week's *Education Guardian*. Easily recognised by catchphrases such as, "Enjoyed your conference paper," "Yes, I'm writing stuff with X in your department." An in-your-face "Got my application yet?" may even be heard on occasion from the most brazen of the type.

The Book-Contract Seeker

Vies with the Jobseeker in the perpetual loser stakes. Characterised by an excess of groveling, the Book-Contract Seeker spends the conference hawking the "big idea" around uninterested publishers. This character may sound plausible in explaining that a huge market exists for "The Party System in Antarctica," but the lack of progress is easily charted. The Book-Contract Seeker begins the week at Oxford University Press, ending with their very own vanity publication.

The Drinker

Mass membership. Tell-tale signs are participation in a welcoming lunch-time session on Day 1; mysterious disappearances from proceedings in the afternoon (siestas); revolutionary fervour when bar threatens to close; copious amounts of fruit juice at breakfast (assuming appearance). Cross-disciplinary.

The Megastar

Possesses some similarities to the Expense Account Merchant, but prefers the good book to the good life. All conference frivolities are beneath such types. The Megastar merely jets in for single paper and disappears, usually before the tedium of a full panel is completed. Book written on the flight home. Refuses to accept research grants below 50k.

The Eternal Graduate

Another type which appears to be on the increase. Characterised by numerous annual appearances at graduate conferences; vagueness when questioned over vita dates and outright evasion when quizzed over age. Physical features often gaunt, due to existing on proceeds of a handful of seminar tuition fees. Good conference company, as they can invariably hold a conversation on absolutely any manner of subjects, often light years away from their research area—a side effect of their departmental teaching demands.

The Freeloader

Perennial scourge of the conference organiser, this is a dangerous beast, possibly growing in numbers. Operating by stealth, the Freeloader declines to pay the conference fee. Instead, this type floats in and out of conference panel audiences, nervelessly asking questions, before drifting into the conference dining area for a free slap-up meal. Lunch and dinner vouchers are invariably "lost," "stolen" or "not issued." Drifts off at close of play in the bar to stay with friends living locally or staying in conference accommodation. Never easy to spot, the Freeloader may be devoid of a conference badge. The breed is most commonly found amongst the postgraduate community, though professorial culprits are not unknown. May be thwarted by the surely imminent creation of a Freeloader Hotline, by which conference-goers can confidentially inform the organiser of suspects.

The Bore

A dismal type, the Conference Bore is perhaps the most easily identified. Tell-tale signs are a talking up of one's own work; wild denigration of the work of others;

an outline of previous exotic conference locations; and a lambasting of colleagues in the profession. An acute strain is found amongst empiricists and their deification of multivariate models, but the Bore extends beyond the parameters of sub-disciplines.

The Recycler

A veteran of conference proceedings, the Recycler spends time between conferences renaming the same piece of work, whilst poring over maps to decide suitable conference venues. The more skilled practitioners may top and tail an article. However, subtlety may confuse seasoned panel members who prefer the cosy familiarity of the annual reading of papers. Usual features? Considerable bonhomie amongst panel members, who take on the appearance of a magic circle. Requirement of outsiders to undertake Masonic-style rituals before penetrating the panel with a paper. Visible signs? Periodic edited books: 1–2 chapters per member of inner sanctum, with contributions "refereed" by the panel chair.

The Academic Conference: An Irreverent Glossary of Terms

James H. Lebovic

The annual meeting of [a professional association] is a time-honored tradition. As it might be an overwhelming experience for the uninitiated, I have compiled a list of key conference terms and their definitions.

Common Areas

The common areas of the conference—lounges, bars, and hallways—create vast open spaces for "trolling," the practice by which conference-goers plant themselves in heavily trafficked areas in an attempt to entrap those of higher rank on the academic food chain, as they walk by. Successful trollers are always poised to "trade up"—dropping smaller fish for a bigger one. Consequently, they must hold conversations while scanning for fresh prey, with eyes that swivel like surveillance cameras. The danger for trollers is that they might unintentionally snag "trash fish" —graduate school classmates who are still looking for their big break (or, worse still, positions at the troller's university), nobodies who want to follow up on a point from the troller's panel, or graduate students under the mistaken impression that the troller is a somebody in the field. Another danger is that a troller will snag a higher-ranked troller who is also on the prowl. Seasoned trollers know that they can only hold someone on the line for so long before it is jerked by a trash fish allowing the big fish to wiggle loose. To practice their craft, trollers must carefully choose their hunting spots. Promising locations include the bottoms of escalators where the unwary can be netted easily as they descend and badges come into view first so that time is not wasted on facial recognition. The best at their craft know that the prime place to snare luminaries is after their panel presentations when they are without their natural defense mechanism—a protective layer of co-authors and graduate students.

Message Board

On the message board, conference attendees can tack scrawled notes addressed to other attendees. Developed as a signaling device during the Peloponnesian Wars, this communication technology continues to prove its value in an age of high-speed internet, cell phones, and voice mail despite an efficiency rivalling that of floating a message in a bottle. Because large bouquets of messages are left for luminaries and few for anyone else, it is obvious that the message board serves both as a repository for fan mail and a pronouncement of who's "in" and who's "out" —the academic equivalent of the "People's Choice" awards.

Panel

Though viewed by the poster presenter (see "poster room") as the "big time," the panel—a forum in which 3–5 authors are expected to present their papers in 12–20 minute flurries to an ostensibly interested audience—is actually the most common means for presenting research results at a conference. The standard panel is composed of the audience, a chair, a discussant, and the panel presenters.

Audience

The role of the audience member is to establish, through "questions" addressed to panelists, that the ideas presented on the panel are derivative of their own or miss the mark, as represented by their own impressive accomplishments in the field. For audience members, posing "questions" to panelists is more efficient than preparing papers for presentation. Unlike panelists, audience members can join a large number of panels and size crowds in advance by carefully picking the venues.

Chair

The chair is the ringmaster for the festivities. The chair's job is to mispronounce the names of the panelists, keep time, and struggle to stay awake. There are no apparent qualifications for the position of chair, other than owning a watch. Chairs enjoy all the prerogatives of the discussant, and more: chairs can comment on the papers without the pretense of having read them. Still, chairs must justify their existence by warning panelists that time has expired using notes of increasing urgency, knowing that it would be easier to stop a speeding train.

Discussant

The discussant's job is to comment on the few papers that were received on time (i.e., at least two hours before the panel). The discussant is obliged: first, to note the diversity and importance of all the papers; second, to compliment the presenters for their attention to detail; third, to relate each paper to the discussant's own research; and, finally, to conclude with predigested comments about the neorealist-neoliberal-constructivist debate and the potential for spurious relationships in the research which fortunately require only a cursory examination of the papers. Discussants thereby conserve their energy for the anonymous peer reviewing of manuscripts, at which point they will not be held publicly accountable for their work ethic.

Presenter

Because no one in the audience will actually read the paper, the job of the presenter is to force-feed the paper to the audience. Although time is nominally a constraint, the task eases conveniently when the presenter is sucked into a black hole that is unregimented by conventional time metrics. The presenter can build the edifice at a leisurely pace—first, cutting and hauling off the theoretical underbrush; then, carefully laying the foundation for the research with homage to disciplinary prophets and saints. With good planning, the official time allocation should expire just as the presenter is preparing to announce the paper topic. Now, the presenter can shift into high gear, tossing out facts, anecdotes, arguments, criticisms, overheads, and footnotes with abandon, stretching the additional "minute" that the chair has allotted grudgingly. Despite the quality of the presentation, the presenter can take comfort in knowing: (a) there will be future engagements (when the paper goes on tour or returns the following year) and (b) it is now time for a snooze. Indeed, the presenter need only appear to listen to the discussant's comments. Miming the recording of these comments is always a nice touch; but a reasoned response to them is neither expected nor appreciated. The discussant is not looking for a fight, or an excuse to prolong the proceedings.

Poster Room

The poster room—a place where presenters can stand next to fragments of their conference paper on display—is an alternative to panels for presenting research findings. By visiting the poster room, one can avoid the two-hour time commitment of attending a panel or an uncomfortable early exit from a panel in progress. For the presenter, the poster room provides an opportunity to present research without sharing the stage with a panel chair, discussant, and panelists or carrying the burden of having to interact with other life forms. The downside is that the presenter must stand for two hours surrounded by people whose ideas were deemed by conference organizers as too revolutionary to debut in a traditional forum.

Publications (Book) Room

The book room, where publishers display their wares, is a place where attendees can cash in on their academic reputations. There, one can reap the rewards of years spent chained to a computer by standing in line for free chocolates, strawberries, and soft drinks or acquiring desk copies of books without any real intention to order them for class. The book room also provides opportunities for personal gratification through the pitching of book "ideas" to a bleary-eyed audience of one. The pitch comes in various self-reverential forms but reduces in essence to a pitiable, "Would you please publish my book?" Learning to pitch thus requires skills opposite to those honed through panel attendance: here, the goal is to present a question in the guise of one's resumé.

On Conferences
Nelson W. Polsby

The American Political Science Association invariably holds its annual meeting in a large commercial hotel in a big city, during the hot muggy days of early September. A couple of thousand people register for four and a half air-conditioned days and evenings of panel meetings, special luncheons and dinners, reunions of far-flung graduates of the various academic departments of political science, plenary sessions, employment interviews, casual hallway and barroom encounters and other exchanges of affection, deference, income, power (Yes!) and so forth. One observer has likened the scene to an assemblage of thousands of dogs, all sniffing about trying to discover who's in heat.

In comparison, as other transatlantic travellers will testify, the PSA of Great Britain puts on an annual meeting more like the decorous and well-mannered Crufts Dog Show. As in America, quite a few of the top dogs stay away, and proceedings appear to be dominated by the energetic young and youngish middle-aged, who evidently find the Association a plausible arena within which to make their scholarly marks. I was told that the nonappearance of most of the holders of professorial chairs in politics or government in the United Kingdom might well be related to an upheaval a couple of years ago in the management of the Association. This was presumably the same revolution that caused the greening of Political Studies, but I prudently forbore to enquire further. If there is one thing to be avoided at an annual meeting it is the discussion of politics.

The relatively small size of the group meant that it was fairly easy to circulate around and say 'hello' to the familiar faces during the numerous breaks for coffee (awful), tea (bracing) and sherry (dry). The panel sessions were surprisingly well attended. In America, one can go to the national convention year after year and never get near a panel. The hallways, lobbies and book exhibits teem with colleagues at all hours of the day and night and it is easy to be distracted from any but the firmest intention to overhear a scholarly presentation. After a while, one scarcely bothers; papers can be purchased or sent for later, and discussion is rarely memorable.

At Warwick, the incentives ran in the other direction. Spaces devoted to casual interaction emptied out during the panels, and my British colleagues dutifully reported to take in one another's intellectual washing. Academic specialization implies that in some panel sessions here I hazard a general guess based on a small sample participants and spectators alike are exceedingly well-known to each other and have already worked out their modus vivendi. In such circumstances, new stimulus may be deeply appreciated or it may be irksome. No doubt some specialty groups are more permeable than others. One or two members of a notably hospitable crowd, the Americanists, remarked on the invisible boundaries around other congregations, their enviable and annoying possession of a common jargon, and their shared but unfamiliar consensus about what constitute acceptable problems and acceptable solutions.

I wandered into a meeting in which it was evidently accepted that for a conclusion to be 'counterintuitive' was a bad thing. Having been raised in a tradition that prized the counter intuitive as possessing novelty, and hence the germ of possible new discovery, I began to harbor the doubts of an outsider. Or was language being used in a slightly but significantly altered way? I recalled that in British and American parliamentary practice to 'table' a motion means more or less opposite things. Without greater experience of British academic culture, I could not resolve the puzzle one way or the other.

British academics, I find, are formidably articulate people. I sometimes think that upper middle class British society must consist of an endless series of oral examinations, and I am constantly running into people who are passing with first class honors. The preoccupation with words, meanings and definitions, the consciousness of accent as a badge of something not casual about one's social identity, the slightly more frequent than random incidence of stammering and other speech impediments all these sorts of thing can be discovered at a PSA meeting, as, one supposes, at any gathering of comparably well educated Britons.

What one finds in addition is a readiness to take intellectual exchange seriously. And, not least, a stereotype-defying–if not downright counter intuitive–collegial friendliness toward at least one bemused stranger.

On Serving as a Panel Discussant

Heinz Eulau

There is a hierarchy of accomplishments by which academics seek to win the esteem and respect, if not love, of their fellow academics. In this hierarchy only being a discussant of learned papers at a panel of some scientific conclave ranks lower than doing a book review.

. . . The panel discussant . . . is the "compleat free rider." First, there really is no need to read the papers in advance because their gist is presented in any case by the paper-giver . . . Second, there is no need to commit anything to paper, though possibly good etiquette suggests scribbling a few remarks-in-response on the back of an envelope while the paper-giver gets to the gist of things. Third, physical exertion in the exercise is minimal because, with usually all-too-many other discussants on the panel, the time allotted to any one discussant is equally minimal. Fourth, even a few minutes after conclusion of the panel the discussant's remarks will have evaporated into thin air, and he or she does not need to worry about having to take responsibility for the gist of the gist as nobody will remember it or, for that matter, the original gist.

Now, these nonexisting costs are compensated for by maximal rewards. First, the discussant gets his or her name into the published program of the meeting, evidence of scholarly commitment that, as the years go by, makes for an increasingly bulky *curriculum vitae*, mostly of interest to university deans who have no time for any reading other than their charges' over-blown if condensed biographies. Second, because discussants, a few deviants excepted, are likely to be polite rather than adversarial in their comments, being on the panel enlarges one's circle of friends, with all kinds of promises for the future, like obtaining a letter of commendation from fellow panelists on the occasion of promotion or a grant application. . . . Third, and probably most rewarding, having been invited to be a discussant or, also likely, having self-selected oneself, guarantees (at least in good times) that one's travel expenses are paid in whole or part by one's college or university. All in all, then, there is nothing to lose and much to gain by being a discussant.

Deviants, of course, pay dearly for their deviance. Opting for the adversarial mode of discussion, they are likely to have read the papers in advance with some care, devoted some time to writing down critical comments, and are looking forward to hot repartee. They soon discover, especially if they are novices, that the few minutes they have to get to the bottom of paper-givers' presuppositions, biases, errors, and other sins are hardly worth the preparatory efforts and hopes.

Practice of Political Science: Administrative Service

On the Theory and Practice of Academic Administration

William J. Keefe

TO: Graduate Students, Staff, and Faculty

FROM: WJK

RE: Still Another Crisis and No Theory

When a crisis develops in the department, I ordinarily turn immediately to theory for guidelines as to its resolution. If the crisis is in "American" I invoke American theory; if the crisis is in International Relations I invoke IR theory; if the crisis is in a subfield I invoke subfield theory. As you know, our discipline is resplendent with theories, all of which can be easily brought to bear and some of which have explanatory power.

Our department is now faced with a crisis for which we have no theory. We will have to go it alone. The hard truth is that we will run out of coffee on Friday or Monday. We do not have sufficient funds to purchase another case. Put another way, we, as the consignee, are in trouble with the consignor. Put still another way, they are going to take the goddamn coffee machine out of here unless we all pay our goddamn coffee bills. If I just had a theory, I would know what to do.

On Recruiting Graduate Students
William J. Keefe

Dear Alan:

It is about that time of year that I write a few rigorously-selected, highly favored, and eminent political scientists a personal letter to ask a small, but important, favor. Would you please be so good as to identify your very best undergraduate major, call him/her into your office, and tell him/her that, in his/her best interests, he/she should send immediately for an application blank for our graduate program? Unless we should decide later on to waive our restriction, we will be able to admit but one student from your institution this year; hence it is in your best interests to offer up your very best candidate. If by chance your very best major is committed to going to Yale, because his/her father/mother went there, we can, under such circumstances, consider your #2 student. You will understand that this is about as far as we can go.

Why would your best student want to come here? The answer is simple: our department, like Pittsburgh the city, is a very exciting and stimulating place in which to live, work, and matriculate. The truth is, our department is so exciting and stimulating that I try to stay home one day a week—on Sunday—just to rest up for the coming week.

No ordinary vocabulary can depict, fully, the intellectual excitement of this place. But let me try by asking you to visualize this extraordinary sight—one I confront each morning at 6 a.m. (even during summer sessions) when I arrive to open the departmental offices. There will be 40–50 students in sleeping bags asleep on the quad near our door; if it is a Monday morning, some of them will have been camped there since Friday, waiting to catch a glimpse of the first faculty to arrive. As I try to open the door, they push, snarl, and shove impatiently; lately the only way I have been able to keep any semblance of order is to bring along Rex, my police dog. Finally, I open the door and they pour in, their eyes round with wonder over what they are about to see and learn. By 7 a.m., when most faculty are at their desks, there will be four or five times as many students gathered—some, interestingly, who are formally enrolled at other universities as far away as 800–1,000 miles.

It is quite beyond me to describe their intellectual frenzy: milling and jostling with each other in the hallways, shouting and cheering as an occasional faculty member arrives late, asking faculty for their autographs, taking snapshots of them, getting them to sign their scrapbooks, rubbing against their luster, taking notes, trying their best to find out what is on their minds. And so it goes all day long: students milling and jostling, trying to warm themselves in the glow of our accomplishments and to eavesdrop on a conversation between faculty members as they go confidently about their business of extending the frontiers of human knowledge. At 1 p.m., when most faculty are ready to leave for the day, there will still be 100 or so students hanging around, some in their pajamas, wistfully watching the faculty stuff their briefcases with manuscripts they intend to work on that night. Truthfully, were it not for our dedication to the life of the mind, all this would be too much.

I honestly wonder how we stand so much intellectual excitement. When our endowed chair-holder arrives for work in mid-afternoon on Tuesdays and Thursdays, sheer pandemonium breaks loose. You have not heard anything until you have heard some 200 pupils screaming in unison, "Doc, tell us what is on your mind today!" I beg him to tell them, and ordinarily he does. It doesn't seem to make any difference which theory the kids scream for him to talk about, he can do it. Usually he begins his talk with impromptu remarks and then, having calmed them, switches deftly and effortlessly into either improvisation or extemporization as he cuts quickly to the heart of the periphery of the theory. "Tour de force," "tour de force," some of the brighter kids chant in Latin as his talk grinds inexorably toward conclusion. Truthfully, the kids eat it up: this is just possibly what graduate education is all about.

On Monday, Wednesday, and Friday, I rely mainly on the dog to calm the pupils. Even then, it is hard to restrain their natural ebullience over learning. So great is the intellectual bedlam that on two occasions this month I have been arrested for running a disorderly house.

As I reflect on our very human conditions, as it were, it is almost as if these students were groupies, though, of course, they are not. They are serious and resourceful young persons bent on smashing the parameters of knowledge and learning just as much as they can, just as fast as they can. Consider this case: last year a graduate student from an Eastern university camped out in the quad and researched and wrote his dissertation in three weeks just from the things he learned from bugging conversations in the faculty lunch room. That meritorious young man, I am happy to report, has just won the Association's outstanding dissertation award. Today he is a member of our faculty, hard at work on his first publication, a textbook for the introductory course.

If you ever had doubts, I trust I have convinced you that this is the graduate department where you should try to place your best student. Others do this as a matter of course. For example, by my count, we have roughly 75 percent of the sons and/or daughters of the last seven Presidents of the American Political Science Association enrolled in our graduate program; a majority of them, incidentally, are doing very well—in our regular, as well as remedial program. Here and there, of course, one can spot a terminal M.A. in this illustrious group.

The best advice I can give you is to tell your best student to apply early. Last year a member of my own family was placed temporarily on the alternate-award list for a teaching assistantship because he/she failed to meet our application deadline.

Sincerely yours,

William J. Keefe
Chairman

Political and Social Theory

The General Theory of Not-gardening:
A Major Contribution to Social Anthropology, Ontology, Moral Philosophy, Psychology, Sociology, Political Theory, and Many Other Fields of Scientific Investigation

Leszek Kolakowski

Those who hate gardening need a theory. Not to garden without a theory is a shallow, unworthy way of life.

A theory must be convincing and scientific. Yet to various people, various theories are convincing and scientific. Therefore we need a number of theories.

The alternative to not-gardening without a theory is to garden. However, it is much easier to have a theory than actually to garden.

Marxist Theory

Capitalists try to corrupt the minds of the toiling masses and to poison them with their reactionary "values." They want to "convince" workers that gardening is a great "pleasure" and thereby to keep them busy in their leisure time and to prevent them from making the proletarian revolution. Besides, they want to make them believe that with their miserable plot of land they are really "owners" and not wage-earners, and so to win them over to the side of the owners in the class struggle. To garden is therefore to participate in the great plot aiming at the ideological deception of the masses. Do not garden! Q.E.D.

Psychoanalytical Theory

Fondness for gardening is a typically English quality. It is easy to see why this is so. England was the first country of the industrial revolution. The industrial revolution killed the natural environment. Nature is the symbol of Mother. By killing Nature, the English people committed matricide. They are subconsciously haunted by the feeling of guilt and they try to expatiate their crime by cultivating and worshipping their small, pseudo-natural gardens. To garden is to take part in this gigantic self-deception which perpetuates the childish myth. You must not garden. Q.E.D.

Existentialist Theory

People garden in order to make Nature human, to "civilize" it. This, however, is a desperate and futile attempt to transform being-in-itself into being-for-itself. This is not only ontologically impossible, it is a deceptive, morally inadmissible escape from reality, as the distinction between being-in-itself and being-for-itself cannot be abolished. To garden, or to imagine that one can "humanize" Nature, is to try to efface this distinction and hopelessly to deny one's own irreducibly human ontological status. To garden is to live in bad faith. Gardening is wrong. Q.E.D.

Structuralist Theory

In primitive societies life was divided into the pair of opposites work/leisure, which corresponded to the distinction field/house. People worked in the field and rested at home. In modern societies the axis of opposition has been reversed: people work in houses (factories, offices) and rest in the open (gardens, parks, forests, rivers, etc.). This distinction is crucial in maintaining the conceptual framework whereby people structure their lives. To garden is to confuse the distinction between house and field, between leisure and work; it is to blur, indeed to destroy, the oppositional structure which is the condition of thinking. Gardening is a blunder. Q.E.D.

Analytical Philosophy

In spite of many attempts, no satisfactory definition of *garden* and of *gardening* has been found; all existing definitions leave a large area of uncertainty about what belongs where. We simply do not know what exactly a garden and gardening are. To use these concepts is therefore intellectually irresponsible, and actually to garden would be even more so. Thou shalt not garden. Q.E.D.

A Desipient Prolegomenon to the Deconstruction of Silence: Neo-postdistanciationalist Approaches

Professor Dr. Dr. Dagobert D. Manteltasche

It is a curious fact that the social sciences pay no attention to silence. Or to state the point in different way, the silence of the social sciences on the subject of silence speaks volumes about its abject ignorance of this important topic. This is a sad and puzzling omission, for silence tells us more—far more—about the world than mere words ever can. Three telling examples illustrate the point.

(1) Glenn Gould's second recording of the Goldberg Variations in 1981 lasts 12 minutes 48 seconds longer than his first of 1956.[1] It is also an incomparably better performance. Why? Bach's notes remain much the same and are produced in pretty much the same order in both recordings, but the silences, pauses, gaps, spacings, and stillnesses that infuse the second performance produce a sublime interpretation of the work. It is not the musical notes that matter but the silences between them, and it is not, of course, the length of the silences but their quality.[2]

(2) Sir Lawrence Olivier recorded "Hamlet" twice, and the second is 52 minutes 37 seconds longer. Why? Not because Olivier's agent negotiated a very favourable contract that paid by the minute of performance time, as suggested by some malicious theatre critics, but because the pauses, discontinuities, hesitations, interruptions, and silences inserted into Hamlet's speeches and soliloquies by Olivier, at the peak of his dramatic art in the second production, make the performance vastly more powerful.

(3) In the 1961 London Sessions (Chess, 1971: CH-60008) Howlin' Wolf delivers a sharp lesson in guitar playing to a callow, young Eric Clapton in the false start to "Red Rooster." "Now come on, man! Always stop at the top. Aw right, let's git on it . . ." Always pause on the high note, the Wolf is saying, always put in that little silent freezing of time, that hanging pause, that hesitation, to get the best effect.

Political science should learn an important lesson from these examples: silences convey more meaning than the slippery, imprecise, ambiguous, dissembling, and inconclusive superficiality of words. We pay far too much attention to what people say, far too little to what they tell us so loudly, clearly, and subtly with their silences.[3]

The Theoreticisation of Silence

A team of the best scientists of the Central Institute for Questions and Answers has been working on silence for a long time. For years, however, we made no progress, no matter what theoretical approach we tried. Marxism, structural-functionalism, discourse analysis, rational/social choice, pluralism, neo-structuralism, post-culturalism, systems theory, macro-dynamic contingency modeling, and even neo-postdistanciationalist politometrics failed to yield any answers.[4] Most puzzling of all, the most powerful analytical tool ever developed in political science, the Schartz-Metterclume Method, made not so much as a dent in the problem.

We were at the point of abandoning the whole project when the blinding realisation hit us that silence is not the opposite of noise, but lies on a completely different dimension of its own. Silence ranges along a continuum with, to put it in plain and simple terms, obmutescence and aphony, at one end, and full-blown reboance and remungence, at the other. Once we understood that words are no more than the frame we put around our silences—all very obvious and straightforward, in retrospect—we made giant strides on two fronts.

On the first front we developed a meta-theory of silence based upon the latest developments in neo-postdistanciationalist theory. We started from the very beginning—literally the beginning of the universe. However, rather than making the common mistake of modern cosmologists, who deal with the first few microseconds *after* the big bang, we took the obvious step of theorising the first few microseconds *before* the big bang.[5] What was there then? There was in the nothingness nothing but silence; there was no light, matter or antimatter, no space, force, or time, not even a perfect vacuum. There was only the total and perfect silence that is the unique feature of the nothing that preceded everything. It follows that the universe, and everything in it, was created from silence alone. Thus, neo-postdistanciationalist theory proves beyond all logical doubt that silence is the origin and the substance of all things. It is a short logical step from this to the conclusion that as the origin of everything, silence is the most important single feature of the world we live in and the basic form of everything in it.[6] The implications of this are as profound and far-reaching for government and politics as for all other fields of scientific inquiry.[7]

The Political Science of Silence

On the second front we developed a less abstract theory of the political science of silence. Content and discourse analyses reveal that silence runs the gamut of human emotions. Among the more important types uncovered by our research are: the Fermata[8]; the Reboant Silence; the Aposiopestic Lapse; the Longanimous Stillness; the Fugacious Hesitation; the Phthistic Intermission; the Pleonastic Gap[9]; the Chrysostomatic Blank; the Deliberative Silence[10]; and the Zeugmatic Space.[11] In this short article, however, we can deal only with the two most common kinds of silence, as revealed by the close analysis of tape-recorded interviews conducted in social science survey research.[12]

The first type of silence in interview responses was first noted by Samuel Katz, the gifted young neo-postdistanciationalist theorist. Lying somewhere between a hesitation and an intermission in length, and known, therefore, as the Katz Pause[13], content analysis reveals two striking patterns of grouping and placing. The Katz Pause is invariably grouped in sets of four, and each member of the group is placed either at the beginning, or the middle, or the end of sentences, or between them. They are remarkably consistent in length, being slightly longer than silences of lesser duration, but curiously shorter than silences that last for a somewhat more prolonged period of time.

Discourse analysis of the Katz Pause shows it to be related to its context and subject matter, to the speakers' understanding of themselves and the social situation in which they find themselves, to the normal conventions of speech patterns at the time, to the particular historical junctures and the totality of dynamic contingencies of the time-frame in which the silence falls, and to whether the speakers are talking to themselves, to others, or in their sleep.[14]

THE NON-RESPONDENT SILENCE

The second of our two main types is the Non-respondent's Silence. As the pace and pressure of modern life intensifies, and questionnaire fatigue sets in, so survey non-response rates rise and the Non-response Silence becomes ever more of a problem. Fortunately, the Schartz-Metterclume (SM) Method enables us to decode silences of this type with greater accuracy than had a meticulous in-depth interview been conducted by a skilled and highly trained interviewer in the first place.[15] This is because Schartz-Metterclume has the capacity to outflank the problems of both the Non-respondent's Silence and the Deliberative Silence by not interviewing respondents at all. We can learn all we need to know about the respondent by analysing their silence with the careful and scrupulous application of the Schartz-Metterclume Method.

The results of this technique are sometimes surprising. For example, it is a well-known fact that about 40% of interview respondents do not agree with their own opinions, and that another 25% do not understand them. SM also reveals that the 60% of non-respondents do not have an opinion about whether they agree with their own opinions. It is notable that owl-simplifiers generally agree with their own opinions, and that lark-knotters typically fail to understand them until they are explained to them by an owl-simplifier, when lark-knotters have a tendency to complicate matters by disagreeing with their own opinions (see Table 1).[16]

To deconstruct the rich and varied meanings of silence is the last and possibly the greatest project of political science. Much work remains to be done, however, and we cannot rest with an understanding of the ways in which spoken words frame silences. We have to go one large step further, and use our fantasy to decode the gaps, blanks, and spaces between the words, sentences, paragraphs, and chapters of the printed word.[17] The Central Institute is even now hard at work on the problem.

Table 1. A Schartz-Metterclume Analysis of Non-respondents' Silence

	Understands Own Opinions	Does Not Understand Own Opinions
Agrees with Own Opinions	Owl-simplifiers: 66.66% Lark-knotters: 11.11%	Owl-simplifiers: 11.11% Lark-knotters: 11.11%
Disagrees with Own Opinions	Owl-simplifiers: 11.11% Lark-knotters: 11.11%	Owl-simplifiers: 11.11% Lark-knotters: 66.66%

Based upon a stratified sample of 1,111 non-respondents. Significant at 0.001%, using a one-tailed test (the use of a one-tailed test is a logical necessity of the Katz Pause).

Notes

1. See the notes for the second recording, Sony SMK 52619.
2. My own attempts at the Goldberg Variation are some 30 minutes longer than Gould's, but I must admit that I sometimes fail to match the expressive quality of his silences.
3. As Sydney Smith said of Macauley, "[He] has occasional flashes of silence that make his conversation perfectly delightful."
4. For a useful introduction to both neo-postdistanciationalism and post-neodistanciationalism see Manteltasche 1999 and Clavicle and Patella 1995.
5. It is worth noting that solving the problem of the initial space-time singularity is best solved by positing a perfect thermodynamical equilibrium of supersymmetric silence before the big bang rather than immediately after it. (Cf. Bogdanov and Bogdanov 2001).
6. We do agree with the thrust of Sokal's argument (1996: 22) about the importance of nonlinearity and discontinuity, but would refine his observation by pointing out that it is the nonlinearity and discontinuity of silence that is crucial. On this point, see Neutics, forthcoming.
7. As Jane Austen observed, "from politics, it was an easy step to silence" (*Northanger Abbey*). I am grateful to Ms. Cara de Klerk for pointing out this valuable quotation.
8. Neo-postdistanciationalist theory confidently predicts the existence of the Fermata, but it has yet to be observed empirically either in the real world or in the laboratories of the Central Institute for Questions and Answers.
9. Some prefer to call this the Epideictic Silence—probably the most irritating of all the types.
10. The Deliberative Silence is when the respondent ruminates while considering what sort of reply the interviewer wants.
11. Needless to say the Zeugmatic Space helps to solve the Great Ballpoint Pen Mystery noted by Clavicle and Patella (1995), and, of course, the fact, noted by Wuffle (1993: 411) that there are more cars than drivers in the U.S.A. The extra cars are all parked in Zeugmatic Spaces.
12. For this purpose a highly specialised technique was developed in which high fidelity recordings were made of formally structured interviews conducted with a stratified sample of 9,459 adults. Sounds of

every kind were cut from the recordings, leaving a smooth, unbroken silence from beginning to end of each interview. These recordings of silence constitute the raw data for analysis. All nonlinear silences were transformed in the normal way.

13. Not be confused with Katz Whispers.

14. People who talk in their sleep often introduce indistinct and blurred silences into their monologues—known, technically, as the Muddy Pause.

15. On the Schartz-Metterclume Method see Manteltasche and Besser-Wisser 2002.

16. On owl and lark theory see Manteltasche 1984, 2002.

17. It is no wonder that Wuffle (1984) failed to answer his own question "Should you brush your teeth on November 6, 1984?" because this is the wrong question to pose in the first place. It should be "Should you brush the gaps between your teeth . . ."

References

Bogdanov, G., and I. Bogdanov. 2001. "Topological Field Theory of the Initial Singularity of Spacetime." *Classical and Quantum Gravity* 18: 4341–4272.

Clavicle, H.Q., III, and H.G.W.J.G.C. Patella. 1995. "The Political Economy of the Automobile—Transient Physical Neo-postdistanciationalism." *Journal of Theoretical Politics* 7: 101–104.

Manteltasche, D.D. 1984. *The History of the Rice Pudding, 1932–1838* (Volume 4). Broadwoodwidger: Last Resort Press.

Manteltasche, D.D. 1999. "Otto I.Q. Besser-Wisser: An Appreciation of the Pioneer of Post-distanciationalist Politometrics." *PS: Political Science & Politics* 32: 730–731.

Manteltasche, D.D. 2002. "Owls and Larks, Knotters and Simplifiers: The Origins of Modern Political Science." *European Political Science* 2: 36–42.

Manteltasche, D.D. and O.I.Q. Besser-Wisser. 2002. "The Schartz-Metterclume Method." *Journal of Theoretical Politics* 14: 129–134.

Neutics, Herman (forthcoming). "Transforming the Boundaries of Social Text." *Journal of Dogmatic Ontology*.

Sokal, A. 1996. "Transgressing the Boundaries: Towards a Transformative Hermeneutics of Quantum Gravity." *Social Text* 14: 217–252.

Wuffle, A. 1984. "Should You Brush Your Teeth on November 6, 1984? A Rational Choice Perspective." *PS: Political Science & Politics* 17: 577–581.

Wuffle, A. 1993. "The Political Economy of the Automobile—Four Approaches." *Journal of Theoretical Politics* 5: 409–412.

Peter Rabbit and the Grundrisse

Rosa Parkin and Charley Parkin

There can be no such thing as an innocent reading of the *Tale of Peter Rabbit*. As that most percipient analyst of the later manuscripts, Enid Blyton, puts it: "We must pose this work the question of the specificity of its object; its relation to its object. The only reading of *Peter Rabbit* which speaks to us through the congealed layers of the past-becoming-present is a symptomatic reading—a reading in which we listen attentively to Beatrix Potter's silences" (Blyton 1968).

So much is of course clear to the average reader of this epochal work, this work which has not only transformed our collective perceptions of rabbitness (*Kaninchenlichkeit*) but which has contributed a new chapter to the political economy of the cabbage patch. It is our contention in this brief monograph that *Peter Rabbit* marks a watershed in Potter's philosophical development, a distinct epistemological rupture from the earlier problematic of the Herne Bay manuscripts (above all, *The Tale of Squirrel Nutkin* and *Jemima Puddleduck*). Nothing more tellingly illustrates the completeness of this scientific metamorphosis than the contrast between the rather schematic hermeneutic of the Nutkin-Puddleduck period and the sure grasp of the principles of comparative political economy manifested in *Peter Rabbit*. The dramatisation of the conflict between Peter and Mr. McGregor in the celebrated garden scene brilliantly pinpoints, in a so brief episode, those acute contradictions and levels of overdetermination characteristic of pre-capitalist cabbage production. The revelatory instance (Potter's favored methodological device) is that "moment" when Mr. McGregor, chasing Peter from the garden, seizes the rake and aims a blow at the fleeing creature. Through an inspired stroke of transformative symbolism, in which the essence of the rake changes from that of tool to that of weapon, Potter lays bare the irresolvable antagonisms of a sub-feudal order in which the role of producer and the role of warrior are indissolubly linked yet totally incompatible in their binary opposition.

It is quite clear from our reading of the unpublished drafts and revisions of the early manuscripts that Mr. McGregor is to be understood as an embodiment (*Traeger*) of that class of small peasant proprietors from whom baronial landlords extracted in direct and unmediated forms surplus value in the dual forms of military service and corvée labour (Poulantzas 1970). However, we must state quite emphatically that despite certain surface similarities the role of Mr. McGregor in the productive process is not to be equated with that of the Seven Dwarfs, as many theorists from Schumpeter onwards have argued.

The extraction of surplus from the productive labour of the Seven Dwarfs by the Royal household (Snow White) was a mediated political form, though ultimately backed up by terror, which is a condition more akin to the Asiatic mode of production than to sub-feudalism. Failure to appreciate this crucial distinction has led to quite understandable confusion among the readers of these works—though unfortunately we cannot go into the important question of whose self-interests are in fact being served by these not accidental attempts at mystification and concealment.

The thesis we wish to advance is that the entire episode between Peter and Mr. McGregor, quite apart from the "rake" scene, is decisive in marking a conjuncture in the transformation of Peter Rabbit from an object of history to the real subject of history. It is precisely at that "moment" when Peter is threatened by the "rake" that he gets his blue jacket caught on the fence, and can only make good his escape by abandoning it. Again, in this capsule statement we have Potter's brilliant portrayal of the self-emancipatory act—the shedding of the "jacket" conveys to us of course the throwing off of servile, anthropomorphic status imposed by the structures-in-dominance of the ideological state apparatus. It is during Peter's tearful monologue in the potting shed that the full significance of his act comes home, to him: i.e., that he has finally and irrevocably entered the realm of history

as a reflexive agent. From this moment on he will be marked out by his kinsmen, Flopsy, Mopsy and Cottontail (who chose to remain in the ever-pre-given-structure of the warren) as a figure of destiny: the singular and heroic figure for which all Potter's earlier works have in a sense prepared us.

None of the previous manuscripts matches the theoretic grandeur and philosophic presence of *Peter Rabbit*—including the much overrated *Tale of Mrs. Tiggy Winkle* which, notwithstanding Lukacs' (1956) extravagant assertions to the contrary, still bears the unmistakable traces of the Herne Bay period. It is quite clear from a symptomatic reading of the Preface to the second edition of the Czech translation of *Tiggy Winkle*, published after the final (Putney) draft of *Peter Rabbit,* that Potter expresses serious reservations about the internal structure of the argument. There is a tacit recognition of the failure to give full weighting to those forces bearing upon Mrs. Tiggy Winkle's actions which can only be accounted for as a result of the over-determination of conjunctive instances within the given totality of the farmyard. What this does in effect is to present us with a completely de-historicized hedgehog-subject. It is impossible to imagine Potter falling into this same trap in any of her later analyses of pre-capitalist economic formations.

Our attempt to produce a correct reading of *Peter Rabbit* deliberately poses the problem of what it is to read. Only in answering this question can we feel confident in our task of rescuing Potter's contribution to science from the hands of those who seek to reduce this work virtually to the level of a fairy tale.

References

Blyton, Enid. 1968. *Live le Peter Rabbit*. Paris: Maspero.

Lukacs, G. 1956. "Weltgeist, Naturgeschichte und Symbolsbegriffe bei *Frau Tiggy Winkle*." *Beatrix-Potter Studien* 8.

Poulantzas, Nicos. 1970. "Hegemony, Surplus and Unproductive Labour in the Cabbage Patch: A Reply to Miliband." *New Left Review* 64.

The House that Polly Sci Built
Gerry Mandering

This is the Marxist theory of state
throwing its dialectical weight
of argument about the rate
of capital accumulation,
to contradict the bourgeois school
which solemnly studies men who rule
using empirical methods and tools,
to criticise the sociological fools
who write of non-decisionmaking
and public policy decision-taking
to show the community power faking
of local influentials.
But this was simply a reaction
against the earlier interaction
of yet another professional faction
(Polsby, Dahl, and others too)
who said that what you have to do
is reassemble, clue by clue—
by way of actual 'key' decisions,
issues, conflicts, and elite divisions—
the polyarchical pattern.
They claimed to show that Floyd Hunter
had got it wrong about Atlanta,
which wasn't ruled just by a junta
of businessmen and property owners.
Then, they said, we put the onus
of proof on the sociologists who claim
that men of wealth and power and fame
control the agenda-setting game.
In turn the elitist and the pluralist camp
had lit a new behaviouralist lamp
by placing an emphatic query
against the old conservative theory
which used the constitutional way
of studying what the statutes say
to understand the full array
of forms of local government.
This, in turn, was something new—
an administrative-legal view—
which in the 1920s grew
from a Fabian, bourgeois hate
of the Marxist theory of state,
which threw its dialectical weight
of argument about the rate
of capital accumulation
against the earlier, liberal view . . .

Research Methods

How to Succeed in Political Science by Being Very Trying: A Methodological Sampler

Lee Sigelman

Daily we are bombarded by advice on how to succeed in political science. We are told what to read—everybody in Philadelphia reads *World Politics*, conclude media watchers Giles and Wright (1975). We are told how to speak—practice phrases like "latent functional isomorphism" and "quasi-longitudinal typology," concludes politico-linguist Betty Zisk (1970), and success will be ours. We are even told where to dine—Tadich's or Sam's for fish in San Francisco, decrees gastronomical heavyweight Richard Brody (1975).

Impeccable reading habits, a finely-honed vocabulary, and proper nutrition notwithstanding, we are in imminent danger of failure as political scientists unless we are able to establish our bona fides as data analysts. This requires that we master some canons of research methodology. Unfortunately, these methodological strictures have yet to be systematically codified.[1] By presenting some basics of proper research methodology, by discussing some more sophisticated techniques (e.g., the Multiplicative N-Extender, the Levitating Measure Raiser), and by cataloguing some even more advanced routines (e.g., the Spontaneous Phylogeny Recapitulator, the Deviant Data Bender), the present exploratory study takes a tentative first step in the direction of a more systematic political science.

Some Basics

(1) **Explore.** Never fail to present your research as a tentative first step toward some new frontier, a tactic that will allow you to deflect unsympathetic criticism with an exasperated "What did you expect? I told you it's only an exploratory study!" Most political scientists are doubtless aware of the *Colonial Corollary*, according to which the title of any respectable scholarly publication must contain a colon.[2] Only slightly fewer recognize that the format of the colonial corollary ("Eyecatcher: Explanatory Subtitle") can readily be accommodated to the spirit of exploration, viz., "The Effluent Society: Prolegomena to a Tentative Exploration of Politics in Gary, Indiana."

(2) **If Paris says wear it, wear it.** Be certain to employ whichever statistical technique is taking Ann Arbor by storm this summer, because it is boorish to be clad in last year's fashions. History shows that this requires true

perseverance. Just when a generation of political scientists was aglee at having mastered chi-squares and product-moments, along came multiple regression. Having finally learned how to tell a *beta* from a *b*, political scientists reeled under the full force of the factor analysis offensive. Now, still scratching our heads over orthogonal versus oblique rotations, we're told that discriminant analysis is *avant garde*. What's next? Smart money is riding on canonical correlation, which produces results so uninterpretable as to be eminently publishable, or on Goodman's log-linear analysis, which seems at this point to be understood only by Goodman; but caution counsels waiting for the fashion pacesetters to bring out their spring line.

(3) **A peek is worth two finesses.** The hypothesis-rejection road to success in political science is long and rocky, so there's no sense in developing an explanatory model until you've had a chance to pore over some computer printouts. If you're getting unexpected results, change your operationalizations. That failing, tinker with the composition of your sample. If your results continue to defy your theoretical expectations, then it's surely time to change your theoretical expectations. Some may castigate this procedure as "betting after the race is over," but peeking is guaranteed to spare you the social stigma of being associated with any rejected hypotheses.[3]

So basic is such advice that it can probably be understood even by advanced graduate students and some full professors. Certain other methodological routines, however, have been mastered only by a narrow elite which by no mere coincidence sits atop the disciplinary totem pole. Modesty forbids sprinkling the following presentation with references to my own research, but I do feel compelled to draw examples from the cross-national research literature. Happily, colleagues in other fields report that these very same routines are used with considerable success throughout political science—most outstandingly, perhaps, in judicial behavior, American state politics, and quantitative international relations.

Beyond Basics, Toward Success

The key to success in political science lies in adherence to "The Let's Pretendency," an integrated system of non-reality-based empirical research methods. "The Let's Pretendency" is so far-ranging in function and application that only a smattering of its key routines—which equip the user with the capacity to transform a single case into several, to turn dubious data into good, and to treat nominal measures as interval—can be reviewed here.

The Multiplicative N-Extender

Success in political science is determined by the ability to publish research, which in turn depends on the use of sophisticated statistical techniques and the attainment of statistical significance, which are themselves functions of the size of one's N. Success in political science, then, demands that one have a large N.

To be sure, the situation has never been entirely hopeless for political scientists who suffer from an undersized N. Those who are adept at camouflaging their stunted case bases have always been able to publish, with Chiswick's (1971) multiple regression analysis of only seven cases serving as an inspiring example of what a dedicated researcher can do to overcome severe shortcomings. Much more encouraging, however, is the recent development of the Multiplicative N-Extender, a routine designed to bolster sample sizes by the proliferation of single cases. This promising technique, devised by students of Western European politics, essentially involves observing a few systems at several different points in time (the higher the ratio of points in time to systems, the greater the utility of the technique), counting each such observation as a separate case, and pooling all the cases into a new, improved sample—large enough to facilitate multivariate analysis and to guarantee statistical significance. The great potential of the Multiplicative N-Extender has been demonstrated by Taylor and Herman (1971), who used it to transform 19 Western democracies into 196, and by Hibbs (1976), who parlayed only 10 European countries into 200. Purist critics who grumble that this routine violates the independence of observations assumption central to statistical analysis can effectively be countered by: (1) reference to the spirit of exploration; (2) metaphysical condescension ("Britain was, of course, a different nation in 1965 than in 1964"); or (3) simple inattention (the preferred solution).

The Double-Barreled Data Enhancer

When confronted with data of dubious quality, unsophisticated researchers are likely to abandon a research project altogether, or at the very least to undertake only the most primitive sorts of data analysis. Both of these strategies are self-defeating, because they entirely eliminate any prospects for publication. Accordingly, the political scientist who aspires to success must become intimately familiar with the Double-Barreled Data Enhancer, a routine for transforming bad data into good. Especially instructive in this regard is the pioneering work of Arthur S. Banks (1971, 1974). At the outset of a longitudinal examination of the course of industrialization in 30 nations, Banks possessed data for only a few scattered years on any industrialization variable for any nation. Unfazed, Banks (1) used the Incremental Missing Data Locator program to interpolate rough estimates of data for each nation-year-variable combination; (2) converted two variables into their U.S. dollar equivalents; (3) subjected five variables to log-10 transformations; (4) computed averages for each nation for each of his eight variables for each seven-year interval; (5) calculated eight arrays of longitudinal z-scores, each encompassing seven-year median data for all 30 nations; (6) performed two orthogonally-rotated P-mode factor analyses, which indicated that the eight variables clustered into four dimensions; (7) averaged the z-scores for each set of clustered variables to form four composite indices; (8) computed group means for industrialized and non-industrialized nations on each of the four clustered, averaged, z-scored variables; (9) computed annual percentage change scores, averaged over each seven-year period; and (10) having created unimpeachably precise variables from his initial crude estimates, began his statistical analysis.

Naive critics may scoff at the Double-Barreled Data Enhancer, charging that the variables it generates are apt to be "polluted."[4] But successful political scientists understand that ecological soundness militates for, not against, the Double-Barreled Data Enhancer; without some such energy-efficient technique, we would never be able to derive maximal benefit from our imperiled natural data resources.

The Levitating Measure Raiser

Success in political science, a nominal discipline with interval pretensions, demands that one establish a reputation for methodological virtue. The political scientist who appears publicly in the company of chi-squares, taus, phis, and their ilk is doomed; one is known by the coefficients one keeps, and such dull statistics impress no one. But the nominal (or at best ordinal) nature of most political science measures would seem to permit no other outcome—a cruel paradox which has stopped scores of political scientists short of the success that could have been theirs.

It is for precisely this circumstance, when matters seem so desperate that the beleaguered researcher laments the fact that he didn't follow his parents' advice and go to law school, that The Let's Pretendency is ideally suited. Rather than trading in his SPSS manual for a torts book, the methodologically virtuous political scientist will extricate himself with the Levitating Measure Raiser.

Because graduate courses in research methodology have always been purveyors of an essentially Aristotelian approach to data analysis, most political scientists still cling to the belief that it is just and good to treat unequal data unequally. The philosophic core of the Levitating Measure Raiser, on the other hand, is the outright rejection of this pernicious doctrine, and the substitution in its place of the methodological equivalent of the biblical Golden Rule: "Treat your data as you would wish to be treated, were you a datum." Following this injunction, rather than singling out a measure for prejudicial treatment solely because conditions have conspired to deprive it of interval status, allows one to get on with the sophisticated business at hand. Operationally, this is quite easy, because the Levitating Measure Raiser consists of three simple steps: (1) one begins by collecting some nominal data, preferably from *A Cross-Polity Survey*—if nominal data can't be located, ordinal will do; (2) one then acknowledges that interval assumptions cannot be made about these data; after which (3) one makes interval assumptions about these data, referring to the spirit of exploration and to any of several articles by Sanford Labovitz (1970). The data having thus been levitated, the sky—path analysis, multidimensional scaling, even canonical correlation—is the limit.

Guaranteeing Success

Success in political science presupposes mastery of the Multiplicative N-Extender, the Double-Barreled Data Enhancer, and the Levitating Measure Raiser. But these routines alone cannot guarantee success, for they are only the most primitive components of the highly sophisticated Let's Pretendency. More advanced techniques, working knowledge of which is still restricted to a narrow methodological elite, include: (1) the Spontaneous Phylogeny Recapitulator, which derives longitudinal conclusions from cross-sectional data; (2) the Oracular Fact Generator, which converts the personal opinions of expert informants into certified judgmental facts; (3) the Unfamiliar Factor Formulator, which facilitates the accumulation of knowledge by repackaging simple reality into complex, unanticipated forms;[5] (4) the Recursive Route Restrictor, which simplifies the analysis of complex causal systems by permitting only undirectional arrowdynamic causation; (5) the Deviant Data Bender, a chiropractic routine for normalizing maldistributed variables by rendering them theoretically uninteresting; (6) the Rapid-Fire Irrelevance Eradicator, which makes indicators which are unusable because they are not related to one's concepts, usable because they are available; (7) the Self-Rising Sow's Ear Silkifier, which melds a set of empirically indefensible assumptions into an elegantly undisverifiable formal model; and (8) the Automatic Article Ender, which cites space constraints to extricate an author from discussing his findings and which, as an optional feature, promises that he will do so in a forthcoming publication. Unfortunately, space constraints preclude a fuller treatment of these advanced routines, which I hope to explicate in a subsequent article.

Notes

1. Singer (1975) has, however, catalogued techniques designed to prevent an unwelcome drift toward cumulation in research findings, and even a sociologist (Shearing 1973) has made a contribution in this regard.

2. Political scientists deserve the heartiest congratulations for their exemplary performance in this vital aspect of the research enterprise. As I shall report more fully in a forthcoming article titled "Colons: Ascending in Political Science, Descending in Sociology, Transverse in Economics," more titles are colonized in the *American Political Science Review* than in any other social science discipline's major journal.

3. For a thoroughly wrong-headed critique of peeking, see Payne and Dyer (1975). I intend to elaborate on the relationship between hypothesis rejection and social stigmatization in a forthcoming monograph entitled "The Cube Law of Rejection: Some Explorations in Logico-Deductive Heuristic Model-Building." The logic underlying the cube law is naturally quite complex, but the law itself can be rendered parsimoniously in the arrowdynamic notation currently in vogue in political science: Rejection of Research Hypotheses → Rejection of Manuscript → Rejection of Tenure Application.

4. This ill-considered epithet is used by Hudson (1973).

5. An encouraging discussion of the theoretical potential of factor analysis is presented by Armstrong (1967).

References

Armstrong, J. Scott. 1967. "Derivation of Theory by Means of Factor Analysis, or Tom Swift and His Electric Factor Analysis Machine." *American Statistician* 21: 17–21.

Banks, Arthur S. 1974. "Industrialization and Development: A Longitudinal Analysis." *Economic Development and Cultural Change* 22: 320–337.

Banks, Arthur S. 1971. *Cross Polity Time-Series Data.* Cambridge: MIT Press.

Brody, Richard A. 1975. "San Francisco in Five Hundred Words or Less." *PS* 8: 173–174.

Chiswick, Barry R. 1971. "Earnings Inequality and Economic Development." *Quarterly Journal of Economics* 85: 21–39.

Giles, Michael W., and Gerald C. Wright, Jr. 1975. "Political Scientists' Evaluation of Sixty-three Journals." *PS* 8: 254–257.

Hibbs, Douglas A., Jr. 1976. "Industrial Conflict in Advanced Industrial Societies." *American Political Science Review* 70: 1033–1058.

Hudson, Michael C. 1973. "Data Problems in Quantitative Comparative Analysis." *Comparative Politics* 5: 611–629.

Labovitz, Sanford. 1970. "The Assignment of Numbers to Rank Order Categories." *American Sociological Review* 35: 515–524.

Payne, James L., and James A. Dyer. 1975. "Betting after the Race is Over: The Perils of Post Hoc Hypothesizing." *American Journal of Political Science* 19: 559–564.

Shearing, Clifford D. 1973. "How to Make Theories Untestable: A Guide to Theorists." *American Sociologist* 8: 33–37.

Singer, J. David. 1975. "Cumulativeness in the Social Sciences: Some Counter-prescriptions." *PS* 8: 19–21.

Taylor, Michael, and V.M. Herman. 1971. "Party Systems and Government Stability." *American Political Science Review* 65: 28–37.

Zisk, Betty H. 1970. "The Compleat Jargoner: How to Obfuscate the Obvious without Half Trying." *Western Political Quarterly* 23: 55–56.

A Young Person's Guide to Positivism
Ronald Herring

If you've been having Doubts
    About the Natural Law,
You can learn to check it out
    By using Kendall's Tau.
If you can't draw from Phenomena
    Their own True Confession,
Trim them till they'll fit
    A Linear Regression.
And if your explanation flounders
    In Conceptual Paralysis,
Convert to Matrices,
    Employ Factor Analysis.
Where the Arts and Humanities
    Are Soft as melted lard,
The Scientist can penetrate,
    Our instruments are Hard.
For the Neophyte-in-Rigor,
    There's no comparable elation
To encapsulate the World
    Within a Standard Deviation.
Now there are a few Precautions,
    And you've always got to heed 'em;

Watch out for Faulty Indices
    And too few Degrees of Freedom.
Before proclaiming new-found wisdom
    In a publishing sensation,
Make certain that you've checked
    For Autocorrelation.
Of course the data's often soft
    And for Science's consumption,
You'll have to plug up holes
    With heroic Bold Assumption;
The leaps of faith you'll make
    Are sometimes downright mystic,
But even non-results
    Are published as Heuristic.
Now the Infidels will charge
    That your models are simplistic,
Conclusions commonplace,
    And methods opportunistic.
But if you really wanna Know
    And that with great facility,
Pick your Paradigm
    To maximize utility.

World Glut of Significant Correlations?
Dick Tator

The daily papers are full of news about the EEC's beef and butter mountains, and its wine and milk lakes, but political scientists in the United Kingdom may not be fully aware that the EEC also has a mountain of significant correlations. The stockpile, thought by some Euro-watchers to be the biggest in the world outside Ann Arbor, is stored in a series of gigantic underground chambers specially excavated for the purpose out of the solid rock of the French and Italian Alps.

The EEC's awareness of the significant correlation problem started in 1980. In June of that year, Dr. Otto Runcible, the powerful and dynamic Commissioner for Ephemera, gave a major speech. He prefaced this by saying: "I would like to make it perfectly clear that no one is more dedicated to the merits of free trade than I. That, after all, is what the EEC is all about—free trade. And that is precisely why my Ministry plans to take a firm control of the most important economic activities of our member states—iron and steel production, coal, agriculture, fishing, the monetary system, and so on."

Dr. Runcible then went on to talk for some three hours about his plans for the careful and detailed regulation of ice cream, sausage, and beer production in the EEC, but of special interest to political scientists were his concluding comments on significant correlations. This is what he had to say.

> Until 1888 not a single correlation coefficient was produced in the entire Western Hemisphere. Now, less than a hundred years later, production has escalated out of control. We have now reached the alarming position when any Tom Hobbes, Dick Rose, or Harry Lasswell can produce his own coefficients. Indeed, any Pearson can now produce them in large numbers without regard for the rights of others, or for the welfare of the correlations themselves. If this continues we are in for a world glut, and I need not dwell upon the truly horrifying consequences for us all.
>
> I have also travelled the length and breadth of the European communities, and it is abundantly clear to me that the great majority of ordinary, decent people do not want a flood of significant correlations flowing into their homes and their private lives.
>
> The Council of Ministers is determined to halt these excesses and to use its democratically elected powers to bring the production and use

of significant correlations under close supervision and control. Insignificant coefficients will be left unregulated because world demand at the moment is very slight, but our plans for significant correlations include the following:

1. Stockpiling coefficients which are surplus to current requirements. They will be treated properly and humanely in specially built warehouses, and maintained at a constant temperature of 65o and humidity of 50o. They will be supervised by properly trained personnel. The Commission has set aside a budget of £500m to meet the costs.

2. Producers of significant correlations will be subsidised at the same level as farmers in the EEC. Surplus production will be purchased from them by the EEC's Bureau of Significant Correlations at 115% of the market price, in standardised European units of account index—linked to the EMS real-price indicator of outturn prices in 1978 deflated by the 1980 projections for 1990 prime rates of production. This is as close to market prices as we can get.

3. Payment will be made in advance of production to encourage the non-production of coefficients which would otherwise have to be produced to qualify for the subsidy.

4. Producers will be paid a once-and-for-all capital sum for the destruction of existing collections of significant correlations. Collections which do not exist because correlations were not produced in order to qualify for the subsidy outlined in paragraph 3 above will only be paid for at 95% of the normal rate.

Dr. Runcible then went on to outline plans for the standardisation of correlation production. He pointed out that there is at present a great deal of diversity and inconsistency in production, and that this was simply confusing to the general public—zero order and partial correlations, and one- and two-tailed tests of significance, three main significance levels, and correction to two, three, four or more decimal places. The EEC, he said, had introduced legislation to eliminate most of these options; henceforth, only correlations of 0.30 or more would be deemed significant.

In question time at the end of his speech Dr. Runcible was asked for some further information about European production of significant correlations, but he pointed out that he was unable to answer this query since the EEC had standardised its social and economic analysis around correlation techniques. According to EEC regulations, any significant correlation produced could not be used, but had to be sent off immediately in specially designed juggernauts to the EEC storage chambers under the French and Italian Alps.

Uncle Wuffle's Reflections on Prediction
A Wuffle

Predictability

The future is always just more of the same, except when it isn't. —Anon.

You know, you never know.—Yiddishism from Kanter (1987)

When in doubt about when to buy and when to sell stocks, look at what the odd-lotters (small investors) are doing—and then do the opposite.—Anon.

Forecasting is very difficult—especially if it's about the future. —Edgar Fiedler, cited in Peter (1979)

Even a stopped watch is right sometimes.—Anon.

Anyone can correctly predict that the Dow will double, since if you wait long enough it will happen. The problem is getting it right as to *when*—and, as recent events have shown, *for how long*.—A Wuffle, April 1, 2009

The surest clue that a trend has crested is when *Time Magazine* celebrates the trend on its cover.—Anon.

Not long after Don Matthews wrote his marvelous description of the Senate as a "gentlemen's club" (Matthews 1960), that description largely ceased to apply.—A Wuffle, April 1, 1986

After twelve years of divided government, Fiorina (1992: 3) wrote that "divided government has the potential to become the new organizing principle of American politics research in the 1990s." At the heart of the belief that divided government was nearly inevitable was the view that the House was likely to remain under Democratic control (as it had for the entire time period from 1932–1990) while the overall weakening of the New Deal coalition made it likely that Presidency (and the Senate) might fall under Republican control. Of course, as we now know, the Republicans take the House in 1994 and hold it for the next 10 years, while Clinton wins in 1992 and again in 1996.—A Wuffle, April 1, 2008

It was long believed that almost the sole exception to the rule "What goes up must come down." was national life expectancy, but the decline in life expectancy in post-Communist Russia showed that, while old clichés never die, the same is not true for Russians.—A Wuffle, April 1, 2004

The fall of the Soviet Union was predicted long before the event by many knowledgeable international relations experts—NOT.—Anon.

Optimist: one who studies Russian. Pessimist: one who studies Chinese.—Hungarian politician Janos Kadar, ca. 1960

The Chase Econometric Model, and econometrics in general, provides convincing proof of the adage that "The more things change, the harder it is to accurately predict them in advance."—A Wuffle, April 1, 1984

The worldwide economic crash of 2009 was warned about in advance by many famous macroeconomists—NOT.—Anon.

Upon learning that an American named Bell had invented a telephone that could transmit human speech, the British set up a parliamentary commission to look at its long-run implications for the British economy. Among the witnesses called was the chief engineer of the British Post Office. Asked whether he thought that this invention will be of any use in Great Britain, the chief engineer replied: "No, sir. The Americans have need of the telephone, but we do not. *We* have plenty of messenger boys."—Arthur C. Clarke, The View From Serendip

The weatherman had been wrong so often in his predictions that he had become the laughingstock of the town. When the teasing became unbearable, he asked for a transfer. "Why?" wrote headquarters, "do you wish to be transferred to another station?" "Because," the man wrote back, "the climate here doesn't agree with me."—Clark (1981)

Give me more variables than there are cases, and I can predict just about anything perfectly—as long as you allow me to do so in retrospect.—A Wuffle, April 1, 1984

He who lives by the crystal ball will end up eating a lot of ground glass.—Lawrence Tribe

That imposition of a testing regime under "No Child Left Behind" with high stakes not just for students but also for school administrators and teachers would create incentives for (a) teachers helping their students cheat, (b) administrators making sure that less skilled students were exempted from testing, (c) a backlash to the tests as unfair to minorities whose failure rate was "unacceptably" high, and (d) a lowering of standards in some states so as to make the test results of no practical consequence, was anticipated by the Republicans and Democrats who joined together to pass the Act—NOT.—A Wuffle, April 1, 2008

The validity of a science is its ability to predict.—Harry L. Schartzeberg, RCA Engineer *(although I doubt he said it first)*

It may be that the race is not always to the swift, nor the battle to the strong—but that's certainly the smart way to bet.—Damon Runyon

Laws of Social Science

Political science does not have any real laws; in contrast, most polities have too many.—A Wuffle, April 1, 2008

Hindsight is the only exact science.—Anon.

Ask a silly question, you get a silly answer.—Attributed to boxer Slapsie Maxie Rosenbloom when, in answer to his question, someone explained the use of fingerbowls to him.

William James had a dream in which the secret of life was revealed. He hastily scribbled it down, and the next morning read:

Higamus, Hogamus, Women are Monogamous,

Hogamus, Higamus, Men are Polygamous.—Quoted in Peter (1979)

Matrimony is the single greatest cause of divorce.—*MAD Magazine*, December 1960

Nobody knows you when you're down and out.—Popular song lyric

Men's buttons button from the left; women's from the right.—Clio Veritas. *The original reason was that women were expected to have a lady's maid to dress them.*

In peace, sons bury their fathers; in war, fathers bury their sons.—Herodotus

If you walk in in the middle, most movies seem so much better than they are—more subtle. Staying over to see the first part of the movie only spoils it.—Paraphrased from dialogue by Pam North in Frances and Richard Lockridge, *The Long Skeleton*.

Mad dogs and Englishmen go out in the noonday sun.—Cole Porter

You never know how many friends you have until you rent a large farm house in Provence.—Anon.

Hot dogs always taste better at the ball park than they do at home.—Anon.

All power enriches, and absolute power enriches absolutely.—Robert Barnard

Power corrupts, and the fear of losing power corrupts absolutely.—David S. Broder

Give a child an inch, and he'll think he's a ruler.—Sam Levenson

References

Clark, David Allen. 1981. *The Giant Joke Book.* Garden City, NY: Doubleday.

Kanter, Rob. 1987. *The Harder They Hit.* New York: Bantam.

Matthews, Donald. 1960. *U.S. Senators and Their World.* New York: Vintage.

Peter, Laurence J. 1979. *Peter's People.* New York: Tower Books.

Cumulativeness in the Social Sciences: Some Counter-prescriptions

J. David Singer

In every social science, there tends to be a recurrent and cyclical preoccupation with the lack of cumulativeness. Some attribute this to the familiar "absence of theory," and lay it at the doorstep of "barefooted empiricism." Others might see the culprit lurking in the conceptual morass that often passes for theory, and would suggest that grand schemata that are not—and usually cannot be—tested will hardly make for greater cumulativeness.

There seems to be more than a germ of truth in both of these suspicions, but let me suggest a third possible source of our disappointment. I refer to certain norms and practices found among *both* the theorizers and the empiricists: those folkways that we pick up in college and graduate school, and are seldom able to shake in the postdoctoral years. On the assumption that an awareness of them and their implications may lead to their gradual extinction, I itemize here a few of what may be our less attractive foibles. While some of them may be peculiar to the field of world politics, most seem to be found all across the discipline.

A—Terminology

1. If our discipline is concerned with global politics, be sure to call it "international relations"; then all will know that we're interested only in the *relations* among *nations*, and not the attributes, relationships, and interactions of all sorts of entities.

2. As long as you precede your efforts with the phrase, "It doesn't matter what we call it, provided we define our terms," feel free to ignore all conventional definitions.

3. Any time you happen across an isolated fact or a welter of verbiage, be sure to label it "data."

4. If we already have a well-accepted word for a generally understood concept, be sure to coin a new one; don't be transparent when you can be prismatic or refractory.

5. When you're not sure which dimensions of a phenomenon you're trying to describe, refer to the "nature of _____."

6. If you're referring to any observed or hypothesized regularity, call it "structure."

7. If you have trouble differentiating among hunches, suppositions, convictions, preferences, and findings, just call them "theories."

8. If you're using the word "relationship," don't let on whether you mean: covariation of variables, similarity between entities, bonds and links between entities, etc.

9. When using the word "paradigm," don't let on whether you mean: model, research strategy, a set of axioms, epistemological criteria, etc.

10. When using the word "parameter," don't let on whether you refer to: the isomorphism between the sample and the population, a constant, a slowly changing variable, a non-measured variable, a boundary condition, etc.

11. If you're unable to articulate an idea clearly, begin to crank out a large number of examples; we'll eventually figure out what you're driving at.

12. Whenever you refer to physics, chemistry, or biology, call them the natural (or exact) sciences; then it'll be clear that we're in an un-natural or in-exact science.

B—Taxonomy and Typology

1. As you shift from one research problem to another, be sure to change your taxonomy in subtle and unreported ways; this reduces the probability of integrating the results.

2. When discussing roles, relationships, or interactions, avoid identifying the social entities that play these roles or experience these relationships and interactions; otherwise, you'll be taken for a stodgy "institutionalist."

3. When constructing a typology, don't use categories that are mutually exclusive, logically exhaustive, or rest on explicit dimensions.

4. When focusing on conflictful interactions, be sure to say that you're dealing with "the conflict system," and when focusing on bargaining in conflict, say that you're dealing with "the exchange system."

5. If you're concerned with the impact of unemployment on national foreign policies, emphasize that you're examining "the economic system," and if unemployment happens to fall unevenly among different ethnic groups, note that this requires study of "the cultural system"; the more "systems" you examine, the less you'll worry about putting your findings together.

6. When one or two attributes of a system show change over time, insist that "it's a completely new system."

7. If the folklore has it that the mitrailleuse or satellite surveillance or public diplomacy have affected the course of world politics, insist that these have led to different and successive systems.

C—Epistemology

1. If you disagree with a colleague's epistemology, tell him how they "do it in physics."

2. If it is suggested that certain attributes of a social system can be described by observing the distribution of certain attributes among its sub-systems, mutter something about "the ecological fallacy" or perhaps "the ecological fallacy in reverse."

3. If a given piece of work doesn't spell out—in mathematical form of course—all the possible relationships among variables that might obtain, observe laconically that "barefooted empiricism remains far from dead."

4. If a colleague's work strikes you as too deductive, remind him of the importance of all those chemists in their labs, and if too inductive, quote Einstein or Bohr.

5. If a colleague's work shows a strong preoccupation with reproducibility and precision, alert others to his or her "indifference to theory."

6. If, after years of urging that insight and intuition have no place in science, you discover the limits of hyper-positivism, announce that science is a failure.

7. If a colleague is not persuaded by the logic and evidence you adduce, invoke a carefully selected metaphor from everyday life; any discontinuities between child-rearing and strategic deterrence, or between driving a car and running a foreign office, will be graciously overlooked.

D—Research Strategy

1. When undertaking a new investigation, don't bother to read prior studies in that area; until you came along, no one did it right.

2. If your methodological repertoire is limited, emphasize that you only employ those methods "appropriate" to the specific inquiry at hand.

3. When you're stymied on the measurement of one of your critical variables, put that project aside and write another essay on what Thucydides really meant.

4. When another's study explicitly focuses on the interaction effects of predictor variables A and B, quickly note his or her "indifference" to variable C.

5. When beginning a new set of investigations, don't be misled by the plausibility of alternative models; pick one that you like and get on with the derivation of "nontrivial deductions."

6. If your model has no recognizable similarities to the referent world, remind your critics that models are supposed to be "useful, not truthful."

7. When a colleague strays into other disciplines for new concepts or models, alert others immediately to these dilettantish tendencies.

8. If you find a colleague working on a given class of problems for several years, point out his or her "lack of breadth."

9. When drawing analogies from inter-personal to inter-national relationships, never go to the findings of psychologists; their experimental evidence might be inconsistent with your argument.

10. If another project has invested considerable effort in identifying a population of nations, IGOs, or other actors, be sure to either ignore their listing or quibble about that South Pacific island that was omitted.

11. When our critics point out the absence of cumulative knowledge about world politics, press the button that says "After all, we're an infant discipline."

12. If several people, at the same institution or not, are unoriginal enough to be working on the same problem (such as the causes of war problem), be sure to observe that they are mere replicas of one another. And if they're working within a common paradigm, ask "Whatever happened to creativity?"

E—Reportage and Communication

1. When publishing more than one paper on a given problem, don't indicate where it falls in your sequence or reports, or whether it represents an extension, refinement, or revision of earlier reports; a little mystery is good for your scholarly reputation.

2. Since it's too much trouble to revise a manuscript to incorporate the comments and suggestions you solicited from others, just tack on the necessary footnotes; the tightness of your reasoning is less critical than the illusion of exhaustive scholarship.

3. If your paper is on the casual side, don't worry about identifying sections and subsections in it; merely insert a numeral—preferably Roman—on every fifth page.

4. In writing up a nice and tight empirical study, don't waste time putting it into a larger context; get right down to the matter at hand.

5. Be sure that the title of your article or book promises considerably more than is delivered.

6. If you've picked up a good idea or insight from someone else's work, be sure to write it up as something brand new and creative.

7. If you're a panel discussant, paraphrase all of the authors' caveats and self-criticisms, being sure to imply that they were oblivious to such problems.

8. Never specify or reiterate the spatial-temporal domain to which you hope to generalize; all propositions are universal.

9. Avoid the rigid tendency of making your opening and closing paragraphs consistent with each other, and in any event, don't let either of them be consistent with the actual operations you carried out.

10. Be sure that the major query of a study is carefully camouflaged, and that the outcome variable remains shrouded in mystery; otherwise, another researcher might be able to refute your findings.

11. Rather than spell out the case for the validity of your indicators, allude to your "auxiliary theory" (citing Blalock, of course), and get on to the important matters.

12. When your student turns in a paper that is incoherent, disorganized, grammatically improper, and replete with errors of spelling and punctuation, ignore such trivial weaknesses and assure him/her that we're scientists, not literary critics.

13. To use your time efficiently, never consider undertaking the construction of a data set, but follow others' work closely, and as soon as you hear of a potentially useful set, request it from the drone who put it together; that kind of scut-work is inappropriate for creative scientists.

14. If, with the support of a public or private funding agency, you generate a useful and high-quality data set, refuse it to others until you've milked it dry; you can always say that the set is not yet complete or clean.

15. If someone proposes the creation of a new journal, or a section in an existing journal, devoted to data-making and index construction, cite Conant to the effect that empiricism is not science, but is merely a poor substitute for good theory.

16. If someone suggests a different way of printing and distributing journals, remind them that we've always done it this way.

17. If you've read a colleague's paper and can't figure out what the hell he did or why, be sure to praise its "heuristic value."

F—Ideology and Policy

1. When a colleague's work is addressed to some minor social inconvenience, such as war, hasten to note his or her indifference to poverty or injustice.

2. If a colleague's empirical findings are inconsistent with your ideological premises, point out that "it is no accident" that his or her research is supported by the _____, or that his nation is the richest (or poorest) in the world, or that he is not a she, an underdog, an African, or untenured.

3. When a colleague uses the same coding categories to describe both Soviet and American diplomatic actions, tell others that you don't worry about his patriotism, but. . . . .

4. When you're challenged as to the accuracy of your facts on the Chinese ABM, tell the critics "if you knew what I know, and had a Q clearance, you'd believe me."

5. If a taxpayer asks whether your research will lead to an improvement in U.S. policy, remind him that you're a scientist, not a politician.

6. If the question of policy implications should arise, put on your other (citizen's) hat and note that social scientists are no different from barbers.

7. When you're trying to account for the difference between the infantry's and the cavalry's share of the defense budget, invest a minimum of 12 man years, and when you're trying to account for the differences between crises that end up in war and those that do not, write a learned essay over the Easter holidays.

8. When examining the ratio between Yale and Harvard men in the Navy Supply Corps, break out your entire methodological armamentarium, but in examining the ratio of military to civilian fatalities, rely heavily on an exegesis of the "just war" doctrine; that's what "normative theory" is for.

9. If, after extolling the virtues of "value-free" science for years, you discover that ethical considerations might just be relevant, denounce scientific method as a hoax perpetrated by the establishment in order to preserve the status quo; allusions to the Karls (Marx and Mannheim) should wrap up the argument.

G—The Clincher

Finally, if by some remote chance, we begin to gather scientific momentum, and there is a real danger that cumulativeness and codification might get out of hand, allude to Kuhn and call for a new paradigm.

Phil's Barber Shop Calendar for 1973–1974: The Ontology of Chronological Modification—A Structural Crisis?

M.F. Parris

You will remember that last month your reviewer looked at THE ASTROLOGICAL TABLES FOR 1973, and concluded that they were full of useful insights, but structurally unsound.

Our current task is a more rewarding one. Quantitative Political Science has come a long way since the days of romanticism and political anecdotage, judgmentalism and bare-faced commonsensism. PHIL'S BARBER SHOP CALENDAR FOR 1973–1974 will take its place among the best and most challenging of the new works in the literature. Here is an analysis, without the ornamentation of political philosophy, without pretensions to metaphysical "explanations," unencumbered by metaphor, analogy, or, indeed, prose at all, which sets out to predict aspects of the future on the basis of observed past patterns, and does it very well. The scope is limited; only certain aspects of the future are dealt with—but they are of profound potential effect upon the polity . . . what, for instance, could be of more impact than the difference between Friday and Saturday, a difference which could cause the whole of Congress to pack its bags and go fishing!

Despite the essential fluidity of the variable with which he is dealing, Phil has constructed a clear and rigorous conceptual model. In each diagram, under the general sub-heading of "Month"—such as OCTOBER—the author has constructed a series of columns, each one representing a "Day-of-the-week"—such as MONDAY, TUESDAY, etc. These columns are then horizontally sub-divided, in each box thus formed being placed Phil's prediction for the "Date" upon which different occurrences of that day-of-the-week will fall. As a combination of structural simplicity with predictive power, this is indeed a tour-de-force.

Some doubts, it is true, remain concerning causality. Does Thursday cause it to be November 1st, or does its being November 1st cause it to be Thursday? Phil does not address this question. In the forefront of his field, he eschews the causal question as probably irrelevant and possibly meaningless. These, surely, are not the interesting questions.

Viewed purely as a conceptual model, PHIL'S CALENDAR deserves every political scientist's acclamation. Some of the leading analysts of our day will wish to stop there, brushing aside the merely factual questions of application. But for those more old-fashioned of us, for whom internal consistency alone is not enough, two questions arise: Is the Calendar true? Is it useful?

Research into the whole question of Today's Date, carried out at Brewster Hall during October, establishes the veracity of PHIL'S CALENDAR almost beyond question. Only on October 29th, when an hour occurred which could not by reference to the Calendar alone be fitted into either Saturday or Sunday, could we find any inadequacy in the model. As to its usefulness, your reviewer, unwilling to stumble into print with a personal value-judgment, made a survey of a representative cross-section of New Haven opinion. Subjects were asked: "DOES PHIL'S CALENDAR, IN YOUR OPINION, SEEM TO BE AN HEURISTICALLY USEFUL TOOL?" Of the replies that were not obscene, a remarkable 87% thought that it was *not*, the remark "It's more what I would call a calendar," being often heard. Far be it from your reviewer to confute a statistical truth by so-called common-sense . . . but surely it is useful to know what day of the week it is? The matter needs more research.

Like every good work in the literature, this study raises as many research questions as it solves. Is there any correlation between day names and date-numbers? A quick glance suggests that there may be. Of the 52 Sundays listed, none of them occurs on the first of the month; while Saturday appears *four times*. The number of firsts-of-the-month occupied by a Saturday OR Sunday, however, equals the number occupied by a Tuesday OR Thursday. Could it be that firsts-of-the-month are awarded to groups starting with the same letter, proportionately with their membership (of one, in the cases of Wednesday, Friday, and Monday) and then dealt out *randomly* within the group? As a theory, this clearly needs refinement; but it could be far-reaching in import.

Another apercu, which I owe to my colleagues, is the fact that, within a given month, the dates upon which a given day-of-the-week falls differ by a multiple of 7. In fact, if y is the date, n the number of times a day-of-the-week occurs within a given month, then

$$y = 7(n - 1) + c$$

(where c is the date of the first occurrence). Critics have remarked that this is due to the fact that there are seven days in the week; but this surely is to miss the point.

Time is an ongoing process. As an important input into the political system, among a welter of cross-cutting cleavages, it is a variable whose cutting edge is ignored at the peril of damage to any viable conceptual framework. In his masterly analysis of the formal but nonetheless important structure of the formal structure, Phil has done all of us in political science a valuable service.

Urban Politics and Sex at Birth

R.S.J. Featherstonehaugh and J.S.R. Cholmondeley

'Lloyd George he knew my mother, my mother knew Lloyd George'
(S.R.J. Mainwaring, *The Folk Songs of Kircudbright, Kilconquhar, Kinggussie and Kilmacolm*).

It is truly remarkable that modern social science has failed to note one of the most interesting and most important patterns of modern society. The fact is, and evidence is accumulating to prove it, that 50 per cent (± 0.5 per cent) of all births in rural areas are male, whereas 50 per cent (± 0.5 per cent) of all births in urban areas are female (see Table 1).

Table 1. Urban Rural Differences and Sex at Birth (percentages)

	Urban Areas	Rural Areas
Male Births	49.0	
Female Births		49.0
Other	0.5	0.5

(Total 100%) N = 4,473,559,500
Note: based on OECD figures for all live births, 1950–2000

Indeed, differences in male and female birth rates in urban and rural areas are so consistent across time and space that they qualify as one of those most rare phenomena—a universal of human existence (Colquhoon and Auchinleck, 1938). The purpose of this brief research note is to explain this remarkable but hitherto unnoticed pattern, using the best theories and methods available to contemporary political science.

Theory

Perhaps the most obvious explanation of the urban-rural sex at birth pattern is a political one. It is well established that party political control of local government has a significant impact on local public policies and tax expenditures; left-wing governments generally spend more on redistributive public policies such as education, housing, and welfare, while right-wing governments tend to have higher expenditures on police, parks, libraries, and fire services (see, e.g., Belvoir and Bicester, 2005). Public policies on gender issues also tend to vary systematically along the left-right continuum in many political systems, so it seems highly probable that the political colour of the party in power locally will also affect sex at birth. However, since left-wing politics tend to prevail in urban areas, whereas the right is often stronger in rural areas, the question is whether it is politics that determines sex at birth, or whether it is the nature of urban and rural society. Strangely, there is very little research on the significance of politics for sex at birth, and we hope our modest little research note will take a small step forward towards filling this striking and important gap in our knowledge.

Methods

A data file was constructed covering all recorded live births in OECD countries between 1950 and 2000, a total of 4,518,746,962. An unambiguous sex at birth was determined in 99 percent of cases, giving in round numbers a total of 4,473,559,500 observations. The politics of the ruling party in local government was coded 2=conservative or socialist, 1=socialist or conservative, 0=other. The normal set of control variables in ecological research of this nature was applied, as follows:

Sex of father: 1=female, 0= male

Sex of mother: 1=male, 0=female

Number of natural parents: Coded 0. . . . n

Age at birth: interval scale in days, months, and years

Politics of child at birth: 2=right, 1=left, 0=other

Size of place: ranges from Leacanabuaile, County Kerry (Pop. 6, all deceased) to Noo Yawk[1] in the USA (Pop. 18,976,457).

First letter of name of place of birth: A=1, B=2. . . . Z=26, other= 27.[2]

Shop opening hours: 24-hour clock standardised on GMT

Percentage owls and larks: 2=owls, 1=larks, 0=cannot make up their mind.[3]

Percentage knotters and simplifiers: 2=knotters (except on Tuesdays between 0800 and 1830 h, unless they are the middle of the two, in which case we took the average price index expressed in constant 1976 dollars in all cases except the blue ones, which were treated in a manner that seemed a good idea at the time), 1=simplifiers, 0=others.[4]

Cosmological constant: the standard Einstein factor of $A=(8\pi G/C2)\omega ac$ was applied to all cases except those measuring more than 0 or less than 10 on the Richter Scale.

Lloyd George Factor: 1=Lloyd George knew mother of the new-born child, 0=Lloyd George did not know mother of the new-born child.

Urban-rural: cities were coded urban, and villages coded rural, and all others were coded both. Urban and rural were determined by a careful analysis of how cities and villages are best coded.

Place name pronunciation: 2=place names pronounced the way they are spelled, 1=place names not pronounced the way they are spelled, 0=place names with no spelling. The data were analysed using the Schartz-Metterclume method, following procedures outlined by Kiltimagh St. John Wriothesley and Sinead Niahm O'Ceallaigh-Woiwode in their standard textbook on the subject.[5]

Results

We do not wish to burden readers with acres of complex and advanced statistical analysis in this short article, preferring to present our main results verbally.

The reader may care to note some interesting and possibly far-reaching implications of the results we obtain. First, place name is an important determinant of the cosmological constant, suggesting that the constant is area-specific right down to the microlevel. However, and perhaps more counter-intuitive, there is a strong tendency (significant at 0.33) for children who are older at birth to have mothers who are female. Notwithstanding this, age at birth is strongly associated with both sex of father and politics at birth. It seems reasonable to conclude, therefore, that political identity at birth is a significant influence on the sex of the father.

Equally, the longer the shopping hours in the place of birth (not withstanding the cosmological constant and the name of the place of birth) the more likely mothers were to be female. The Lloyd George factor is strong, explaining no less than 0.00000011 per cent of the variance. What matters, however, is not whether Lloyd George knew your father, but whether he knew your mother, and it is surprising how many he did know.

The regressions show that urban-rural differences have a significant influence. Socialist cities are strongly and negatively correlated with conservative villages (r=-.99), suggesting that they may be mutually exclusive categories. Last, age at birth is significantly associated with sex at birth, suggesting that there is a high probability of those born in their first year of life being either male or female, but not both.

The regressions also show that politics matter. The statistically significant and positive association between both socialist cities and conservative villages, and male or female sex at birth is strong confirmation of our hypothesis that the political control of local jurisdictions has a powerful influence on sex at birth. In other words, whether one is born in a socialist city and/or a politically conservative rural area strongly influences one's chances of being either male or female at birth. However, we cannot rule out the possibility of a reverse pattern of causal relations—that is, sex at birth may determine the political control of the local jurisdiction. More research on this question is urgently needed.

Conclusions

We are all too aware that our work barely scratches the surface of this important topic, and that we have raised more questions than we have answered. At the same time our results show how politics pervades every corner of human existence down to the smallest detail of how many fathers and how many mothers we have, and whether Lloyd George knew our mother or not. We recommend that the wider social science research community focuses its attention on the matters raised here, and that in the interest of scientific progress in this and other fields you give strong support to the campaign to award us a Nobel Prize next year.

Notes

1 We are given to believe that this place is not pronounced as it is spelled (and vice versa), but then, as the Murrican writer, Mawk Twine, observed, "Furriners allus pronownz better'n'ey spelt."

2 On the importance of place names as determinants of party political control see Siobhan Cichan-Enroughty's fascinating volume (2012).

3 On owl and lark theory see Menzies and McCaughey (2001), though a far more intelligent treatment of the subject is found in Manteltasche and Besser-Wisser (2002b).

4   On knotters and simplifiers see Wymondham (1632).

5   On the higher mathematics of the Schartz-Metterclume method see Marjoribanks and Woolfardisworthy (1987) but note that this book largely plagiarises the later work of Manteltasche and Besser-Wisser (2002a).

References

Belvoir, R.S.J, and J.S.R. Bicester. 2005. *Making Public Policies: A Comparative Study of Greenwich, Happisburgh, Rievaulx and Mousehole*. Towcester: Geoghagen Publishing Co.

Cichan-Enroughty, S.R.J. 2012. *What's in a Name?* Rutherfordton, NC: The Leveson-Gower and Buccleuch-McCaughrean Publishing Co.

Colquhoon, S.J.R., and R.J.S. Auchinleck. 1938. *Live Births in the OECD, 1950–2000: An Empirical Study*. Alnwick: Oswaldtwistle Books.

Manteltasche, D.D., and O.I.Q. Besser-Wisser. 2002a. "The Schartz-Metterclume Method." *Journal of Theoretical Politics* 14: 129–134.

Manteltasche, D.D., and O.I.Q. Besser-Wisser. 2002b. "Owls and Larks, Knotters and Simplifiers: The Origins of Modern Political Science." *European Political Scientist* 2: 36–42.

Marjoribanks, J.R.S., and S.R.J. Woolfardisworthy. 1987. *How Many Beans Make Five?* Trottiscliffe, Kent: Tywhitt-Tywhoo University Press.

Menzies, S.J.R., and R.S.J. McCaughey. 2001. *Larking About with Owls*. Youghiogheny, PA, and Taliaferro, MA: Hawick, Costessy, Wriothesley and Chrichton and Co.

Wymondham, S.R.J. 1632. *What's in a Name?* Boyounagh, County Durham: The Leveson-Gower and Buccleuch-McCaughrean Publishing Co.

THE SCHARTZ-METTERCLUME METHOD*

Dagobert D. Manteltasche and Otto I.Q. Besser-Wisser

This article is a short, layman's account of what is quite probably the most brilliant breakthrough in social science methodology since Pearson invented the correlation coefficient in 1888. Known as the Schartz-Metterclume Method (SM), it is a highly effective but parsimonious statistical method of deducing everything that can be known about the unknown by analysing anything that happens to be known about the known (Carlotta 1995). For a critical appraisal of SM, see Quabarl (1996). That is, SM analyses whatever data are readily to hand and uses it as the foundation for a method that uncovers causal relationships among variables about which nothing is known. The great beauty of the method is that the less that is known, the more powerful SM is and the more precise and robust the statistical results it produces. It is not necessary even to have particularly reliable factual information to start with, although it is true that wholly inaccurate information presents some tricky statistical problems for the method.

Given its remarkable capacities, it can be confidently predicted that within a few years the great majority of leading political scientists will have abandoned their current theories, methods and approaches in favour of SM. Indeed, by using the SM method itself we can predict with absolute certainty that within the next ten years all leading political scientists will have abandoned all other theories and methods in favour of SM.

It should be noted that the method is based on the most advanced statistics and mathematics; and that it draws upon the synergies of rational choice, discourse analysis and neo-postdistanciationalist theory to provide its epistemological and ontological foundations.[1] Consequently, it takes exceptional intellectual ability and many years of advanced training to be able to understand the logic of the method and many years of experience to use it satisfactorily. This article is merely a taster to prepare you for your future.

BACKGROUND

Information about the world is sometimes incomplete. For example, most data sets are inadequate: they lack crucial variables; miss a battery of vital questions; cover the wrong years; are not compatible with each other; are cross-sectional not time-series, or time-series not cross-sectional; not refined enough; have large amounts of missing data; are based upon samples that are too small or poor to sustain any generalizations; suffer from interviewer bias, bad questionnaire wording or question-order contamination; ask the wrong questions; aggregate data in the wrong way; were never pilot-tested properly; are poorly coded; classify and categorize incorrectly; were not adequately cleaned; or have incomprehensible codebooks, if they have codebooks at all. Probably the single most important complaint of social scientists is that information is inadequate for the task in hand. This is a source of agony to all empirical researchers. SM is specially designed to satisfy their every desire.

The Method in Outline

At the start, SM requires only one bit of information about one variable at a single point in time—known as a Data Singularity (DS). More information makes the job easier (while making the results less precise and reliable), but one piece of information is entirely sufficient. The DS is first subjected to dodecaphonic log-log-linear orthogonal factor analysis (DLLOFA) to establish its deep sedimented structure. This process is repeated on the deep sedimented structure, but in the reverse order, to establish the second, even deeper tessellated, fractal structure of the first layer of the deep sedimented structure. Only in this way can we probe beyond the superficial and apparent nature of the world to get to its real, underlying core. Then, by means of many trillions of binary-digital permutations a Complete Known Data Matrix (CKDM) is calculated—that is, a complete data matrix of all known information about a given phenomenon at any point in time.

From this simple and straightforward procedure it is only a short step to create a matrix for the Coefficient of Relations for all Known Variables (CRKV), which maps the causal relations between all known data at all points in time. So far the method uses conventional statistical techniques to understand the known world, but the real challenge, of course, is how to extrapolate from the CRKV to an exact and precise calculation of the Coefficient of Influence of the Unknown Variables (CIUV).[2]

There are several steps in this process:

First, all exogenous variables are endogenized, and all endogenous variables exogenized. Though easier said than done, this transformation works by a series of logico-inductive and empirical-deductive steps that triangulate on what is termed the Coefficient of Potential of Unknown Variables (CPUV). That is to say, knowing everything about the DS and hence everything about the Complete Known Data Matrix and the Coefficient of Relations for all Known Variables, it is possible to parameterize a Complete Unknown Data Matrix (CUDM). It helps in this process to ignore all non-linear relationships.

Useful though this is, it does not get us far in the determination of the causal matrix of all unknown variables. To move from the CPUV to the CIUV is the crucial step, and this is where the main power, originality and sheer aesthetic beauty of SM lies. There are two important statistical processes: (1) The ratio of explained to unexplained variance for each pair of known and unknown variables is estimated, using the conventional iterations of stochastic algebraic geometry. (2) Each of the resulting statistics is individually standardized by using the Schartz-Metterclume Normalization Procedure (SMNP)©. This is the social science equivalent of Einstein's Cosmological Constant, so it cannot be subject to any criticism from mere political scientists, although some have tried unsuccessfully (see the discussion between Wuffle [1992, 1993] and Clavicle and Patella [1995]).[3]

By standardizing the ratio of explained to unexplained variance by using the SMNP, and summing the resulting statistics, it is possible to calculate the exact contribution of the Complete Known Data Matrix to the explained variance. It follows logically that it is possible to calculate the exact contribution of the Coefficient of Potential of all Unknown Variables (CPUV) to the unexplained variance.

Last, by subjecting the complete matrix of the CPUV to analogue nonparametric infraction (not analogue parametric infraction, as some might assume) at very high temperatures it is possible to extract the essence of the problem—that is, the CIUV.

For the technically minded the SM formula can be presented thus:

SM = DS(V_1, t_1; V_2, t_1 V_n, t_n...)ϖ

⇔⇒⊄ψ<=>{DLLOFA}□C□✝□✝📖♦✠"📭"💱☒♌

⇒CKDM⌘☸◁e_T⇒🔼🔽☯ [λ≥⊄Ξℜ℘{ ℘CRKV}]

⇔χ∀≥≈⊃ϖΩM{(CUDM]/CRKV)} ę àα(Ω

⇔⇒ ℘Σ(CPUV)⚖♌⚖/CPUV♠✳□ [□9❹]Æ

⇔ΓρΞ(CUDM) ⓞ Ⱡ̃ÑMÐ✣

↔ℵφΠΣ (CPUV/R^2 (EV)%Œ ³📇⁑📡∦⋇ - CPUV/ R (uv)]

= CPUV ÐÞå œ f9ANPI)/📇✏SMNP™ ∋⇔Φςℜ

= CIUV˙

For the most advanced mathematicians this may be reduced to

$SM=BS^2$

Some political scientists trapped in pre-postmodern and linear modes of thinking, and unskilled in advanced rational-choice, discourse analysis, neo-post-distanciationalist theory and statistical methods have frankly doubted the capacity of SM to move from a small amount of known information to the vast world of the totally unknown (however, see Abramson [1997] for a qualitative approach similar in many respects to SM). It is, of course, perfectly understandable that members of the older generation should want to stick to the straight and narrow-minded. Nevertheless, they must acknowledge that the SM method has been subject to the most rigorous and exhaustive analysis. Indeed, it has been tried and tested against the best of the exciting range of new approaches to political science currently being developed in the laboratories of the Central Institute for Questions and Answers—including mess and simple survey research, focused gropes, astro-illogical studies, double-bind experiments, qualitative guesswork, scuzzy-set analysis, bald assertion, post-hoc theorizing, self-contented analysis, fashionable choice theory, algorithms and reggae rhythms, multidimensional failing, macro-dynamic contingency modelling and Wuffle's post-rational analysis. Even New Labour and Genetically Modified Foods (to say nothing of British Nuclear Fools) have not tested their products as thoroughly. We are pleased to report that on every occasion it has been tested, SM has produced better results than any of these new approaches, even on Monday mornings before the first cup of coffee and on wet Friday afternoons.

Notes

* Sadly, Otto I.Q. Besser-Wisser passed away shortly after finishing this article. For an appreciation of the great man and the great intellectual debt we all owe him, see Manteltasche (1999).

1. For a useful account of neo-postdistanciationalist theory see Clavicle and Pattella (1995).

2. We are happy to acknowledge a great debt to Sokal (1996), whose brilliant exegesis of transformative hermeneutics prompted a breakthrough in our own thinking about the conceptualization and measurement of the unknown. At the same time, however, we disagree entirely with his account of Derrida's discussion of non-linear space-time diffeomorphisms. For reasons that will be obvious to the intelligent reader by the end of this article, the crucial feature of Newton's G is not its variance (as Sokal seems to suggest) but the invariance of the variance around its variance. At the risk of pointing out the obvious, the same is not true of Einsteinian theory, where variance around the invariance of the variance approximates infinity. If this were not the case, then obviously Shartz-Metterclume could, in principle, merely approximate measurement of the unknown, rather than producing exact and precise measurement. In all modesty, however, we can only claim to have developed Shartz-Metterclume to a Newtonian level of approximation: the field awaits its Einstein.

3. As Clavicle and Patella (1995) observe, Wuffle's work cannot always be taken seriously, given that he has admitted to driving a Toyota Corolla.

References

Abramson, P.R. 1997. "Probing Well Beyond the Bounds of Conventional Wisdom." *American Journal of Political Science* 41: 675–682.

Carlotta, L. 1995. "Schartz-Metterclume, or Why the Unknown Is Not Unknowable." *Journal of Dogmatic Ontology* (August): 2014–2683.

Clavicle, H.Q, III, and H.G.W.J.G.C. Patella. 1995. "The Political Economy of the Automobile—Transient Physical Neo-postdistanciationalism." *Journal of Theoretical Politics* 7: 101–104.

Manteltasche, D.D. 1999. "Otto I. Q. Besser-Wisser: An Appreciation of the Pioneer of Post-distanciationalist Politometrics." *PS: Political Science & Politics* 32: 730–731.

Quabarl, M. 1996. "Jumping over Your Own Shadow in the Dark." *Journal of Phlogiston Sciences* 6: 34–41.

Sokal, A. 1996. "Transgressing the Boundaries: Towards a Transformative Hermeneutics of Quantum Gravity." *Social Text* 14: 217–252.

Wuffle, A. 1984. "Should You Brush Your Teeth on November 6, 1984? A Rational Choice Perspective." *PS: Political Science & Politics* 17: 577–581.

Wuffle, A. 1993. "The Political Economy of the Automobile—Four Approaches." *Journal of Theoretical Politics* 5: 409–412.

Public Policy Analysis

> "Things are more like they are now than they ever were before.
> —Dwight Eisenhower
>
> The difficulty with all policy analysis is not the known knowns, or the known unknowns, not even the unknown knowns, but the unknown unknowns.
> —Donald Rumsfeld"

Get Your Tongue Out of My Mouth 'Cause I'm Kissin' You Goodbye: The Politics of Ideas

Kenneth J. Meier

The seminal work of Derthick and Quirk (1985) argues that public policy changes when the intellectual debate of ideas establishes that policy options are legitimate and current policies are ineffective.[1] Overlooked in their otherwise exceptional analysis is the role that country music plays in the politics of ideas.[2] The thesis of this article is that country music is a crucial part of the politics of ideas, and, in fact, many policy debates are resolved in country music well before the intellectual community of policy analysts reaches a consensus. This article will recap some of the key policy debates in which country music set the agenda,[3] established the key policy alternatives, or resolved the policy debate and permitted the adoption of public policy (Anderson, 1994).[4]

Criminal Justice Policy

Perhaps the most noteworthy contribution to public policy has been country music's framing of the death penalty debate after *Furman v. Georgia*. On the one side is the classic argument for deterrence by Roger Miller (1964):

> Dang, me. Dang, me.
>
> They ought to take a rope and hang me, high from the highest tree.

Miller was effectively debated by Willie Nelson in his Red-Headed Stranger essays (Nelson, 2000):

> You can't hang a man for killin' a woman,
>
> who's trying to steal your horse.

Criminal justice policy—and country music in fact—was the inspiration for Paul Sabatier's (1988) theory of policy learning.[5] The entire Sabatier theory was borrowed from (Waylon) Jennings, and (Johnny) Cash and their commentary on Southern corrections:

> Yes, momma,[6] we're learning lots of things down here,
>
> like, there ain't no good in an evil hearted woman;
>
> I ain't cut out to be no Jesse James,
>
> You don't go writing hot checks, down in Mississippi,
>
> and there ain't no good chain gang. (Cash & Jennings, 1978)

The contribution of country music to criminal justice policy is evident in some of the major policy proposals by scholars. Quite clearly James Quince Wilson borrowed his theory that crime is a function of demographics, specifically young males, and that demographic change would eventually resolve some of the crime problems from Hank Williams Jr. (1982b), who noted:

> Nobody wants to get drunk and get loud,
>
> All my rowdy friends have settled down.

On a more intellectual level, Ray Wiley Hubbard (1973) has argued that a person's environment is a major determinant of criminal behavior:

> He was born in Oklahoma,[7]
>
> his wife's name is Betty Lou Thelma Liz.
>
> He's not responsible for what he's doing,
>
> his mother made him what he is,
>
> and it's up against the wall, redneck mother . . .[8]

The impact of dysfunctional families on crime was reinforced by Hank Williams Jr. (1979):

> Hank, Why do you drink? Why do you roll smoke?
>
> Why must you live out the songs that you wrote?
>
> . . . If I get stoned and sing all night long,
>
> It's a family tradition.

Even the famed insanity defense was effectively rebutted by Texas's own Kinky Friedman singing with the Texas Jew Boys about Charlie Whitman, best known for climbing the library tower at the University of Texas with a rifle and engaging targets of opportunity:

> There was a rumor about a tumor,
>
> nestled at the base of his brain.
>
> He was sitting up there with his .36 magnum,
>
> who are we to say the boy's insane (Friedman, 1973c).

Finally, convincing evidence suggests that Ronald Reagan decided to launch his war on drugs after listing to the songs of Kris Kristofferson (1970b):[9]

> The law is for protection of the people,
>
> rules are rules as any fool can see.
>
> We don't need no druggies like Joe Stewart,
>
> scarin' decent folks like you and me.

Reinventing Government

Well before there was a Grace Commission or Albert Gore, country music was concerned with government efficiency and how it could operate better. David Allen Coe (1976) was in the forefront of the debate questioning the precursor to educational voucher systems. Speaking of his father:

> He bought the house on the GI Bill,
>
> but it wasn't worth all he had to kill to get it.
>
> . . . coal burning stove, no natural gas,
>
> if that ain't country, I'll kiss your ass.

Similarly, the HUD scandal involving section 8 rehabilitation programs under Ronald Reagan was first brought to national attention by David Frizzel (2000a):

> I'm gonna hire a wino to decorate our home.[10]

Family Values

Although family values is a Republican euphemism for "Democrats have more fun," it has set several issues related to families on the national agenda. All these issues have been debated by two advocacy coalitions in country music (Sabatier & Jenkins-Smith, 1994),[11] including:

1. The importance of male role models: (Moe Bandy & Joe Stampley, 2003)

   > Tell ole' I ain't here, he better git on home
   >
   > or else he's gonna find me and the baby gone.

2. The effort to deify Pat Nixon as a role model: (Merle Haggard, 1999)

   > Back before microwave ovens, when
   >
   > a girl could still cook, still would . . .

Or more succinctly put by Kinky Friedman (1973a):

> This women's liberation has gone to your head,
>
> get your biscuits in the oven and your buns in bed.

Friedman (1973a) also set the stage for the classic Brady and Stampley essay "Ladies in Pink" by stating:

> if you can't love a male chauvinist,
>
> you better cross me off your Christmas list.[12]

This idealized version of Ozzie and Harriet (or Waylon and Jessie) permeates the politics of ideas in country music, Merle Haggard and Willie Nelson (1982a) state:

> We're looking for a home life with clean smelling sheets
>
> and all the soft places to fall.

The male focus on family values has not gone unchallenged. In fact, the second advocacy coalition contains the roots of the feminist movement and is a clear reaction to the effort to impose these family values. In the words of Kitty Wells (1995): "It wasn't God who made honky-tonk angels."[13] A similar statement with a different short-term strategy was expressed by Emmy Lou Harris (1978): "It's midnight and I'm all right, 'cause I got two more bottles of wine." Linking these issues to spouse abuse is Linda Ronstadt (1974), who noted: "I've been cheated, been mistreated, when will I be loved?" Similar positions were noted on family values by Loretta Lynn (1967), "Don't come home a drinkin' with lovin' on your mind" and by Lorrie Morgan (1995):

> I'm not interested in romance
>
> or what you had in mind,
>
> What part of "no" don't you understand?

These arguments often were used in response to Kenny Rogers's (currently a pitcher for the Texas Rangers) question about why Ruby took her love to town. The debate was effectively ended by Loretta Lynn (1990) who stated:

> All these years I stayed at home,
>
> while you had all your fun. . . .
>
> It's gettin' dark, it's roosting time,
>
> tonight's too good to be real.
>
> But daddy don't you worry none,
>
> 'cause momma's got the pill.

Immigration Policy

Country music both anticipated the current debate over immigration policy and the current scholarly emphasis on regulatory enforcement originated by Dan Wood. In the words of Merle Haggard and Willie Nelson (1982b):

> All the federales say, they could have had him any day,
>
> they only let him slip away, out of kindness, I suppose.

Welfare Reform

The 1980s debate over welfare reform was effectively set on the agenda by Charles Murray in his book *Losing Ground*,[14] which contends that the decline in the work ethic was responsible for the persistence of poverty. Murray, of course, borrowed this line of reasoning from Johnny Paycheck (1999): "Take this job and shove it, I ain't workin' here no more."

Federalism

The question of federal-state relations triggering the Reagan administration's attempt to devolve federal regulatory authority was borrowed from Waylon Jennings's (1975) treatise, "It don't matter who's in Austin. Bob Wills is still the king."[15]

Environmental Policy

Environment policy is a second policy area in which country music has spawned two advocacy coalitions, one based on development and the other on conservation and protection. On the development side are the advocates of industrialization, especially important infrastructures such as railroads and trucking. The list of important contributions is endless: Roy Acuff ("The Wabash Cannon Ball," 1955); C.W. McCall ("Convoy," 1975); Glen Campbell ("I Love My Truck," 2000),[16] Arlo Guthrie ("The City of New Orleans": "I got the disappearing railroad blues," 1972).

The leading spokesperson among the conservation people is Hank Williams Jr. (1982c), who targets cities as the major problem. In regard to New York City he argued, "If this is the promised land, then I've had all I can stand." Williams essentially advocates a back to nature policy: "I got a shot gun, rifle, and a four wheel drive, a country boy can survive" (Williams, 1982a). The issue of overgrazing federal lands was effectively raised by Nelson and Jennings (2003): "Mommas don't let your babies grow up to be cowboys," and seconded by Kinky Friedman (1973b): "Ride, Ride 'em Jew Boy, ride 'em all around the old corral."

This coalition actually grew out of the endangered species movement formed by Roger Miller (1991): "No, you can't roller skate in a buffalo herd."[17] The threats to humankind from failure to recognize the need for endangered species was summarized best by Buck Owens (1965):

> I've got a tiger by the tail, it's plain to see.
>
> I won't be much when she gets through with me.
>
> I'm losing weight and looking kind of pale.
>
> Looks like I got a tiger by the tail.

So Conway Twitty was really advocating a saner toxic waste policy when he contended, "Mister, there's a tiger in these tight fittin' jeans" (1981).

Education Policy

The current debates over the rigor of higher education and the movement toward political correctness was also initiated by Kinky Friedman's "Ballad of Charlie Whitman." About the students at the University of Texas, he stated:

> some were dying, some were weeping
>
> some were studying, some were sleeping,
>
> some were shouting Texas #1 (1973c)[18]

Education as the means to compete in world markets is recognized by Billy Joe Shaver's song about trade relations with Japan:

> I got a good Christian raisin',
>
> and an eighth grade education,
>
> ain't no need yawl to treat me this a way. (1993)

Bureaucratic Policies

Some policies are initiated and adopted by bureaucracies rather than the major political institutions.[19] Bureaucracies are also influenced by the politics of ideas as expressed in country music. Quite clearly the U.S. Department of Agriculture decided to revise its food and nutrition chart after being persuaded by the arguments of Kris Kristofferson (1970a):

> I woke up Sunday morning
>
> with no way to hold my head that didn't hurt.
>
> The beer I had for breakfast, wasn't bad
>
> so I had one more for dessert.[20]

Similarly, the Federal Communications Commission's effort to reregulate cable television was triggered by a policy analysis done by Hank Williams Jr. (1982d):

> There are some preachers on TV, with a suit, and a tie, and a vest. They want you to send your money to the lord, but they give you their address.

Finally, the Department of Health and Human Services policy on organ donors was taken directly from Janie Fricke (2002): "I don't want your body, if your heart's not in it."

Conclusion

This article has effectively demonstrated that country music sets the agenda for the politics of ideas. In case after case, it is country musicians debating major changes in public policy and coming to a resolution that sets the pattern for the policy debates in Congress, the bureaucracy, and the executive branch. That this will continue into the future is not in doubt.[21] In the words of Kris Kristofferson (1970c):

> There's lots of drinks that I ain't drunk,
>
> Lots of pretty thoughts that I ain't thunk,
>
> There's still a lot of wine and lonely girls,
>
> in this best of all policy advocacy worlds.

Notes

The article title comes from a 1995 unpublished John Denver song. Copyright by John Denver. I would like to thank Jack Daniels, if you please (Coe, 1983); Jose Cuervo, who is a friend of mine (West, 1994); the beer that made Milwaukee famous (and made a loser out of me) (Lewis, 1968); and a great speckled bird for inspiration.

1. If you think that my interpretation of Derthick and Quirk is wrong, remember the words of Hank Williams Jr. (1981), "I got a right to be wrong."

2. One might wonder how the *APSR* has missed this important political phenomenon. A journal must have priorities and everyone admits the *APSR* has published and continues to do so all the seminal works on Thucydides on war.

3. The agenda setting literature flourishes because it lacks a falsifiable hypothesis. So here's one: No issue is ever placed on the agenda unless Willie Nelson sings about it. Whether this is more useful than policy windows coinciding with policy streams, and the like, I leave to future research.

4. It is unusual to cite Anderson in regard to country music since his position is that music is the food of gods, see Anderson (1994).

5. By now most people will recognize that all my work contains a gratuitous footnote to Paul Sabatier. This is it.

6. We should point out that the phrase "yo momma" is considered complimentary in country music.

7. This is clearly a necessary condition, and may well be a sufficient condition. Note that there is a related literature on slander by David Frizzel and Shelly West: "You're the reason God made Oklahoma" (Frizzel, 2000b).

8. In the words of Willie Nelson (1978): "I gotta get drunk and I sure do dread it, 'cause here's what I'm gonna do, I'm gonna spend all my money callin' everybody 'honey,' and wind up singing the blues."

9. This would have been the only case in which Reagan got any intelligent policy advice on the war on drugs. See Shull (1985).

10. There is also some truth to the rumor that the HUD scandal was called to the attention of the General Accounting Office when an accountant heard David Frizzel's song and recalled that he had approved a HUD voucher for such decoration.

11. This is a second gratuitous cite to Paul Sabatier; most country music people think an advocacy coalition is a form of group sex.

12. See Brady (1988).

13. Wells was of course rebutting Hank Thompson, who was thanking God for honky-tonk angels, which was probably the first effort to establish that family values means that a woman's job is to stay home and take care of the kids and keep the family operating while the man's function is drinking, cheating, and lying. More recently this perspective has been used by Shepsle (1993) to create a formal model of Congress.

14. If you're looking for a cite on Murray, forget it. I don't have time to look up every book you're interested in the library. Do it yourself.

15. For a more scholarly look at this question see Wood (1988). For an alternative view, see Eisner (1990).

16. There are those misguided souls who think that Campbell is advocating the repeal of laws that declare relationships that are not heterosexual illegal. See Stewart (1986). Stewart's argument is based on the oft-heard statement, "I'd rather push a Ford than drive a Chevy."

17. Others contend the origin of the conservation movement was a concern with clean water, see Ringquist (1997).

18. See Sheffield (1991).

19. If you don't know this, you ought not be in public policy.

20. Kristofferson is also attempting to influence the Food and Drug Administration policy on prescription drug approvals. Here he triggers the debate on whether the FDA should permit folk remedies even if they violate the general research standards needed to demonstrate that the drug is safe and effective. See Savage (1991).

21. It should be noted that all references that are not included in the reference list (i.e., footnotes, in-text citations) may be marginally inaccurate due to a slight touch (well, maybe a heavy dose) of poetic license on the author's part.

References

Acuff, Roy. 1955. The Wabash Cannonball. On *Songs of the Smokey Mountains*. Dualtone Music Group.

Anderson, James. 1994. "Lutefisk, Leftse and Ja Sure Ya Betcha: The Role of the Accordion in Public Policy Analysis." *Journal of Norwegian Studies* 1: 1–23.

Bandy, Moe, and Joe Stampley, Jr. 2003. Tell ole' I ain't here, he better get on home. On *Moe and Joe: The Ultimate Hits Collection*. Audium.

Brady, Da Willie. 1988. "Ladies in Pink and Pink Ladies." *Journal of Pastels* 37: 374–396.

Campbell, Glenn. 2000. I love my truck. On *Super Hits*. Atlantic.

Cash, Johnny, and Waylon Jennings. 1978. Ain't no good chain gang. On *I Would Like to See You Again*. Columbia Records.

Coe, David Allen. 1993. Jack Daniels, if you please. On *Superhits*. Columbia.

Coe, David Allen. 1976. If that ain't country. On *Longhaired Rednecks*. Bear Family.

Denver, John. 1995. Get your tongue out of my mouth, I'm kissing you goodbye. *Unpublished Song*. Copyright John Denver.

Eisner, Marc Allen. 1990. "Bob Wills Was Just a Bureaucrat." *Journal of Obscure Public Administration* 1–4.

Fricke, Janie. 2002. Your heart's not in it. On *Live at Billy Bob's Texas*. Smith Music.

Friedman, Kinky. 1973a. Get your biscuits in the oven and your buns in the bed. On *Sold American*. Vanguard.

Friedman, Kinky. 1973b. Ride 'em, Jew Boy. On *Sold American*. Vanguard.

Friedman, Kinky. 1973c. The ballad of Charles Whitman. On *Sold American*. Vanguard.

Frizzel, D. 2000a. I'm gonna hire a wino (to decorate our home). On *Best of the Best*. Federal.

Frizzel, David. 2000b. You're the reason God made Oklahoma. On *Best of the Best*. Federal.

Guthrie, Arlo. 1972. The city of New Orleans. On *Hobo's Lullabye*. Koch.

Haggard, Merle. 1999. Are the good times really over? On *For the Record: 43 Legendary Hits*. BNA Records.

Haggard, Merle, and Willie Nelson. 1982a. All the soft places to fall. On *Pancho and Lefty*. Legacy Records.

Haggard, Merle, and Willie Nelson. 1982b. Pancho and Lefty. On *Pancho and Lefty*. Legacy Records.

Harris, EmmyLou. 1978. Two more bottles of wine. On *Quarter Moon in a Ten Cent Town*. Warner Brothers.

Hubbard, R.W. [songwriter]. (1973, ca.) Up against the wall, redneck mother. Performed by Jerry Jeff Walker on *Viva Terlingua*. MCA.

Jennings, Waylon. 1975. Bob Willis is still the king. On *Dreaming My Dreams*. Buddha Records.

Kristofferson, Kris. 1970a. Sunday mornin' comin' down. On *Kris Kristofferson*. Monument Record Corp.

Kristofferson, Kris. 1970b. The law is for the protection of the people. On *Kris Kristofferson*. Monument Record Corp

Kristofferson, Kris. 1970c. The best of all possible worlds. On *Kris Kristofferson*. Monument Record Corp.

Lewis, Jerry Lee. 1968. What made Milwaukee famous (has made a loser out of me). On *Another Time, Another Place/Walking the Floor*, Raven Records.

Lynn, Loretta. 1967. Don't come home a drinkin'. On *Don't come home a drinkin'*. Decca.

Lynn, Loretta. 1990. The pill. On *Loretta Lynn: Country Music Hall of Fame Series*. MCA.

McCall, C. W. 1975. Convoy. On *Greatest Hits*. Mercury.

Miller, Roger. 1991. You can't roller skate in a buffalo herd. On *Roger Miller: His Greatest Hits*. Curb Records.

Miller, Roger. 1964. Dang me. On *Dang Me*. Tree Publishing Company.

Morgan, Lorrie. 1995. What part of no. On *Greatest Hits*. BNA.

Nelson, Willie. 2003. Mamas don't let your babies grow up to be cowboys. On *A tribute to Willie Nelson*. Tribute.

Nelson, Willie. 2000. Red-headed stranger. On *Red-headed stranger*. Sony.

Nelson, Willie. 1978. I gotta get drunk. On *Willie and family life*. Legacy Recordings.

Owens, Buck. 1965. I've got a tiger by the tail. On *I've got a tiger by the tail*. Sundazed Music.

Paycheck, Johnny. 1999. Take this job and shove it. On *16 biggest hits*. Epic.

Ringquist, Evan. 1997. "The Young Pioneers and Cool Clear Water." *Journal of Sewage Treatment* 36: 124–189.

Rogers, Kenny. 1983. Ruby, don't take your love to town. On *20 greatest hits*. Capitol Nashville.

Ronstadt, Linda. 1974. When will I be loved? On *Heart like a wheel*. Capitol/EMI Records.

Savage, Robert. 1991. "It's Not Just for Breakfast Anymore: Beer as the Next Wonder Drug." *Journal of Medical Intoxication*.

Shaver, B.J. 1993. Georgia on a fast train. On *Tramp on your street*. Zoo/Volcano.

Sheffield, Jimmy Joe Bob. 1991. "Texas #1: The Legacy of Longhorn Football." *Journal of Ancient History* 7: 26–47.

Shepsle, Kenneth. 1993. "Alphonse D'Amato's Preference Curves Are Convex to the Origin." *Public Choice* 27.

Shull, Steven. 1985. "If Nancy Reagan Just Says 'No': How Come She's Anorexic and Glassy Eyed?" *Presidential Studies Quarterly*.

Stewart, Joseph, Jr., 1986. "Consenting Adults, Pickups, and Sodomy." *Motor Trend*, 47: 2–14.

Twitty, Conway. 1981. Tight fittin' jeans. On *Red neckin' love makin' night*. Universal Special Products.

Wells, Kitty. 1995. It wasn't God who made honky-tonk angels. On *It wasn't God who made honky-tonk angels*. Universal Special Products.

West, S. (1983). Jose Cuervo. On *Alone and together*. Universal MCA.

Williams, Hank, Jr. 1982a. A country boy can survive. On *Greatest Hits*. Curb Records.

Williams, Hank, Jr. 1982b. All my rowdy friends (have settled down). On *Greatest Hits*. Curb Records.

Williams, Hank, Jr. 1982c. Dixie on my mind. On *Greatest Hits*. Curb Records.

Williams, Hank, Jr. 1982d. The American dream. On *Greatest Hits*. Curb Records.

Williams, Hank, Jr. 1981. I got a right to be wrong. *Rowdy*. Curb Records.

Williams, Hank, Jr. 1979. Family tradition. On *Family Tradition*. Curb Records.

Wood, B. Dan. 1988. "Bob Wills: A Principal-Agent Model." *Music City News*, 24–30.

The Political Economy of the Automobile—Four Approaches

A Wuffle

The aim of this brief note is to contribute to a much neglected topic: the study of collective movement. Earlier work[1] has dealt with vertical movement; here our focus is on the horizontal. We adapt models representing the views of four different schools of economics: (1) the Chicago school, (2) the rational expectations school, (3) the Malthusian school, and (4) the Veblenian school. We seek to represent these models in a form from which their commonsense plausibility will be apparent.

The Chicago School

At the heart of Chicago economics is the "law of the invisible bumper." The law of the invisible bumper states that "if every person drives in whatever direction he or she wishes at whatever speed he or she finds convenient, everyone will get to their destination with the least total expenditure of gas." Closely related to the "law of the invisible bumper" is the postulate that what any given car does cannot matter, since no single car can significantly affect either the direction or the speed of the "prevailing traffic."[2] In the view of Chicago-trained economists, that the assumptions of a model are completely unrealistic is not of relevance to its probable accuracy, since the test of a model does not lie in its assumptions.[3] In particular, in modeling the behavior of cars and drivers as a free market, it is appropriate to neglect the fact that automobiles are by and large driven on roads built by governments, with speed limits and other rules of the road enforced by government officials.

While criticized by John Kenneth Galbraith for their failure to take into account traffic fatalities and smog in evaluating the potential merits of traffic regulation (by focusing only on what minimizes gas consumption), Chicago-trained economists have convincingly replied that whatever may be the drawbacks of roads without speed limits, automotive pollution control devices or policemen, government attempts to make things better would only make things worse. Indeed, this view that "government can do no good" is an article of faith of neoclassicists, and they have devoted a great deal of effort to abolishing the On-road Safety and Highway Administration, an arm of the federal government whose efforts they have ridiculed. However, their negative view of government has recently been challenged by economists of the "rational expectations" school.

The Rational Expectations School

Unlike the more old-fashioned Chicago school, which merely believes that "all human behavior can be viewed as involving participants who maximize their utility from a stable set of preferences and accumulate an optimal amount of information and other inputs in a variety of markets" (Becker, 1976:14),[4] the rational expectations school believes that drivers are rational not just in their own behavior but in their ability to anticipate the behavior of the other drivers. In particular, because they accept the Chicago view that every driver will drive perfectly, drivers can also anticipate perfectly the behavior of other drivers. Thus, it is a central tenet of the rational expectations school that no improvements to highway safety can result from government intervention, since if the accident could have been anticipated it logically could not have occurred in the first place. However, the really critical difference between the rational expectations school and the Chicago school comes in how they view the possibility that government action can make things worse. Chicago-trained economists, of course, hold the view that "that government is best which regulates traffic least";[5] rational expectations economists, in contrast, believe that government can do no nothing that will in any way affect the flow of traffic, since any regulation that government can impose will be anticipated and thus have no discernible consequences.

The Malthusian School

The central tenet of the Malthusian school is that "the population of cars expands geometrically, while roads expand only linearly; thus, there will always be fewer lanes than there are cars to fill them." This school is especially strong in California and on Long Island. There is considerable empirical support for the central tenet of Malthusian doctrine: For example, from 1970 to 1980, highway mileage went from 3,730,000 miles to 3,955,000 miles, a rate of growth of only 0.6 percent per year (*Statistical Abstract of the United States*, 1989, Table 1003). In contrast, from 1970 to 1980, motor vehicle registrations increased from 108,418,000 to 155,796,000, a rate of growth 8 times greater than that of highway mileage (*Statistical Abstract of the United States*, 1989, Table 1012).

During the oil crisis of the 1970s, economists of the Malthusian school were heard making the claim that is was no use blaming the Arabs, rather it was Mother Nature who was to blame for the fact that the car population had outstripped the fuel resources needed to support it. Further support for the Malthusian view has been found in my own empirical work showing conclusively that, in this century, the US population of cars has expanded faster than its population of people. For example, in 1987, over 7 million cars were born in the USA,[6] whereas the US population grew by only slightly more than 2 million (*Statistical Abstract of the United States*, 1989 Tables 1013, 23 and 27).[7,8]

The Veblenian School

While few contemporary economists are willing to admit that Thorstein Veblen was an economist despite his having held an academic position in that discipline,[9] Veblen's insights into the consumer society have striking applications to our present topic. In particular, Veblen's third law, "As you drive so shall you be judged,"[10] might seem to be the only way to account for the fact that some people actually pay more for their cars than what other people have paid for their homes.[11] However, Chicago-trained economists have propounded an alternative explanation for America's love affair with the automobile by appealing to the principle of utility maximization (distance minimization) in accord with Euclid's famous postulate of California geometry: "The shortest distance between any two points passes through an automobile."[12, 13]

Notes

1. See, e.g., Wuffle (1982).

2. Chicago-trained economists also tend to neglect the fact that there are some very large trucks on the road, whose behavior other drivers have to pay attention to.

3. If subjective factors (such as politics or psychology) are admitted into the models of Chicago-trained economists they do so by making the only realistic assumption possible about human behavior—positing that all human beings behave exactly like Chicago-trained economists.

4. Yes, Virginia, he really said that.

5. Few are aware that the famous phrase "laissez-faire" is only the first half of a longer expression: "laissez faire, laissez passer" (Galbraith 1987, 51). Fewer still are aware that the latter phase was first used in French chariot races of the Middle Ages by drivers seeking the right of way.

6. Actually, many of them were born in Japan and Korea and came as immigrants into the US.

7. As of 1986, there were only 158,494,000 licensed drivers in the US, but 181,000,000 registered motor vehicles (*Statistical Abstract of the United States*, 1989, Tables 1013 and 1023). An intriguing empirical question is "Who is driving the extra 22,506,000 vehicles?"

8. Related work has been done by Grofman (1988).

9. Economists generally consign him to the same category as that of former Ambassador John Kenneth Galbraith, namely that of pop sociologist.

10. At Prego's, an ultra-posh Italian restaurant in Irvine, drivers of BMWs and Porsches have their cars valet-parked prominently in front of the restaurant, while those who (like me) drive 1981 Toyota Corollas have their car parked far away so as to be well out of sight of potential restaurant patrons.

11. However, it was not Veblen, but I who first noted that "If wishes were horses, California beggars would drive very powerful cars."

12. It is important to understand that, in California, distance is measured in minutes, not miles. For example, the answer to the question "How far is it between UCI and UCLA?" is "A little over an hour, if traffic is moving."

13. Other economists, inspired by evolutionary analogies, have proposed that automobiles, like dinosaurs, have lost their niche, and should be replaced by smaller and more flexible vehicles, e.g., bikes. George Orwell, not normally thought of as an economist, uttered what has become the rallying cry for groups as diverse as environmentalists and the Hell's Angels: "Two wheels good, four wheels bad."

References

Galbraith, John Kenneth. 1987. *Economics in Perspective: A Critical History*. New York: Houghton Mifflin.

Grofman, Bernard. 1988. "The Supply Elasticity of the American Indian Population, 1950–1980." *Public Choice* 57: 85–88.

Wuffle, A. 1982. "The Pure Theory of Elevators." *Mathematics Magazine* 55: 30–37.

The Political Economy of the Automobile—A Fifth Approach Transient Physical Neo-Postdistanciationalist Theory

Hiram Q. Clavicle, III, and H.G.W.J.G.C. Patella

This is probably the most important article in political science of the post-war period. It argues that the theory of transient physical neo-postdistanciationalism can explain everything in need of explanation in politics and things that need no explanation at all. The theory is parsimonious yet powerful, and solves some timeless mysteries of human existence, including the theory of escalators, ball point pens, and Murphy's Law Number 283.

We are frankly astounded that A Wuffle (1993) chooses four outdated theories to explore the political economy of the automobile. We are not surprised that someone so far behind recent theoretical developments should drive a 1981 Toyota Corolla. Not only does Wuffle fail to theoreticize the dynamic historical totality of the postmodern world, but his four theories fail to explain why there are more than 22 million more registered cars than registered drivers in the USA. The simple fact is that there is a major fifth theory which solves at one and the same time all the theoretical loose ends of his four approaches, and explains everything that has happened in the past. This is the theory of transient physical neo-postdistanciationalism. For his sake, and that of readers, we outline the theory below.

Distanciationalist Theory

The central tenet of distanciationalist theory is that the objectified distance between two or more points in any given physical environment and within any given time frame is directly related to a positivistic estimation of the temporal elapse incurred in transposition between them, whereas the subjectified distance between any two points in any given social environment and within any given time frame is directly but exponentially related to the socially engendered desire for transposition between them (Schleist, 1923).

It becomes clear from this formulation of the problem of physical and social movement that Wuffle's approach is merely a special case of a more general theoretizational project concerned with the explication of movement in both physical and social environments. As such, it encompasses the topics of both horizontal and vertical physical movement (e.g., by elevator and automobile) and horizontal and vertical social movement (e.g., moving between concurrent social roles and social climbing).[1, 2]

Transient Physical Distanciationalism

The original distanciationalist theorem developed by Otto Schleist has passed through several stages of conceptual and theoretical refinement—neo-distanciationalism, post-distanciationalism, post-neodistanciationalism and, most recently, neo-postdistanciationalism—but for present purposes we will concentrate on the two main contemporary schools of thought.

These are the transient physical neo-postdistanciationalisms, led by Chitinous, Gastropod, Arachnid and others (see Chitinous and Gastropod 1952) and the social neo-postdistanciationalism of Patella, Clavicle and Zygomatic (Reticle 1989).

Both schools recognize the crucial importance of Schleist's hypothesis of the "nevernessless of the physical-social continuum" but differ on the diurturnity of the first, and the intransientnessless of the second. Naturally, the diuturnitalist school was primarily responsible for the claim that we are currently witnessing the twilight of the discourse-analytical mode of discourse. This is now universally accepted in advanced theoretical circles (Butter, 1984).

However, we are mainly concerned in this short article with transient physical neo-postdistanciationalism (hereafter TPNP) and especially the problem of intransientlessness in any given space-time continuum. By means of advanced mathematical calculations too complex to explain to political scientists, we have established that there was not one big bang which created our universe, but 27 big bangs each creating a separate universe with its own alternative virtual reality. Furthermore, by means of irrefutable logical deduction we have succeeded in proving that each universe is the natural home for a different variety of physical objects which will migrate there from other universes in which they find themselves. That is, they will migrate if they have the chance but doing so requires them happening upon a correct hole in the space-time continuum by which they can exit from one universe and move to their desired universe. Hence TPNP is concerned not merely with physical movement within our own universe but also with physical movement between parallel universes.

"Oh ho," you (the reader) might say, "this is all very good in theory. But where is the evidence?" The theory of TPNP does, indeed, have a good deal of prima facie plausibility, but notwithstanding this, we have devoted most of our research time over the past 30 odd years to collecting cast-iron proof for it. First we will start with an observation by Wuffle himself.

Item

Wuffle observes in passing that the number of licensed vehicles exceeds the number of licensed drivers in the United States and asks, "Who is driving these extra vehicles?" By implication he admits that none of his four theories can even begin to tackle the question. But TPNP has the answer, and the answer is "No one"; our own universe is simply the natural home for vehicles which relocate here from other universes. The 22 million extra vehicles have obviously moved here because our universe constitutes their natural home. It is to be hoped that none of the 26 other alternative universes happen upon their own form of Henry Ford. Moreover, our theory explains another mystery. A short walk around any city in the world (particularly car parks, canals and bits of waste land) will show a large number of excess supermarket trolleys. Where do these come from? The answer, of course, is that our own universe is also the natural home of trolleys, and the excess has migrated here from other universes. Thus TPNP not only solves the Wuffle Mystery, but also The Great Supermarket Trolley Mystery as well.

Item

Our recent article in the *Ball Point Manufacturers and Retailers Monthly Review* shows that each literate adult person in our universe buys an average of 1.628677 ball points every calendar month, and yet has only 0.976377 ball points in their possession at any given point in time. What has happened to the missing ball points? TPNP shows that they have moved to their "natural" universe. The inside pockets of men's suits and the discarded purses of women are, we have shown beyond all shadow of doubt, access points to other universes.

Item

Murphy's Law No. 283, states that "If you put into your washing machine six pairs of black socks, a couple of coloured T-shirts and a pair of jeans, you will get out three pairs of black socks, three odd socks, a tartan shirt and a washed, bleached, shrunk and largely destroyed bank note" (Wall 1982). This law has been empirically verified over and over again, but no explanation found for it until now. The answer, we know from TPNP, is that washing machine doors cover holes in the space-time continuum which open out into alternative universes.

Item

There has been much discussion of late about "phantom withdrawals" from bank cash points. People put in their cheque card, punch in a request for 100 units of money and at irregular intervals something like 289,632 units of money disappear from their bank account. Banks have hired very expensive accountants, advertising executives, psychologists, lawyers and electronic engineers to prove that this does not and cannot happen. But around the world many thousands of people know full well that it can and has happened to them. The answer is that the money has gone to its natural home in an alternative universe, and that cash points are the doors in the space-time continuum by which it leaves our own universe.

Conclusion

We have outlined the main features of transient physical neo-postdistanciationalist theory. It explains not just horizontal and vertical physical movement in our own universe (of the kind considered by Wuffle) but all kinds of physical movement in all known universes. The theory is parsimonious but has a powerful explanatory potential. Not only does it explain things which cannot be otherwise explained, but it explains things which need no explanation at all. We have not had the time, space or inclination to elaborate all our evidence but we might add, in passing, that this includes (1) the fact that a very high proportion of political scientists wish to be in a Department other than their current one, (2) the fact that very close to 50 percent of live births in urban areas are female, while close to 50 percent of live births in rural areas are male (Harrow and Tator, 1978), and (3) that almost exactly half of all married people are male. We recommend the theory to all readers in this and other universes.

Notes

1. It seems not to have occurred to Wuffle that there are special theoretical difficulties entailed in forms of physical movement which combine the horizontal and the vertical at the same time—e.g., by escalator. But that is a different story.

2. On social climbing see Parkin and Parkin (1974).

References

Butter, Roland. 1984. *Fast Food for Thought.* London: Hole in the Corner Press.

Chitinous, Hubert, and Vladimir Orlando Gastropod. 1952. "The Functions and Powers of the Rural District Clerk: A Transient Physical Neo-postdistanciationalist Approach." *Rural District Review* 34: 38–342.

Harrow, Tom, and Dick Tator. 1978. "Urban Determinants of Sex at Birth." *Journal of Phantasmogorical Studies* 34: 2–4.

Parkin, Rosa, and Charley. 1974. "Peter Rabbit and the *Grundrisse.*" *European Journal of Sociology* 15: 181–183.

Reticle, Theo. 1989. "Theories of the World Tell Us More about the Theorists than about the World." *Central Institute for Questions and Answers, Very Occasional Papers,* Number 897.

Schleist, Otto. 1923. "Do Taller Men Wear Longer Trousers, and If So Why?" *Journal of Reject Studies:* 204–313.

Wall, Walter. 1982. "The Significance of the Fitted Carpet in Modern Political Thought." *Tiler and Grouter Quarterly Review* 18: 36–57.

Wuffle, A. 1993. "The Political Economy of the Automobile—Four Approaches." *Journal* of *Theoretical Politics* 5: 409–12.

Voting Behavior and Party Competition

Should You Brush Your Teeth on November 6, 1984? A Rational Choice Perspective

A Wuffle

American educators have long been concerned about whether our citizens brush their teeth. In our schools children are exhorted to brush their teeth and warned that dangerous consequences will follow if they do not. Nonetheless, the rate of toothbrushing seems to have fallen in the general population (1980 is a partial exception), and the blame can't be attributed solely to poor dental care socialization of the younger generation. Rather the decline in toothbrushing appears among a wide range of citizens. This decline has been blamed on a variety of causes, including a growing lack of respect for the role of teeth in our society, which some scholars believe to have been intensified by the Wonderbread scandal.

One group of scholars, using what they call a rational choice approach, has developed a model to explain the conditions under which people will brush their teeth, and also to explain which of the two American styles of toothbrushing, U (up and down) and S (side to side), citizens will adopt.[1] Any single day's brushing will have an imperceptible effect on whether or not the citizen does or does not get C_0, zero cavities, or C_1, one cavity. Hence, on any given day, rational citizens should not brush their teeth.

This "rational choice" view has distressed a number of scholars, since it seems to imply that *nobody* will brush their teeth. (Clearly, it is costly to brush one's teeth in time and energy, not to speak of the cost of periodically buying a new toothbrush.) Since most citizens still do brush their teeth, this "rational choice" view quite obviously makes little sense (cf. Grofman 1983). On the other hand, some scholars (see, for example, Niemi 1977) have rebutted by pointing out that many people actually get pleasure from brushing their teeth and that toothbrushing is a topic of family conversation and, thus, in many ways a social rather than an individual act.[2,3] Moreover, one classic empirical study in the *American Dental Science Review* (Riker and Ordeshook 1968) showed that many people feel that brushing their teeth is a duty, regardless of its effect on tooth decay. Indeed, this perception of duty was more important than other instrumental factors.

Other scholars in the rational choice tradition have sought to show that brushing can sometimes be rational if you have a strong fear of tooth decay and don't care about probabilities, but only about worst possible cases. This minimax-regret model has, however, never been felt to be particularly convincing by anyone other than its propounders.[4]

We believe the usual analysis of the rational choice model of toothbrushing is misguided on three counts. First, empirical work on the rational calculus of toothbrushing has been marred by an emphasis on front teeth. Most of work on the perceived relative desirability of side-to-side vs. up-and-down styles, and (for reasons incomprehensible to me) virtually all work on brushing vs. nonbrushing, has been confined to the perceived impact of brushing on the upper front teeth only, completely neglecting the fact that the ordinary person generally brushes a number of teeth at once and is at least somewhat concerned (albeit not equally) with all of them. (Cf. "All I want for November is my two front teeth.")

A second difficulty with the usual rational choice analysis is that it treats toothbrushing as a one-shot decision. Since citizens are confronted with a large number of occasions on which they must decide whether or not to brush (and a reasonably large number of teeth which might be brushed on any given occasion), looking at the decision from a rule-utilitarian rather than the customary act-utilitarian perspective seems to be the more sensible approach.[5] This point is reinforced by Weisberg and Grofman's (1981) finding that an excellent predictor of front-two-teeth toothbrushing is previous brushing history; i.e., the decision to brush or not to brush one's two front teeth on any given day seems to reflect a considerable element of choice of a long-run rule for action.[6] For example, Weisberg and Grofman (1981) found that 76.5 percent of such decisions in 1976 could be predicted simply by predicting that those who usually brush would continue to do so and those who usually didn't wouldn't. From a rule-utilitarian perspective, individuals (perhaps in terms of some form of *long-run* utility maximization) choose a rule to live by, and only sometimes do they deviate from it.[7]

Third, and most importantly, we must recognize that, for most individuals, the most crucial decision in toothbrushing is probably whether or not to buy a toothbrush.[8] For example, Traugott and Katosh's (1979) Tooth Validation Study shows that 92.4 percent of the decisions to brush or not to brush one's two front teeth in 1976 could be correctly predicted by knowing who owns a toothbrush and predicting that those who do will brush and those who don't won't (cf. Erikson 1979).[9] The importance of toothbrush purchase for the decision to brush might be explicable in rational choice terms, since the main cost component of the toothbrushing decision is the decision for many individuals to buy or not to buy a (new) toothbrush.[10]

To see why taking into account toothbrush purchase changes the citizen's decision calculus, we need to think of the costs of brushing as having two components, fixed cost (toothbrush purchase) and variable cost (toothbrushing). Having purchased a toothbrush, one can brush whenever one thinks it important enough to do so; while the cost of toothbrush purchase can be amortized over a number of brushings. In particular, once one owns a toothbrush, any given decision to brush or not to brush requires incurring only minimal *additional* costs. Furthermore, the decision to purchase a toothbrush is made in advance of *particular* day-to-day decisions to brush or not to brush and is based on a calculation of the desirability that one *may* at some time or times *in the future* wish to brush.[11, 12] It is not, as in the usual analysis of the expected value of brushing on any single specified occasion, an event-specific decision. Thus for many citizens, *once having decided to buy a toothbrush*, brushing their teeth is as habitual an act as brushing their teeth (cf. Boyd 1981).

Of course, we now have to account for why some people choose to buy a toothbrush while others do not!

Notes

1. Even dental scientists are not in agreement on which style of brushing is best. Indeed, some believe in the merits of regular alternation.

2. E.g., "Jimmy, did you brush your teeth today?" "Aw, gee, mom, do I have to?" Laurily K. Epstein has pointed out (personal communication) that some citizens have dentists, dental technicians, or toothbrush salesmen in the family who check to see whether your toothbrush has been used and help you get a new toothbrush if your old one gets broken.

3. Other more philosophically minded scholars have argued that each citizen is concerned not only with his own decision to brush or not to brush but with that of millions of other citizens. Thus, a citizen is motivated to brush on any given day not solely because of the consequences of that decision for the prevention of tooth decay but for the inspiration it will provide to other citizens. Unfortunately, that argument doesn't seem very compelling since the causal nexus between one citizen's toothbrushing activities and that of another seems nonexistent. Indeed, even if we think of the citizen as concerned not with decisions of others but only with decisions of his many future selves, under some philosophic views (e.g., existentialism), there is no causal nexus between an act of not toothbrushing today and an act of not toothbrushing tomorrow. Of course, some might argue that we are what we have been, and that in Brody's felicitous phrasing, "toothbrushing is a self-reinforcing process" (Brody 1977). This is particularly true in those climates where a failure to brush several times in a row renders your toothbrush inoperable.

4. Indeed, there is suspicion that at least one of its authors doesn't believe it.

5. The distinction between "rule" and "act" utilitarianism is an important (although controversial) one in the contemporary literature on social ethics. (See Rawls 1955; Smart 1956; Kaplan 1961.) To achieve a reasonably high probability of clean teeth, it may be necessary to brush *most* of the time, even though no given toothbrushing is likely to contribute significantly to this end.

6. In like manner, the decision to buy or not to buy a toothbrush may reflect a decision about the merits of brushing *in general*, not merely on any given day. See discussion below.

7. Explaining such deviations may require short-run factors, but the issue becomes accounting for deviations *from the rule* the citizen has chosen.

8. Without a toothbrush, it is impossible to brush either up and down or sideways.

9. Since citizens are known to lie through their teeth to survey researchers about whether or not they own a toothbrush, I would propose some probing questions to determine who really does own a toothbrush, e.g., "Where did you buy your toothbrush?" "How long ago did you buy it?" "How long do you think it will last?" (cf. Traugott and Katosh 1979).

10. We are not arguing that if toothbrushes were free or if everyone were given a toothbrush that would last a lifetime that everyone would brush his/her teeth. Rather, we are noting that of the costs of toothbrushing, purchase of a toothbrush is a major factor. In many states governmental inefficiency makes it difficult to buy toothbrushes most days of the year and most hours of the day and restricts their availability to a limited number of locations. It is well known that reducing the price of toothbrushes close to zero may not dramatically up the incidence of toothbrushing (Smolka 1978). In terms of this approach, such a phenomenon can be accounted for if many of those who don't brush are those for whom toothbrush purchase costs are not the principal cost component in their decision to brush or not to brush, are those with especially high variable costs, are those who assign low value to prevention of tooth decay, or are those who attribute low efficiency to brushing.

Note also that our analysis suggests that people who go on trips (and who may not have a toothbrush with them) are less likely to brush, because brushing will necessitate purchase of a new toothbrush.

11. Citizens may also be prey to something akin to the "gambler's fallacy" of believing that past events affect future probabilities even for independent events (i.e., if 3 reds appear in a row on the roulette wheel, then the next time is more likely to be black than red). The analogue to the gambler's fallacy would be the belief that the more times you brush, the more likely it is that your *next* brushing will be efficacious.

   Bernard Grofman (personal communication) has conjectured that individuals who brush their teeth and don't get cavities are more likely to continue to brush than those who brushed but get cavities anyway, even though their brushing cannot be shown to have been responsible for their absence of cavities. (Among sociologists this is known as "superstitious behavior.") In like manner, Grofman has conjectured that individuals who haven't brushed and still don't get cavities will be unlikely to bother acquiring a toothbrush or bother to brush even if they happen to already own one. This notion of toothbrushing as responsive not so much to rational calculations as to previous history of positive reinforcement for brushing/not brushing is, in my view, one which ought to be explored in the future by adding a question to the usual surveys to obtain both recollected previous brushing history and the historical linkage between brushing and the occurrence of cavities. It is rooted in an operant conditioning view of dental socialization.

12. It is also well known that citizens overestimate the impact of their own brushing activities on the incidence of cavities.

References

Boyd, Richard W. 1981. "Decline of U.S. Voter Turnout: Structural Explanations." *American Politics Quarterly* 9: 133–160.

Brody, Richard. 1978. "The Puzzle of Political Participation in America." In Anthony King (Ed.), *The New American Political System*, 287–324. Washington: American Enterprise Institute.

Erikson, Robert. 1979. "Why Do People Vote? Because They Are Registered." Paper presented at the Conference on Voter Turnout, San Diego.

Ferejohn, John, and Morris Fiorina. 1974. "The Paradox of Not Voting: A Decision Theoretic Analysis." *Legislative Studies Quarterly* 51: 625–635

Ferejohn, John, and Morris Fiorina. 1975. "Closeness Counts Only in Horseshoes and Dancing." *American Political Science Review* 69: 920–925.

Grofman, Bernard. 1983. "Models of Turnout: An Idiosyncratic Review. *Public Choice* 41: 55–61.

Kaplan, Morton A. 1961. "Restricted Utilitarianism." *Ethics* 71: 301–302.

Niemi, Richard. 1976. "The Costs of Voting and Nonvoting." *Public Choice* 27: 115–119.

Rawls, John. 1955. "The Concepts of Rules." *Philosophical Review* 64: 3–32.

Riker, William, and Peter Ordeshook. 1973. *An Introduction to Positive Political Theory*. Englewood Cliffs, N.J.: Prentice-Hall.

Riker, William H., and Ordeshook, Peter, 1968. "A Theory of the Calculus of Voting." *American Political Science Review* 62: 25–42.

Smart, J.C.C. 1956. "Extreme and Restricted Utilitarianism." *Philosophical Quarterly* 29: 344–354.

Smolka, Richard G. 1978. "Possible Consequences of Election Day Registration." Delivered at the Annual Meeting of the Midwest Political Science Association, Chicago.

Traugott, Michael, and John P. Katosh. 1979. "Response Validity in Surveys of Voting Behavior." Paper presented at the Conference on Voter Turnout, San Diego.

Weisberg, Herbert, and Bernard Grofman. 1981. "Candidate Evaluations and Turnout." *American Politics Quarterly* 9: 197–219.

The "Minimax Blame" Rule for Voter Choice: Help for the Undecided Voter on November 8, 1988

A Wuffle

Consider an election in which all the choices are dismal, albeit some perhaps even more dismal than others.[1] How should voters in such an election choose whom to vote for or whether or not to vote?

It has been suggested (Riker and Ordeshook 1973; cf. Weisberg and Grofman 1981) that a voter is unlikely to vote if no choice exists whose election would yield him any appreciable degree of delight. Such a voter is alienated from the system. Consider, now, an election whose outcome is virtually certain. The conventional wisdom is that such certainty as to outcome should depress turnout, since *ceteris paribus*, voters who come to see their vote as making no difference, should be less likely to vote than when they saw themselves as having a chance, however remote, to influence the outcome.

We believe that there are circumstances under which voter alienation and an election whose outcome is certain are both conditions which will increase rather than decrease turnout. Following the insightful lead of Ferejohn and Fiorina (1974; cf. Wuffle 1984; Grofman 1983) we wish to propose a minimax blame theory of voting. "Minimax blame" voters believe that whichever candidate will be elected will do an *awful job*. For such voters *the object of the voting act is to avoid voting for a winning candidate, lest one be accused of having helped to elect him*. If we, for simplicity, neglect the intrinsic costs and benefits of voting, the calculus of voting for "minimax blame" voters is straightforward; they seek to minimize the blame they'd get, on the assumption that, if they voted for a candidate who won, they'd have to take *full* responsibility for that candidate's election.

There is clear empirical evidence that the set of minimax-blame voters is not an empty set. Mary McGrory (February 1984), in a syndicated column on the 1984 New Hampshire Democratic Primary, notes that three registered voters in the small New Hampshire town of Nashua "will not vote at all, because," as one distracted young mother said, "then you don't need to worry about picking the wrong one."

Clearly,

Expected Maximum Blame

(Voting for c_i) = $p_i D(c_i)$

where p_i is the probability that the ith candidate, c_i, will be elected and $D(c_i)$ is the disutility of electing that candidate, i.e., $D(c_i)$ = -utility (c_i).

Hence, if they vote at all, rational "minimax blame" voters vote for that candidate for whom $c_i D(c_i)$ is minimum. If $D(c_i) = D(c_j)$ for all i and j, then "minimax blame" voters vote, if they vote at all, for that candidate who is least likely to get elected. More precisely, "minimax blame" voters vote for c_i rather than c_j if

$$\underline{D(c_i)} \neq \underline{P_j}$$
$$D(c_j) \neq P_i$$

The value of abstention is equally straightforward.

$$\text{Expected Maximum Blame (Abstention)} = \Sigma\, p_j D(c_j)$$

In other words, "minimax blame" voters act as if they believe that a voter who stays at home will be fully blamed for whatever happens, since the voter didn't do anything to prevent it.[2]

Under these assumptions it is easy to prove that, for "minimax blame" voters, the closer the election, the lower the turnout.[3]

Notes

1. The nature of the correspondence between this picture and any recent/forthcoming election(s) is left to the reader's imagination.
2. As in the usual minimax regret argument (Ferejohn and Fiorina, 1974), we posit that voters neglect the probability of certain events and focus only on their possibility. For a defense of this seemingly ridiculous point of view, see Ferejohn and Fiorina (1975).
3. Of course, if we neglect the net *intrinsic* costs/benefits of voting, rational "minimax blame" voters always vote.

References

1. Ferejohn, John, and Morris Fiorina. 1975. "Closeness Counts Only in Horseshoes and Dancing." *American Political Science Review* 69: 920–925.

Ferejohn, John, and Morris Fiorina. 1974. "The Paradox of Not Voting: A Decision Theoretic Analysis." *American Political Science Review* 68: 526–535.

Grofman, Bernard. 1983. "Models of Voter Turnout: A Brief Idiosyncratic Review." *Public Choice* 41: 55–61.

Riker, William, and Peter Ordeshook. 1973. *An Introduction to Positive Political Theory*. Englewood Cliffs, NJ: Prentice-Hall.

Weisberg, Herbert, and Bernard Grofman. 1981. "Candidate Evaluations and Turnout." *American Politics Quarterly* 9: 197–219.

Wuffle, A. 1984. "Should You Brush Your Teeth on November 6, 1980? A Rational Choice Perspective." *PS* 17: 577–580.

Why the Democrats Lose Presidential Elections: Toward a Theory of Optimal Loss

(with apologies to A Wuffle)

Robert S. Erikson

In 1988, as in four of the previous five presidential elections, the Republicans won the White House with remarkable ease. Pundits have been busy explaining the inevitability of this result. Many attribute the Republican victory to ideology, repeating the familiar line that the Democrats now are too liberal to win a national election. Another popular explanation is the economy. The incumbent party never loses, we are told, when the economy is prosperous. Some even blame the Electoral College. Other explanations have been offered as well (e.g., Sigelman 1988). Despite this disagreement on the details, two things appear certain. The Democrats had no chance in 1988. And the Democrats are in the throes of a painful electoral decline.

But is any of this conventional wisdom correct? If we ignore the presidency, the current Democratic Party enjoys a period of national hegemony perhaps unequaled since the Era of Good Feeling. For the past quarter century, the Democrats have almost continuously controlled more state legislatures and governorships than the Republicans. And the Democratic hold on Congress is even stronger than its hold on state government. After enjoying majority control for over three decades, the Democrats' lock on the U.S. House never was safer. Following the recent interruption of Republican control, the Senate now seems safely Democratic too. Add to all this a continuous Democratic plurality in party identification and one cannot doubt that the Democrats are the dominant party in the U.S. today and have been for decades.

So maybe we are asking the wrong question. The right question is not why the Democrats are in hopeless decline. The right question is instead: why does a party that is so powerful choose to run presidential campaigns that are so amateurish and disorganized that they are almost guaranteed to fail?

Fortunately, advancements in political science provide an answer. From a "rational choice" perspective, only one explanation is possible for the Democrats' decision to run losing presidential campaigns. Obviously, it must be in the Democrats' electoral interest to lose presidential elections. We need only to find out why.

I will show that by passing up the largely ceremonial office of the presidency, the Democrats maximize their real goal—control of Congress. At first glance, this theory makes no sense whatsoever. One objection is that presidential candidates still have coattails, so that congressional candidates are helped rather than hurt when their party makes a good presidential showing. Admittedly, this objection may have some merit. But Democratic strategists are not so myopic to settle for the short-term reward that would accrue from successful presidential coattails. Instead, they sacrifice the short-run benefit of coattails for much greater future rewards.

The Democrats look beyond the presidential year to the next midterm, when losing the presidency brings its first payoff. As has been documented (Jacobson and Kernell 1983, 63), each party is better off at midterm when the other party controls the presidency. So losing the presidency is a stepping stone to midterm victory. But the payoff for a presidential loss does not stop there. As any time series analyst would anticipate, the rewards at midterm carry over to the next on-year vote (neutralizing any coattails) and indeed cascade still further into the future. Winning the presidency, on the other hand, only brings future congressional misery.

Naturally, this result can be demonstrated with the help of some statistical models. First, we must recognize that presidential years and midterms are different, so we model each type of election separately. For the 10 post–WW-II presidential years (not counting 1988), the best model of the national congressional vote is:

Equation 1

Dem. Pres. Year House Vote = 27.5 + .37 x Presidential Vote (.07) + .18 x Dem. Midterm House Vote (.15) - 2.43 x Dem. President Dummy Var. (1.15)

Adjusted R squared = .790. SEE = 1.19. N = 10. (Standard errors in parentheses.)

This equation makes a lot of sense. The presidential vote and (to a lesser extent) the previous midterm vote shape the congressional vote in presidential years. But the equation also shows the first hint of why controlling the presidency is dangerous—a small but almost statistically significant (prob. < .08) penalty for controlling the presidency, even in presidential years. Put positively rather than negatively, the equation shows the electoral reward for being out of power. Fortunately for the Democrats, this 2 percentage point reward for not controlling the presidency cushions the blow of adverse presidential coattails. Now look at the postwar midterm equation:

Equation 2

Dem. Midterm House Vote = 5.0 - .24 x Presidential Vote$_{t-2}$ (.11) + 1.18 x Dem. Pres. Year House Vote$_{t-2}$ (.28) - 6.31 x Dem. Pres. Dummy Var. (1.83)

Adjusted R squared = .819. SEE = 1.52. N = 11. (Standard errors in parentheses.)

This equation brings nothing but good news for the Democrats. The equation shows a highly significant (prob. < .01) six-point penalty for the party in power, reflecting the presidential party's midterm slump. The midterm vote is surprisingly responsive to the congressional vote in the prior presidential year (b > 1.0). But most votes lost in presidential years from adverse coattails (b = .37 in Equation 1) are restored at midterm, as indicated by the negative -.24 coefficient at midterm for the previous election's presidential vote (Equation 2).

Fortunately for the Democrats, the benefit from the favorable midterm vote extends even into the future. As Equation 1 shows, the midterm vote feeds into the next presidential year vote. And if the Democrats are fortunate enough to lose this next presidential election as well, the benefits add extra fuel to the next midterm triumph. Clearly, an uninterrupted series of presidential "losses" can be the engine to drive a party to perhaps unimaginable heights of electoral success.

But how big is the Democrats' gain from forfeiting the presidency? We can find out easily enough by doing some simulations. Suppose we simulate the long-term congressional outcome if the Democrats were to lose every foreseeable presidential election by the same 54 to 46 percent margin that they lost by in 1988. Assume the 1986 starting point of 55 percent Democratic.

Taken together, Equations 1 and 2 forecast a Democratic vote for 1988 of 54.4 percent, which is a slight undercount.[1] Thus, if anything, the model is conservative in its projections of Democratic success. Even so, the model forecasts that the Democratic vote should rise to a near historic 58.2 percent Democratic at the 1990 midterm. From there on, the Democratic vote moves upward in a sawtooth pattern—down in presidential years but increasing to new heights at every midterm. By early in the 21st century, the Democrats achieve a regular 55 percent of the vote in on-years and 59 percent in off-years. Averaging these two numbers, let us label 57 percent Democratic as the equilibrium outcome. With a favorable swing ratio, 57 percent Democratic ought to be sufficient to elect Democrats to two-thirds of the House seats, for a veto-proof Congress.

Of course a series of 54 to 46 Republican presidential "victories" is not the only available scenario. Tracking the resultant equilibrium House vote as a function of the presidential vote across the continuous range of repeated presidential outcomes produces a best outcome for the Democrats—a minimal presidential "loss"—in the range of 49 to 51 percent. Barely losing the presidency can push the equilibrium vote up to the 58%+ range.

To be sure, this equilibrium result can be matched or exceeded following a string of outsized Democratic presidential "victories" as well as by slim "defeats." But for the Democrats to win as much by "winning" the presidency as they can accomplish by the easier task of "losing" requires presidential victories too large to be attainable. The Democrats would need to win over 70 percent of the presidential vote in order to achieve the level of congressional hegemony they achieve by losing the presidency by a slim margin.[2]

Tempting as 49 to 51 percent presidential "losses" might be, however, this target of losing by a slim amount is too dangerous for the Democrats to attempt. There is a serious peril of overshooting and actually winning the presidency. The parties sometimes converge toward the center, and sometimes do not converge. But one party never converges while the other does not. The "victory" zone would reduce the equilibrium Democratic vote to barely above 50 percent. The Democrats would do worse only by winning less than 30 percent of the presidential vote. It should not surprise, therefore, that the Democrats chose more comfortable loss margins and may even be living dangerously when they aim for a "loss" in the range of 54 to 46 percent.[3]

This paper has accounted for why the Democrats lose the presidency. A theory was presented which predicts that the Democrats lose the presidency because it is in their electoral interests to do so. Empirical tests were conducted and found to be consistent with the theory.

Only one puzzle remains. Theories of party competition generally are symmetric. The motives that determine one party's behavior ought to determine the behavior of the other. For example, spatial models of party competition demonstrate that parties should try to lose the presidency.[4] Therefore our remaining puzzle is the following: while the Democrats try to lose the presidency because it is in their interest to do so, why do the Republicans continue their mistaken course of trying to win?

Notes

1. Unfortunately, the national two-party vote for congressional elections is never reported in timely fashion. The exact 1988 verdict probably will not be known until publication of the 1990 *Statistical Abstract*. However, given the modest Democratic seat gains in 1988, one can infer that the 1988 Democratic vote is probably greater than the 55 percent Democratic reported for 1986.

2. Some accounts of congressional elections find that the presidential party is especially vulnerable during the midterm year of its second four-year term, as if the electorate has a "six-year itch." But "six-year itch theory" anticipates only part of the electoral momentum from being the party out of "power." To see the consequences of ten years in "power," check what happened to the Republicans in 1930. Note also that FDR's four sequential presidential victories only resulted in the Republicans' triumphant midterm landslide of 1946 and the fabled "Do Nothing" Eightieth Congress. (The less clear examples of 1942 and 1950 do not count because they are war years.)

3. This finding helps account for the unusual animosity which congressional Democrats held toward Jimmy Carter during his presidency. We now know that this animosity was structurally driven. Carter's narrow victory only added to the electoral vulnerability of congressional Democrats, whose numbers had swollen following Watergate.

4. This motivation to lose undermines the traditional Downsian prediction that party positions should converge toward the median voter. Indeed, the well-known fact that parties rarely converge toward the center serves to support the theory proposed here. While the theory proposed here is not the only theory that accounts for parties not converging, it does hold a clear advantage in terms of parsimony. One important task is the development of models of the ideological locations of candidates.

References

Jacobson, Gary C., and Samuel Kernell. 1983. *Strategy and Choice in Congressional Elections*. New Haven: Yale University Press.

Sigelman, Lee. 1988. "Are Democrats Stupid?" *Journal of Irreproducible Results* 33: 2–4.

Why Democrats Shouldn't Vote

(with acknowledgements to R. Erikson)

A Wuffle and Christian Collet

Controversy persists over the link between turnout and the likelihood of success of Democratic candidates, with the common wisdom being that higher turnout helps Democrats (e.g., Burnham 1965, 1982; Tucker and Vedlitz 1986; Piven and Cloward 1988; Radcliff 1994), but some arguing that voters and non-voters are not really that different from one another in their partisan preferences (Texeira 1992), and some arguing that high turnout is actually likely to help the minority party, whichever party that may happen to be (DeNardo 1980, 1986; Grofman *et al.* 1995). Contrary to everything ever written on this topic, we provide conclusive evidence that higher turnout actually benefits Republicans, and preliminary evidence that the same is true for higher registration.

We look at several different data sets, beginning with data on elections to the California Assembly.

We first regress turnout proportion among registrants on Democratic vote share (percentage) for the 80 districts in the California Assembly, in each of the elections over the 1962–92 period. Results are shown in Table 1.

All the correlations in Table 1 are negative, and all results are statistically significant.

Next, we look at state-level data for US Senatorial elections pooled for the years 1950–90. The correlation between Democratic vote share and turnout among (estimated)[1] voting age population is again negative, -.44, and statistically significant.

Next, we compare national election year net Democratic House seat gains and losses with pooled national level turnout from 1950 to 1992. We again obtain negative correlations: -.15 in presidential years, and -.34 in off-years.[2] When we do analysis for recent individual years using state-level data, the same pattern appears: the higher the ratio of turnout to voting age population, the less well the Democratic presidential candidate does. For example, in 1992, the correlation between Clinton's statewide vote share percentage and percentage turnout among voting age population in the state is -.32 ($p = .02$), with a regression line of -.185 * TURNOUT% + 55.3.

Finally, when we examine registration levels rather than turnout among registrants or turnout among eligibles, we obtain similar results: the higher the registration as a percentage of voting age eligibles, the less well Democratic presidential candidates do: the correlation is -.42 ($p < .01$), with a regression line of -.301 * REG% + 59.2.

Discussion

The data we have presented show conclusively that, for legislative elections in the US House, the US Senate and the California Assembly, and for presidential elections, the higher the turnout in the contest the less well Democrats do. *Since higher turnout has been shown to benefit Republicans, it is obvious that voters sympathetic to the Democratic cause should stay home.* Indeed, while less definitive on this point, our work on the link in 1992 between registration levels (relative to eligibles) and Democratic presidential success strongly suggests that Democrats should not register, either.

Our work is in a recent tradition of paradoxical findings that are derived from what Alec Stone (1995) has aptly called the "Wuffeauldian" research paradigm of "post-rationalist" theory. Key works in this tradition include Wuffle (1992), which shows that it is easier to find your way around if you do not have a map; Wuffle (1984), which accounts for class bias in voting by showing that only people who find it rational to brush their teeth should also find it rational to bother to vote; and Wuffle (1988), which shows that voters who do vote will often find it optimal to support candidates that they do not *wish* to see elected—a result extended by Erikson (1989), who shows that Democrats should not vote for Democratic nominees for President lest such candidates actually win.[3] We believe that the findings in this brief research note further significantly advance the Wuffeauldian program of revealing the fallacies of rational choice modeling, quantitative analysis, and anything not written in French.

*Table 1. Correlations Between Democratic Vote Share and Turnout as a Proportion of Registration: California Assembly, 1966-90**

Year	Correlation
1966	-.54
1968	-.34
1970	-.46
1972	-.44
1974	-.62
1976	-.42
1978	-.58
1980	-.64
1982	-.19
1984	-.65
1986	-.28
1988	-.67
1990	-.61

All values are statistically significant at least at the .01 level.

Notes

1. We use a straight line projection to interpolate voting age population in non-census years.

2. National level turnout figures are estimates by Burnham (1987) and Texeira (1992). The first of the two correlations reported above does not reach statistical significance.

3. Some might interpret Erikson's (1990) analysis as being in the rational choice tradition because he notes that subsequent midterm losses might cost the Democrats control of Congress but, since Downs (1957) posits that each election is entire unto itself and that voters have no foresight, this would make Erikson a heretic.

References

Burnham, Walter Dean. 1965. "The Changing Shape of the American Political Universe." *American Political Science Review* 59: 7–28.

Burnham, Walter Dean. 1982. *The Current Crisis in American Politics*. New York: Oxford University Press.

DeNardo, James. 1980. "Turnout and the Vote: The Joke is on the Democrats." *American Political Science Review* 74: 406–20.

DeNardo, James. 1986. "Does Heavy Turnout Help Democrats in Presidential Elections?" *American Political Science Review* 80: 1298–1304.

Downs, Anthony. 1957. *An Economic Theory of Democracy*. New York: Harper & Row.

Erikson, Robert. 1989. "Why the Democrats Lose Presidential Elections—Towards a Theory of Optimal Loss (with Apologies to A Wuffle)." *PS* 22: 30–35.

Grofman, Bernard, Christian Collet, and Robert Griffin. 1995. "Do Democrats Do Better in Higher Turnout Elections?" Paper prepared for delivery at the Annual Meeting of the Public Choice Society, Long Beach, CA.

Piven, Francis Fox, and Richard A. Cloward. 1988. *Why Americans Don't Vote*. New York: Pantheon Books.

Radcliff, Benjamin. 1994. "Turnout and the Democratic Vote." *American Politics Quarterly* 22: 259–76.

Stone, Alec. 1995. "Of Wuffle and Truffles: Gastronomic Expeditions in the Neighborhood of the 1995 ECPR Meetings in Bordeaux." Unwritten manuscript, School of Social Sciences, University of California, Irvine.

Texeira, Ruy. 1992. *The Disappearing American Voter*. Washington: Brookings Institution.

Tucker, Harvey J., and Arnold Vedlitz. 1986. "Does Heavy Turnout Help Democrats in Presidential Elections?" *American Political Science Review* 80: 1291–8.

Wuffle, A. 1992. "A Corollary to the Third Axiom of General Semantics." *Journal of Theoretical Politics* 4: 238–40.

Wuffle, A. 1988. "The Minimax Blame Rule for Voter Choice: Help for the Undecided Voter on November 8, 1988." *PS* 21: 639–40.

Wuffle, A. 1984. "Should You Brush Your Teeth on November 6, 1984? A Rational Choice Perspective." *PS* 17: 577–80.

Are Democrats Stupid?

Lee Sigelman

> I never said all Democrats were saloonkeepers; what I said was all saloonkeepers were Democrats. —Horace Greeley

In 1972, when the Democrats' fortunes fell to rock bottom, the core support for the hapless George McGovern came from those who had dropped out of school before seventh grade. Curiously enough (or perhaps not so curiously, given the liberal leanings of most American political scientists [Ladd and Lipset 1975]), no serious analyst concluded at the time that one had to be stupid to vote for McGovern. But as one watches the Democrats stumble from election to election, somehow managing to parlay their sizable lead in sheer numbers into loss after loss on election day—six of the last nine presidential elections having now gone to the Republicans—one cannot help but wonder if perhaps, just perhaps, the Democrats aren't a bit on the slow side.

Of course, it is well known that the typical Democrat is less educated than the typical Republican, and, presumably as a consequence, Democrats are less at home in the world of ideas (Nie, Verba, and Petrocik 1976). But the suspicion lingers that Republicans enjoy a mental edge over Democrats even beyond what would be expected on the basis of educational differences alone.

The purpose of this paper is to determine whether Democrats are—not to put too fine a point on it—stupid. However, as a question "Are Democrats stupid?" ranks alongside "How's your wife?" for both leave unspecified the frame of reference: "Compared to what?" Let me therefore restate the issue as: "Are Democrats stupider than Republicans?" But even now the question is too vague. The ideology of the Democratic Party, such as it is, is aimed toward society's downtrodden. That ideological appeal, then, creates a social base of the underprivileged, and the mean intelligence of Democrats might be expected to be lower than that of Republicans solely because the two parties appeal to rather different segments of the population. So we must try to isolate the more or less "pure" linkage between partisanship and intelligence, laying aside any intellectual deficit attributable to social and economic differences. Clearly, then, education and occupation will have to be held constant when intelligence levels are compared across parties; that way, if a partisan differential does emerge, we will be able to tell whether Democrats are stupid as such or whether the Democratic Party simply has a disproportionate number of stupid types of people in it.

The data for this analysis come from a series of General Social Surveys of the adult population conducted in 1974, 1976, 1978, 1982, and 1984 by the National

Opinion Research Center (Davis and Smith 1983). Respondents in each of these surveys were given a shortened version of an intelligence test devised by Thorndike (1942; Thorndike and Gallup 1944) for use in survey research. This ten-item multiple choice vocabulary test may outwardly seem to be no more than a test of verbal achievement, or perhaps verbal ability, but there is considerable evidence that brief vocabulary tests like this one perform quite well as measures of general intelligence. Surveying the results of several dozen studies, Miner (1957) found a median correlation of .83 between scores on short vocabulary tests and measures of general intelligence based on the Stanford Binet, Wechsler, and other standard 10 tests. This correlation compared quite favorably with the median correlation between various measures of general intelligence (.73), meaning, as Miner concluded, that vocabulary test scores correlate at least as well general intelligence scores as general intelligence scores do with one another.

The number of respondents in each General Social Survey is approximately 1,500, but the analyses reported here are for whites only, and are also restricted to those who identified as members of either the Democratic or the Republican Party; independents, including partisan-leaning independents, have been eliminated from the sample along with those who identified with another party or with no party, bringing the total number of cases to 3,599. Besides intelligence, the variables in the analysis include: party identification—0 = Democrat, 1 = Republican; level of education—number of years of school completed; occupational status—score on the Hodge-Siegel-Rossi occupational prestige measure; and region—appropriately enough, a dummy variable, with 1 = respondents who grew up in the South (the South Atlantic, East South Central, or West South Central section) and 0 designating those who grew up outside the South.

Findings

The mean intelligence score of the 3,599 white Democrats and Republicans in the combined set of five General Social Surveys is 6.17 on the 0–10 scale (standard deviation = 2.15). Consistent with the notion that Democrats are less mentally acute than Republicans, there is a difference of almost six-tenths of a point in the Republicans' favor (mean intelligence = 5.94 for the Democrats, 6.52 for the Republicans)—a difference significant well beyond any conventional level ($F = 63.84$, $df = 1, 3598$, $p < .0001$).

As a group, then, Democrats are significantly less intelligent than Republicans. On the other hand, intelligence is strongly related to both level of education ($r = .522$) and occupational prestige ($r = .401$) and is significantly related to region ($r = .153$), with Southerners, as expected, being slower. So some or all of the .58 partisan differential in intelligence could be due simply to compositional differences between the two parties.

One way to isolate the partisan difference in intelligence is to correlate party identification and intelligence after the impacts of education, occupation, and region have been removed from each. The third-order partial correlation between intelligence and party identification is .051, considerably below the simple correlation of .132 but still highly significant (p < .001). Thus we conclude that even though the "pure" partisan link with intelligence is lower than the simple correlation between the two, this link is real, not spurious.

A somewhat more refined perspective can be achieved by including party identification as one predictor of intelligence in a multiple regression analysis, alongside education, occupational prestige, and region. The results of that analysis are summarized in Table 1, where one result in particular stands out: the unstandardized regression coefficient for party identification of .190 (p < .01) means that even when the effects of education, occupational status, and region on intelligence are held constant, there is an intelligence difference of approximately two-tenths of a point between Democrats and Republicans.

Table 1. Multiple Regression Summary: The Predictors of Intelligence

Predictor	b	s.e.	Sig.
Education	0.296	0.012	.001
Occupational status	0.025	0.001	.001
Region	-0.529	0.066	.001
Party identification	0.190	0.062	.01
Multiple R = .552, R2 = .305			

Conclusion

Are Democrats less intelligent than Republicans? Yes, by almost six-tenths of a point on a ten-point scale. Can this gap be attributed to the different social bases of the two parties? To some extent, yes, but a significant component of the gross partisan difference in intelligence remains even after education, occupational prestige, and region are taken into account. Is this difference large enough to make a difference? Perhaps. Elections are often won or lost by very narrow margins, and what a candidate says during a campaign can be decisive. Candidates who campaign on dumb slogans like "I'll never tell y'all a lie" or "Where's the beef?" in effect shoot themselves in the foot, undercutting any chance they might otherwise have had of being elected. If the Democrats could draw upon a less depleted gene pool, they might be able to field candidates who would not be so likely to say stupid things and who would therefore win more elections. By the same token, the massive blue-collar defection from the Democrats in 1980 suggests that many rank-and-file Democrats are incapable of calculating where their self-interest lies. If they were even a little smarter, they might be able to resist the blandishments of the Republicans, voting the straight Democratic ticket instead of being tricked time and again into supporting the Republicans. (On the other hand, if these Democrats were much smarter, they would probably be Republicans in the first place, given the correlation we have observed between partisanship and intelligence.)

Unfortunately, the findings reported here leave unresolved the key issue of whether stupidity causes one to be a Democrat, or whether being a Democrat causes one to be stupid. Hence we leave as a task for future research the exploration of the link between partisanship and intelligence in a developmental, a quasi-experimental, or even an experimental context. Developmentally, one might expect long-time Democrats like Tip O'Neill to be even dumber than those who have been party members for only a short while; on the other side of the coin, Ronald Reagan is fast becoming one of the smartest men in the world. An interrupted time-series design holds out even more promise for settling issue of causality: if being a Democrat causes stupidity, then one would expect former Democrats like Strom Thurmond, John Connally, and Phil Gramm to have gotten smarter as a result of joining the Republican Party.

If developmental, quasi-experimental, and experimental studies fail to turn up the expected differences in intelligence, then the only remaining possibility will be that stupidity leads to Democraticness, not vice-versa. Should that turn out to be the case, the parties might well begin to reposition themselves on several key domestic policy issues. For example, even though early childhood enrichment programs like Head Start have traditionally been spearheaded by the Democrats, Republicans would probably want to assume the lead role, calculating that stupid children, if left to their own devices, would grow up to be Democrats, but that smarter children would mature into Republicans.

The findings reported here will doubtless discomfit some Democrats, but there may be a silver lining. The Republican Party is growing more and more popular, especially in the South, as the GOP attracts large numbers of people who once considered themselves Democrats. Accordingly, it can be predicted with some confidence that the partisan gap in intelligence will shortly be closing. In this sense, what we are presently witnessing is not only the massification, but also the stupification, of the Republican Party. Just as brute numbers have not always paid dividends for the Democrats, the Republicans may now be undermining their electoral prospects by reaching out to increase their head counts and thereby diluting their per capita brain power.

References

Davis, James A., and Tom W. Smith. 1983. *General Social Surveys, 1972–1981* (machine-readable file). Principal Investigator, James A. Davis; Senior Study Director, Tom W. Smith. NORC ed. Chicago: NORC, producer; 1983; Storrs, Conn.: Roper Public Opinion Research Center, University of Connecticut, distributor. 1984. 1 data file (17052 logical records) and 1 codebook (483 pp.).

Ladd, Everett C., and Seymour Martin Lipset. 1975. *The Divided Academy: Professors and Politics.* New York: McGraw-Hill.

Miner, J.B. 1957. *Intelligence in the United States.* New York: Springer.

Nie, Norman H., Sidney Verba, and John R. Petrocik. 1976. *The Changing American Voter.* Cambridge, MA: Harvard University Press.

Thorndike, R.L. 1942. "Two Screening Tests of Verbal Intelligence." *Journal of Applied Psychology* 26: 128–135.

Thorndike, R.L., and George H. Gallup. 1944. "Verbal Intelligence of the American Adult." *Journal of General Psychology* 30: 75–85.

Toward a Stupidity-Ugliness Theory of Democratic Electoral Debacles

Lee Sigelman

For the fifth time in its last six tries, the Democratic Party has managed to parlay its massive lead in party identifiers into another presidential election debacle. One shameless Democratic apologist, groping for a face-saving excuse, has hit upon the bizarre idea that the Democrats lose presidential elections time after time because, being rational political calculators, they find it in their partisan self-interest to do so (Erikson 1988). This tortured theory overlooks the obvious: Democrats are too stupid to calculate their self-interest.

Although this conclusion may seem unduly harsh, science has proven that Democrats are significantly dumber than Republicans, even when the differing social bases of the two parties are held constant (Sigelman 1988). This intellectual deficit helps explain why, time and time again, the Democrats find themselves hopelessly out-organized, out-strategized, and out-maneuvered—in short, out-thought—by the wilier Republicans.

Still, the Democrats may have more than a shortage of gray matter to blame for their electoral misadventures. In the television age, what really matters is not what candidates have to say about the great issues of the day, which makes remarkably little difference to anyone, but how they look when they are saying it (see, e.g., Rosenberg, Bohan, McCaffery, and Harris 1986). In the sage words of Thackeray: "A clever, ugly man every now and then is successful, . . . but a handsome fool is irresistible." Is it possible, then, that in addition to being intellectually overshadowed, the Democrats have been aesthetically outflanked? In plain English, are the Democrats ugly as well as stupid?

Data and Methods

Any natural-born citizen who has lived in the United States for fourteen years and is at least 35 years old is formally eligible to become president. In practice, however, those without experience in high public office need not apply. Of the 61 active candidates in the last five presidential campaigns, only Alexander Haig, Jesse Jackson, Pat Robertson, and Sargent Shriver failed to list on their résumés at least one term as governor or member of Congress (updated from Abramson, Aldrich, and Rohde 1987).

The issue, then, is whether the Democrats are at a disadvantage because the Republicans have a more eye-pleasing pool of potential presidential candidates from which to choose. In order to find out, the 50 governors, 100 senators, and

435 House members pictured in *The Almanac of American Politics 1988* (Barone and Ujifusa 1988) were rated on an ugliness scale ranging from + 5 ("Yummie") to - 5 ("Yecch").[1]

Findings

Very few high officeholders in either party are downright repulsive. Even so, these data contain some worrisome portents. Of the five most hideous officials, four hail from California. So if, as is so widely assumed, it is in the Golden State that the future of American politics takes shape, we seem to be in for a long ugly spell.

Now, what about the inter-party ugliness differential? The data confirm the hypothesized glamour gap. It is the extremely rare Democrat (only three of 338) who scores above +3 on the ugliness scale, but more than ten percent of the Republicans (28 of the 247) do so. Meanwhile, 25 of the 26 most unsightly officials are Democrats. Overall, the Republican mean of +1.2 falls significantly above the Democratic mean of -.5 ($p < .001$).

Of course, this difference could be spurious. For example, Democratic officeholders may be older than their Republican counterparts, and it is well known that old people are ugly.[2] Moreover, the intense competition for gubernatorial and senatorial seats may weed out more of the truly abominable than do House races, few of which are closely contested; if so, then appalling looks may not be an attribute of Democratic officeholders *per se*, but rather of members of the House, where the Democrats predominate.

The regression-based investigation of these possibilities summarized in Table 1 reveals that older officeholders are indeed significantly uglier than their younger colleagues. Also as expected, there is significantly greater per capita pulchritude in governors' mansions and the Senate chambers than there can be found on the floor of the House. But the crucial question is whether the interparty ugliness differential remains when age and position are held constant. The answer is that it does: controlling for these factors lowers the gap only by one-tenth of a point, from 1.7 to 1.6.

Discussion

In spite of the profusion of gleaming pates, sloping foreheads, crossed eyes, flapping ears, prominent proboscises, and cascading chins among them, it would be incorrect to conclude that the Democrats have cornered the market in grotesquerie. There are ugly Republicans, too.

Still, the Democrats possess, in truly awesome abundance, physical attributes that torment the eyes of the beholder. Compared to the ugly duckling Democrats, the Republicans are comely Quayles.

Since looks matter so much in modern electoral politics, the Democrats enter each election year at a severe competitive disadvantage. In order to meet the

Republicans head to head, so to speak, the Democrats would have to choose their candidates with consummate care. But it is here that cruel reality intercedes, for stupidity and ugliness actually impose a triple burden: (1) Because there are so few intelligent Democratic contenders to choose from, the Democrats nominate mental lightweights who conduct silly campaigns. (2) Because there are so many ugly Democratic contenders to choose from, the Democrats select standard-bearers who are not only dumb but ugly. (3) And because the Democrats are so dense, they have no inkling of how much better off they would be if they deliberately nominated someone the voters could bear to look at and listen to. Having chosen a candidate who spends the fall saying stupid things and looking stupid saying them, the Democrats are then invariably shocked when, in November, the Republicans register yet another handsome victory.

Table 1. Multiple Regression Summary—Determinants of the Ugliness of Officeholders

Predictor	b (s.e.)	t	beta
Age (in years)	-.08 (.01)	-11.4***	-.40
Senator (0=no, 1=yes)	.79 (.20)	4.0***	.14
Governor (0=no, 1=yes)	.86 (.26)	3.3**	.11
Party (0=Democrat, 1=Republican)	1.57 (.15)	10.6***	.36
Constant	3.77 (.40)	9.5***	
p<.01. ***p<.001. N=685. Multiple R=.57. R2=.32. s.e.=1.8. F=68.6*.			

Notes

1. The rating was done by a middle-aged woman who has an inordinate fondness for looking at pictures of men. She is a known sympathizer of "l-word" causes, and her knee jerked uncontrollably throughout the exercise. This information should allay any suspicion that the ratings may have been "cooked" to support the research hypothesis, a strategy that, I hasten to assure the reader, never even occurred to me.

2. Hatfield and Sprecher (1986: 287) summarize the link between age and physical attractiveness as follows: Q. What is this? "10, 9, 8 . . ." A. Bo Derek growing older.

References

Abramson, Paul R., John H. Aldrich, and David W. Rohde. 1987. "Progressive Ambition among United States Senators: 1972–1988." *Journal of Politics* 49: 3–35.

Barone, Michael, and Grant Ujifusa. 1988. *The Almanac of American Politics 1988*. Washington: National Journal Press.

Erikson, Robert S. 1988. "Why the Democrats Lose Presidential Elections: Toward a Theory of Optimal Loss." Mimeo.

Hatfield, Elaine, and Susan Sprecher. 1986. *Mirror, Mirror . . . : The Importance of Looks in Everyday Life*. Albany: State University of New York Press.

Rosenberg, Shawn, Lisa Bohan, Patrick McCafferty, and Kevin Harris. 1986. "The Image and the Vote: The Effect of Candidate Presentation on Vote Preference." *American Journal of Political Science* 30: 108–127.

Sigelman, Lee. 1988. "Are Democrats Stupid?" *Journal of Irreproducible Results* 33: 2–4.

The Hobbesian World of Democrats
Lee Sigelman

Democrats are stupid (Sigelman 1988) and ugly (Sigelman 1990). This much is certain. From these hard but uncontestable truths it is but a small step to an image of Democrats as bottom feeders in a dismal swamp, relegated by the flatulence of their intellects and the unsightliness of their visages to the bottom rungs of a societal pecking order in which looks and smarts are what count.

Until now, there has been no hard evidence—merely logic and common sense—to indicate that Democrats are miserable failures in life. In the grand tradition of social science, my purpose here is to confirm what everyone already knows, or at least *should* know. However, because social scientists are themselves notorious Democrats (Ladd and Lipset 1975), it is never safe to assume that they know what they should.

My argument is simple: Compared to respectable Americans, i.e., Republicans, Democrats can be expected to inhabit a Hobbesian state of nature, a world in which life is poor, short, solitary, brutish, and nasty (Hobbes 1968). My method is equally simple: I compare Democrats' and Republicans' answers to questions about their lives that have been asked in the ongoing NORC General Social Survey, 1972–1993 (Davis and Smith 1993).[1]

Findings

Poor

I will begin by saying what goes without saying: Democrats are substandard wage earners. The mean family income of all 1972–93 Democratic GSS respondents was 25% below that of their Republican counterparts—$21,900 versus $27,300 ($p<.001$).[2] This means that most Democrats can only dream about the really great stuff that the average Republican can buy every day—nougahyde recliners, gas barbecue grills, vacations at Disney World, and the like.

Short

Many dead people vote a straight Democratic ticket—the so-called graveyard vote that has been responsible for so many Democratic victories over the years. The preponderance of cadavers among Democrats could conceivably be taken as evidence that people put themselves at risk of dying by being Democrats, but I prefer a more conservative interpretation: people put themselves at risk of becoming Democrats by dying.

What evidence, then, is there that Democrats have short lives? Because most survey respondents are alive when they are interviewed,[3] it is somewhat awkward to use survey data to try to establish that Republicans live longer than Democrats do. However, once we realize that healthy people live longer than unhealthy people do, the facts begin to fall into place. Democrats are significantly less healthy ($p<.001$) than Republicans: Asked to describe their own health as "excellent," "good," "fair," or "poor," Democrats, on average, fall between "fair" and "good" (1.9 on a scale on which 0 denotes "poor" and 3 equals "excellent"), while Republicans fall between "good" and "excellent" (2.1 on the same scale). Democrats are also better bets to take their own lives. Birds of a feather flock together, and when asked how many people they know who have committed suicide, Democrats average .26, Republicans a mere .08 ($p<.05$). But the single most compelling datum is simply that the average Republican is a full year older than the average Democrat (47.5 years versus 46.6, $p<05$), which must mean that Republicans live longer than Democrats do.

Solitary

Democrats—impoverished, sickly, suicidal, doomed to an early death—are hardly the sorts of people any rational individual would seek out for companionship. Accordingly, they are significantly less likely than Republicans to be married (58% versus 63%, $p<001$), and, if they have ever been married, are significantly more likely to have been separated or divorced (31% versus 24%, $p<001$).

Nasty

So far, we have seen that about all Democrats have to be thankful for is their relatively short life span. Reflecting the wretchedness of their lives, they also have lousy dispositions. Only 31% of Democrats, but 39% of Republicans, describe themselves as "very happy" ($p<001$), and 13% of Democrats, but only 8% of Republicans, consider themselves "not too happy" ($p<001$). They also have a dismal view of human nature: Asked whether "most people would try to take advantage of you if they got a chance" or would "try to be fair," 40% of Democrats but only 30% of Republicans see people as predators ($p<001$); asked whether "most of the time people try to be helpful" or "are mostly just looking out for themselves," 49% of Democrats but only 40% of Republicans see people as self-serving ($p<001$); and asked whether "most people can be trusted" or "you can't be too careful in dealing with people," 61% of Democrats but only 50% of Republicans endorse distrust ($p<001$). In short, by comparison to Republicans, Democrats are curmudgeonly misanthropes; in this light, it is little wonder that so few people are willing to marry them or stay married to them.

Brutish

As noted above, it has already been established that Democrats are stupid and ugly, two prime characteristics of brutishness. Moreover, they are singularly lacking in self-control and are apt to be involved in all sorts of mayhem and disreputable behavior. For example, 37% of them smoke, as compared to only 30% of Republicans ($p<001$), and 23% of them have seen an X-rated movie within the past year, as compared to only 17% of Republicans (p<001). These differences might be pooh-poohed as lifestyle choices,[4] but during their adult lives Democrats are also significantly more likely than Republicans to have been hit (p<.001), shot at (p<.01), robbed (p<.01), and burglarized (p<.01), and no normal person *chooses* to be hit, shot at, robbed, or burglarized.

Conclusion

Might these differences between Democrats and real Americans be spurious? For example, Democrats are disproportionately poor, and many of the uncivilized attitudes and feral behaviors considered here are known to be linked to social class. So is it possible that the differences catalogued above say less about the kind of people Democrats are than about the kind of people who are Democrats?

To these questions I offer two responses. First, when all the differences reported above were reanalyzed with statistical controls instituted, as appropriate, for income, race, and age, only the differences in age and in the probabilities of being shot at, robbed, and burglarized declined to nonsignificance. All the other significant differences—13 of the 17—remained. Based on this evidence, I conclude that the great majority of the differences reported above reflect the kind of people Democrats are, not the kind of people who are Democrats. Second, no matter whether these differences reflect the kind of people Democrats are or the kind of people who are Democrats, the differences are real: Democrats are the dregs of society.

What, then, does the future hold for Democrats? The answer, I believe, is that the differences documented here will only widen. Because no respectable person wishes to mate with someone who is not only stupid and ugly but also diseased and desolate, Democrats are fated to continue in-breeding, producing new generations that are even stupider, uglier, and more pathology-ridden than the last.[5]

Notes

1. I classify Democrats and Republicans according to their answers to the GSS party identification question: "Generally speaking, do you usually think of yourself as a Republican, Democrat, Independent, or what?" It has been argued that, no matter how they themselves feel about it, "weak" Republicans and Democrats should be reclassified as independents, and partisan-leaning independents should be reclassified as Republicans or Democrats (Keith, Magleby, Nelson, Orr, Westlye, and Wolfinger 1992); I strongly suspect that this is a dumb Democratic attempt to make Democrats seem less stupid.

2. In the GSS data file, family income is given in categories, e.g., "$5,000–$5,999," rather than in raw dollars. To calculate means, I expressed each respondent's income as the midpoint of his or her category. For the highest category, which is open-ended ("$25,000 or over"), I arbitrarily assigned a value of $50,000; if anything, this should understate the Democrat-Republican income gap, as there are certainly more rich Republicans than rich Democrats.

3. This proposition may be controversial. Study after study has established that most citizens are impervious to new political information. The assumption that most survey respondents are dead provides a powerful, yet parsimonious, explanation of this phenomenon.

4. A position with which I myself concur. If Democrats wish to behave like animals, then I consider it their right as Americans to do so.

5. The 1992 shift in the Democratic locus of power to the state of Arkansas was an obvious step in this direction.

References

Davis, James A., and Smith, Tom W. 1993. *General Social Surveys, 1972–1993* [machine-readable data file] Principal Investigator, James A. Davis; Director and Co-Principal Investigator, Tom W. Smith; sponsored by National Science Foundation. —NORC ed.—Chicago: National Opinion Research Center [producer]; Storrs, CT: The Roper Center for Public Opinion Research, University of Connecticut [distributor], 1993.

Hobbes, Thomas. 1968. *Leviathan*, ed. C.B. Macpherson. Harmondsworth: Penguin.

Keith, Bruce E., David B. Magleby, Candice J. Nelson, Elizabeth Orr, Mark C. Westlye, and Raymond E. Wolfinger. 1992. *The Myth of the Independent Voter.* Berkeley: University of California Press.

Ladd, Everett Carll, and Seymour Martin Lipset. 1975. *The Divided Academy: Professors and Politics.* New York: McGraw Hill.

Sigelman, Lee. 1988. "Are Democrats Stupid?" *Journal of Irreproducible Results* 33: 2–4.

Sigelman, Lee. 1990. "Toward a Stupidity-Ugliness Theory of Democratic Electoral Debacles." *PS: Political Science & Politics* 23: 18–20.

Vindicating Anthony Downs

Mark M. Gray and A Wuffle

Positive turnout rates in the United States and elsewhere are widely considered "an embarrassing limitation of the economic approach to politics" because, for any one voter, "the costs of casting a ballot in any large election are almost always greater than the potential benefits, which are dependent on the unlikely occurrence of casting the winning or tie vote in an election" (Knack 1992, 133). Green and Shapiro (1994), whose scathing critique of the rational choice field centers on the work of Anthony Downs (1957), trenchantly put it: "Rational choice theorists have trotted out an astonishing variety of conjectures about the costs and benefits of voting, in the process generating an enormous literature, possibly larger in terms of academic citations and sheer bibliographic length than any other rational choice literature in American politics" (47–48), yet they still have no answer as to why people vote when, according to their arguments, reason says they ought not.[1] Grofman (1993), paraphrasing Morris Fiorina, has referred to the failure of rational choice theory to explain turnout as the "paradox that ate rational choice."[2]

We disagree. Our rejoinder is a simple one. Downs was right. You shouldn't vote. And, as more people come to recognize that fact, they'll stop.

Our proof proceeds in four parts. First we demonstrate that Downs is rising in importance in the academic literature on voting and turnout relative to classic works emphasizing civic duty (Berelson *et al.* 1954; Almond and Verba 1963) or partisan attachments (Campbell *et al.* 1960). Second, we demonstrate that the rise in Downs' influence relative to these other works is accompanied by a general decline in voting in the U.S., with the increased turnout in the 2004 election an easily explainable minor blip. Third, we provide limited but suggestive evidence that those who presumably know Downs best and are most likely to find his arguments credible—economists—are much less likely to vote than their level of education might predict. Finally, we account for the fact that people still vote by providing compelling evidence that most people have never heard of Downs, and thus are unlikely to be familiar with the ideas that made him "famous" (sic!).

(1) Downs Is a Rising Star

That Downs is a rising star in academia is undisputed. Still, evidence never hurts. For the period 1956 through 2004, citations of *An Economic Theory of Democracy* trended steadily upward, rising from single digits to 160 or so per year. By contrast, citations of three other classic books on voting and political participation, *Voting*, *The Civic Culture*, and *The American Voter*, all peaked in the mid-1970s and have been on the decline ever since then (data adapted and extended from Wattenberg [1991]).³

(2) As Downs Goes Up, U.S. Turnout Goes Down

In a little-known 1980 article⁴ that inspired the present work, Brunk (1980) reported results of a quasi-experimental study in which he discussed Downs' model with his undergraduate classes and checked to see if their willingness to vote had subsequently decreased.⁵ His findings are clear: "An introduction to rational participation has a major impact on the attitudes of individuals towards elections. As a result of discussing a model of participation a month earlier, the number of individuals who indicated that they would vote in various contests decreased. Interest in the outcome of an election was no longer sufficient to insure voting" (561–562). While his study was limited to the college classroom, Brunk hypothesized that his results would generalize. "If rational participation were routinely discussed, individuals would be better able to maximize their personal utility. They would do so by choosing not to vote in many elections. This would result in an accelerated decline of voter turnout" (561).

Turnout in the United States has indeed been in decline from its high point of 63% of the voting age population (VAP) in the 1960 presidential election to a low in 1996 of 49%. The patterns of change correlate well with citations to Downs. Explaining 61% of the variance in voter turnout during the 40-year period. the average number of citations of Downs (1957) in the four-year period preceding a presidential election is perhaps the most impressive single predictor of change in turnout identified to date.⁶ It would thus seem that, as more people read Downs, more people get the message.⁷

Although the slight increase in turnout in 2004 as compared to 2000 may seem an anomaly, it is easy to explain within the Downsian framework.⁸ Downs predicts higher turnout in elections where the possibility that any individual's vote could be decisive increases. Following the 2000 election, where essentially the margin of victory was zero, and with polls indicating similar closeness between Bush and Kerry in 2004, some of those who had closely read Downs may have realized that this might be one of those rare elections where their vote could actually matter.⁹ We expect this effect will wane significantly in 2008 as the memories of 2000 continue to fade, especially since the margin of victory in the 2004 presidential election returned to more "normal" proportions.

Moreover, there is another intriguing argument as to why presidential turnout may have been higher in 2004 than in 2000. Downs (1957) was out of print in 2001 and, while it did come back into print before the 2004 election, it was only in the form of a reprint that cost $47.00. The higher cost of his book may have deterred some voters from learning about the Downsian cost-benefit analysis of turnout. Indeed, exactly as Downs (an economist) might have expected, as we report below, purchases of *An Economic Theory of Democracy*, did fall off with this price increase.

We can provide further evidence of Downsian impact by looking at turnout levels among political scientists as compared to economists. Economists are those likely to be most exposed to Downsian views and most likely to find them credible. Frank, Gilovich, and Regan (1993) have found some evidence of more rational, self-interested behavior among those studying to be economists. We take this one step further and compare the voter turnout rates for a selected set of economists and political scientists. Our key hypothesis is that economists will vote at lower levels than political scientists; but we also expect that, in departments exposed to Downsian ideas, even political scientists will have a turnout less than 100%.

Using official voter history data collected by Gray (2003) from registrars of voters in Los Angeles and Orange counties (California) we analyze the voting behavior of permanent faculty members in the economics and political science departments at three Ph.D.-granting institutions, the University of California, Irvine; the University of California, Los Angeles; and the California Institute of Technology.[10] We look at turnout data for three different types of elections: the 2003 special state election that led to Arnold Schwarzenegger replacing Gov. Gray Davis, and general elections in 2000 (a presidential election year) and in 2002 (a mid-term election year).

In each of the three elections, turnout among economists was lower than that among political scientists. For economists, the turnout values (as a proportion of potential eligible voters) for 2000, 2002, and 2003 were 61%, 50%, and 70%, respectively; while, for political scientists, the corresponding turnout figures were 82%, 66%, and 80%. Only in the recall election was turnout among political scientists not at least 20 percentage points higher than that among economists. And, we can readily explain that narrowed gap once we recognize that (a) this special plurality-based election included a field of 135 candidates and was expected to be relatively close and (b) the University of California faculties were, in essence, selecting their boss.

In these elections turnout among economists is well below what we would expect among individuals of their education level.[11] For the 2000 election, *economists teaching at elite southern California institutions of higher education had turnout levels comparable to what we would expect of junior college graduates.*[12]

However, we can at best give only two cheers for the political involvement of the political scientists in our sample. Southern California political scientists with Ph.D.s teaching at elite institutions do not vote at rates higher than others with doctorates. Either a career focused on the study of politics does not motivate greater political participation (or may even inhibit it, thanks to the greater knowledge of the true nature of political competition),[13] or we are observing contamination effects from the presence of rational choice scholars at these institutions.[14]

(3) Explaining the Limited Impact of Downs

While we have clearly established the impact of Downsian ideas both on the general electorate and among economists, two important questions remain. First, why have rational choice ideas not yet driven turnout nearer zero?[15] And second, when, if ever, might we expect to see this occur?

The first question has an obvious answer. While Downs may be a "best seller" as academic tomes go, in the real world that doesn't mean much. *An Economic Theory of Democracy* has been in and out of print in recent years. Even taking account of used book sales it ranked as only 81,242 on the Amazon.com sales rankings in 2001. And, after it went out of print and was reprinted with a new price of $47, its rank slipped to 225,075 in 2005.[16] Thus, the Downsian penetration of the market has been far from strong.

Hence, few citizens are acquainted with Downs' compelling arguments against wasting your time voting. Thus, it's not at all surprising that so many are still voting.[17] Moreover, as Ledyard notes, the self-evident rationality of abstention must compete with "political activists" who, in his apt phrasing, "operate to interfere with the natural forces" (1984, 37). We might expect that only until Downs becomes as widely known and popular as some of these political activists such as, for example, Sean "P. Diddy" Combs and his "Vote or Die" campaign of 2004, could we expect turnout to decrease more substantially.[18]

Conclusion

The influence of Downs is undeniable on those who know him best. If the positive time trend in citations to Downs continues, then, absent another pipsqueaker like 2000, we should look forward to a continuing very slow decline in average levels of turnout in U.S. elections.[19]

Notes

1. There have been various attempts at reworking the calculus to solve the paradox (Riker and Ordeshook 1968: Ferejohn and Fiorina 1974), but these attempts are widely seen as having fallen short of the prize— leading some to have lost faith; e.g., Aldrich (1993) asserted that the economic approach just is not going to work with turnout. Green and Shapiro sarcastically refer to this retreat as a "peace with honor" solution (1994, 58). For a strongly contrary point of view to that of Green and Shapiro, see Hanks and Grofman (1998); Grofman (1996); cf. Grofman (2004).

2. Of course, in fairness, rational choice theory is not the only theory that turnout might have been said to have eaten. For example, survey-based studies of turnout have long associated a respondent's education level with their likelihood of casting a ballot (Verba and Nie 1972; Verba, Schlozman, and Brady 1995). Yet education levels have risen in the U.S. (and worldwide) while turnout has generally decreased.

3. Data are taken from the *Social Sciences Citation Index* (SSCI).

4. Brunk's article averages less than one citation per year.

5. An initial survey of student attitudes was done near the start of the semester.

6. Perhaps the next best single predictor already in the literature is the square root of the number of federal, state, and local laws overturned by the Supreme Court (Klinkner 1993). The Klinkner time series, involving a longer timeline (1840–1988) than our work, achieves a very respectable adjusted R^2 of 49.5%. (Of course, correlation is not causation—but when has that caveat ever prevented regression results from appearing in print?)

7. Of course, we do have to be careful with our operationalization of the independent variable. That an academic cites Downs doesn't necessarily mean that he or she has read him.

8. Excluding 2004, the regression line shifts to $y = -0.0848x + 61.626$ with an R^2 of 77.5%.

9. The 2000 election complicates the calculus of voting slightly because it is now evident that the margin of error for counting votes in the United States is significantly larger than one vote. Thus, no presidential election, using the current voting equipment, can ever realistically be decided by one vote; unless, of course, the only votes that count are those of the nine Supreme Court justices.

10. We exclude visiting faculty, adjuncts, instructors, and professors emeritus not currently teaching as they may not be permanent or current residents. We searched for each faculty member in the entire registration and history files. We also reviewed each faculty member's publicly available biography and/or curriculum vitae to evaluate the voting eligibility of those who were not registered to vote—removing those who either explicitly indicate that they are non-citizens or those with any indication that they may not be a citizen (degrees from universities abroad). CVs were also used to gauge when these professors were present in southern California (time and place of appointments). Additionally, we include seven other economists and political scientists located at other graduate-degree–granting universities within the Los Angeles and Orange County area who presented papers at the Public Choice Society annual meetings in either 2004 or 2005. This provides an N of more than 110 potential voters for each election.

11. Moreover, the difference in turnout levels between economists and political scientists was contrary to what we would expect from party affiliation. Democrats vote at lower rates than Republicans, but the economists in our sample were more likely to be registered as Republicans than were the political scientists in our sample (26% versus 11%). One in ten economists was registered under a "third party" (Libertarian, Green, or American Independent) whereas no political scientists were. Economists were less likely to be registered as Democrats (49% versus 73%). About 15% of political scientists and economists each decline to state a party affiliation.

12. The data are taken from Current Population Survey (CPS) estimates. Although survey respondents in general are slightly more likely to indicate voting, of all the polls measuring turnout, the CPS has the smallest problem of over-reports. McDonald and Popkin (2001) estimate that 55.6% of the voting eligible population (VEP) cast ballots in 2000 and the Census CPS for this election estimates 60% participation (over-report of 4.4 percentage points). Even if one subtracts 4.4 percentage points to each of the CPS estimates, the economists are only about as likely to vote as an American with an associate's degree or some college.

13. Cf. the famous quote about "making sausages."

14. The three southern California universities that make up the bulk of our data are each ones where we might expect rational choice ideas to have had some impact on the political science faculty, since each has a significant concentration of modelers and game theorists in political science, and a graduate focus in at least one area related to rational choice modeling. Moreover, each of these universities includes at least one faculty member who has made significant contributions specifically on the issue of turnout. Unfortunately, our small sample size does not allow us to meaningfully compare the turnout rates of the political scientists in our sample who have rational choice leanings with the turnout levels of their peers who lack such inclinations.

15. We use "near zero" turnout in reference to game theoretic models (Ledyard 1984; Palfrey and Rosenthal 1983) that postulate small positive turnout rates when voters are acting strategically. In particular, if nobody else was voting, then you really could be the pivotal voter!

16. As noted above; this drop in sales may in part explain the slight increase in turnout in 2004 compared to 2000. But we, perhaps, should not make too much of a blip in a time trend. Visual inspection of the regression line reveals six elections which fall below the line and six which are above it, including 2004.

17. And, of course, there is another possible explanation we might suggest: Keynes long ago noted that everyone is the slave to some dead economist. But Downs is still alive. (One of us (Wuffle) has characterized this as the *Paradox of the long-lived economist*: "If an economist lived long enough to see the impact of his/her work s/he wouldn't.")

18. Yet, even some of the celebrity turnout activists in southern California have had trouble motivating themselves for every election. For example, a well-known actress and producer who starred in a documentary film for MTV in 2004 specifically designed to increase participation among young people had not cast a ballot in either the 2003 recall or the 2002 general election. Similarly, a young heartthrob actor (a former Bostonian now living in Los Angeles) described his get out the youth vote campaigning with John Kerry as "a once in a lifetime experience" (quoted in Rosen 2004)—which is similar to his voting history between November 2001 and October 2003, since he only cast a ballot in the 2002 general election.

19. Heckelman and Whaples (2003) trace the close parallels between the views of randomly chosen economists and those of Public Choice scholars in both economics and political science. Hence, one obvious way we might do even better at lowering turnout than having them read Downs, would be to persuade more Americans to study economics. (Still we must be careful about the direction of causality. The distinguished European Public Choice economist Bruno Frey recently conducted a study showing that business students gave less money to charity than other students. But, that study also showed that their behavior "is not due to their education in economics. Rather, persons choosing to study business are less inclined to help others even before they have been subject to any economics teaching" (Frey 2005).

References

Aldrich, John H. 1993. "Rational Choice and Turnout." *American Journal of Political Science* 37: 246–278.

Almond, Gabriel, and Sidney Verba. 1963. *The Civic Culture*. Boston: Little, Brown.

Berelson, Bernard R., Paul F. Lazarsfeld, and William N. McPhee. 1954. *Voting: A Study of Opinion Formation in a Presidential Campaign*. Chicago: University of Chicago Press.

Brunk. Gregory C. 1980. "The Impact of Rational Participation Models on Voting Attitudes." *Public Choice* 35: 549–564.

Campbell, Angus, Phillip E. Converse, Warren E. Miller, and Donald E. Stokes. 1960. *The American Voter*. New York: Wiley.

Downs, Anthony. 1957. *An Economic Theory of Democracy*. New York: Harper.

Ferejohn, John, and Morris Fiorina. 1974. "The Paradox of Not Voting: A Decision Theoretic Analysis." *American Political Science Review* 68: 525–536.

Frank, Robert H., Thomas Gilovich, and Dennis T. Regan. 1993. "Does Studying Economics Inhibit Cooperation?" *Journal of Economic Perspectives* 7: 159–171.

Frey, Bruno. 2005. "Letter to the Editor." *The Economist*, March 5, 16.

Gray, Mark M., and Miki Caul. 2000. "Declining Voter Turnout in Advanced Industrial Democracies, 1950 to 1997: The Effects of Declining Group Mobilization." *Comparative Political Studies* 33: 1091–1122.

Gray, Mark M. 2003. "In the Midst of Fellows: The Social Context of the American Turnout Decision." Ph.D. dissertation, University of California, Irvine.

Green, Donald, and Ian Shapiro. 1994. *Pathologies of Rational Choice*. New Haven: Yale University Press.

Grofman, Bernard. 1993. "Is Turnout the Paradox that Ate Rational Choice Theory?" In *Information, Participation and Choice: 'An Economic Theory of Democracy' in Perspective*, ed. Bernard Grofrnan. Ann Arbor: University of Michigan Press, 93–103.

Grofman, Bernard. 1996. "Political Economy: Downsian Perspectives." In *The Handbook of Political Science*, eds. Robert Goodin and Hans-Dieter Klingemann. New York and London: Oxford University Press, 691–701.

Grofman, Bernard. 2004. "Downs and Two-party Convergence." In *Annual Review of Political Science*. ed. Nelson Polsby. Palo Alto, CA: Annual Reviews, 25–46.

Hanks, Christopher, and Bernard Grofman. 1998. "Turnout in Gubernatorial and Senatorial Primary and General Elections in the South, 1922–90: A Rational Choice Model of the Effects of Short-run and Long-run Electoral Competition on Turnout." *Public Choice* 94: 407–421.

Heckleman, Jac C., and Robert Whaples. 2003. "Are Public Choice Scholars Different?" *PS: Political Science & Politics* 36: 797–799.

Klinkner, Philip. 1993. "Dwarfing the Political Capacity of the People? The Relationship between Judicial Activism and Voter Turnout, 1840–1988." *Polity* 25: 633–645.

Knack, Stephen. 1992. "Civic Norms, Social Sanctions, and Voter Turnout." *Rationality and Society* 4: 133–156.

Ledyard, John. 1984. "The Pure Theory of Large Two-Candidate Elections." *Public Choice* 44: 7–41.

McDonald, Michael P., and Samuel L. Popkin. 2001. "The Myth of the Vanishing Voter." *American Political Science Review* 95: 963–974.

Palfrey, Thomas R., and Howard Rosenthal. 1983. "A Strategic Calculus of Voting." *Public Choice* 31: 7–43.

Putnam. Robert. 2000. *Bowling Alone: The Collapse and Revival of American Community.* New York: Simon & Schuster.

Riker, William, and Peter Ordeshook. 1968, "A Theory of the Calculus of Voting." *American Political Science Review* 62: 25–42.

Rosen, Hanna. 2004. "From Beantown to Bentown," *Washington* Post (July 27).

Verba, Sidney, Kay Lehman Schlozman, and Henry E. Brady. 1995. *Voice and Equality: Civic Voluntarism in American Politics.* Cambridge: Harvard University Press.

Wattenberg, Martin P. 1991. *The Rise of Candidate-Centered Politics in Presidential Elections in the 1980s.* Cambridge: Harvard University Press.

Voter Advice in the Presidential Election of 2008: A Guide for the Perplexed

A Wuffle

This short note is a contribution to the recent work on voter assistance aids (VAAs), such as the "Who Should I Vote For Presidential Candidate Quiz" http://www.dumbspot.com/ and "Electoral Compass USA" http://electoralcompass.com/ both designed for the 2008 U.S. Presidential election, which have become available on the Internet to help voters make election choices.[1] Customarily these aids work by asking a set of questions about the voter's policy preferences and then matching the voter's answers to the presumed policy positions of the candidates or parties, and then devising some method of weighting/combining the various questions so as to develop an overall assessment of voter-candidate or voter party proximity in one or two dimensions. The voter is then advised which candidate or party s/he is closest to.[2] Some VAAs, such as Compass, also include candidate evaluations scales about trust, competence, etc.

Here we offer our own contribution to the VAA literature, one that is rooted in the KISS principle that less is more.[3] Thus we focus on a single five-item discriminator as our preferred VAA for vote choice in the 2008 U.S. Presidential election. Also, rather than focusing on policy positions that might be located in candidate position statements or party platforms, to make sense of partisan choice we seek a more indirect and unobtrusive measure. In particular, adapting an idea from the use of instrumental variables in two-stage least squares, we chose a variable that is not directly found in any presidential party/candidate platforms, namely attitudes toward moose.[4] Carefully conducted experiments with both business executives and students[5] fully validate the predictive power of this instrument.

Respondents were instructed as follows:

HOW TO VOTE IN 2008

The Moose Opinion-ometer

A GUIDE FOR THE PERPLEXED

I will offer you five statements—about Moose.

Identify the <u>one</u> you agree with most.

You must pick one — and not more than one.

The Wit and Humour of Political Science

> And, once you know which one you picked, it will be clear to you how to vote in the 2008 Presidential election.
>
> *The five choices are as shown below—circle the number of your <u>one</u> choice*
>
> **1** The only good moose is a dead moose.
>
> **2** Helicopters were intelligently designed to carry moose.
>
> **3** Field dressing a moose is like putting a sweater on your dog when it gets cold.
>
> **4** I never met a (chocolate) mousse I didn't like.
>
> **5** Moose who've been to Alaska long enough deserve the right to vote in local elections—especially for governor.

Decoding the answers is straightforward. Those who pick either item 1 or item 2 should vote Republican; those who pick either item 4 or item 5 should vote Democratic. Item 3 is added as a reality/reliability check. Anyone who picks that answer should be discarded.[6]

Notes

1. Electoral Compass is headquartered in the Netherlands and has developed sites in a number of countries, including Portugal; http://www.smartvote.ch/ is a German-language website that allows one to access VAAs for a number of elections in Switzerland. Walgrave, Aelst, and Nuytemans (2008) study the use of a VAA in Belgium.
2. More sophisticated VAAs also inform voters of the degree of policy proximity to the different candidates/parties.
3. This view is also associated with Mies van der Rohe.
4. We are highly skeptical about most other VAAs since appropriate weighting of issues is not at all obvious and, in any case, probably should be voter-specific, and the assignment of "true" positions to the candidates/parties is likely to be problematic, especially if it is derived from scientific research by political scientists. Also there are potential biases in issue selection. By not bothering to select more than one issue, and focusing on an issue not discussed in platforms, it is clear that we can completely avoid these problems.
5. The n of our combined sample was three. Three businessmen reported the fit of our predictions to their actual preferences; in each case the prediction was perfect. The *n* for students was, however, zero, since we forgot to collect the completed questionnaires.
6. For the record, field dressing a moose involves gutting it from gullet to anus and then draining the blood. It has nothing to do with sweaters.

References

Walgrave, Stefaan, Peter van Aelst, and Michiel Nuytemans. 2008. "'Do the Vote Test': The Electoral Effects of a Popular Vote Advice Application at the 2004 Belgian Elections." Acta Politica 43: 50–70.

Legislatures

Leaving Office Feet First: Death in Congress

Forrest Maltzman, Lee Sigelman, and Sarah Binder

> Death is stronger than all the governments because the governments are men and men die and then death laughs: now you see 'em, now you don't.—Carl Sandburg, "Death Snips Proud Men"

Charlie Wilson (D-TX) described his decision to retire from the U.S. House of Representatives as the best of the three options open to him: "To get defeated, to get carried out feet first, or to . . . start another life" (Gerhart and Groer 1995). Although much research has been undertaken on electoral defeat (Collie 1981; Ferejohn 1977; Jacobson 1992; Mann 1978) and voluntary retirement (Gilmour and Rothstein 1996; Groseclose and Krehbiel 1994; Hall and Van Houweling 1995; Hibbing 1982; Kieweit and Zeng 1993; Schansberg 1994), research on death is still in its infancy. Indeed, rather than staring death in the face, political scientists have buried the issue. In one recent study, for example, mortality is treated as a form of retirement: "Members of the House leave for a number of reasons, most prominent among them being electoral defeat and retirement. Other avenues of departure include death and expulsion. . . . Simplifying somewhat, we categorize all departures as either the result of electoral defeat or the result of 'retirement'" (Gilmour and Rothstein 1996, 56).

Of course, some deaths—suicides—are voluntary. However, although many members of Congress die in office, suicide is extremely rare.[1] Accordingly, we caution against treating death as a form of retirement. Otherwise, members of Congress must be presumed to engage in such implausible calculations as the following: "Let's see now. How shall I spend the next few years? I suppose I'll run for re-election. But maybe I should retire so I can spend more time playing golf. Or, since I'm thinking of retiring, why don't I just shuffle off this mortal coil, cross over Jordan's bank to the Stygian shore, pay my debt to nature, and join the choir invisible?"

Why Study Death?

Members' deaths have both immediate and long-term political repercussions. It was the untimely passing of 14 members, including Speaker Nicholas Longworth (R-OH), that enabled the Democrats to elect one of their own as Speaker during the 72nd Congress (1931–1933) even though the Republicans had won a majority of House seats in the 1930 elections. Besides affecting partisan control of Congress, death has proven vital to the political advancement of women. As Kincaid (1978, 96) explains, "For women aspiring to serve in Congress, the best husband has been a dead husband, most preferably one serving in Congress at the time of his demise."

Since the first session of Congress, the roll of members who have died in office numbers 1,084. Thus, of the approximately 11,500 individuals who have served in Congress, almost one in ten has succumbed to the ultimate term limit—more than have forsaken the House for the Senate, resigned, been expelled, or been appointed to higher office. As a consequence, death ranks third, behind retirement and electoral defeat, as a cause of congressional departure.[2] Over the years, the incidence of death has been extremely uneven, with the Grim Reaper cutting a wide swath through some sessions while avoiding others like the plague. Whereas 29 members were struck down during the 76th Congress (1939–41), only three breathed their last during the 103rd (1993–94). These fluctuations reflect more than accidents, for only two members of the unprecedentedly lethal 76th Congress died by accident; all the others died on purpose.[3] The long-term trend—a mounting annual death toll for the first four decades followed by a steep decline over the remainder of the century—is obvious, as are numerous short-term fluctuations around it.

'Til Death Do Us Part: Explanations of the Body Count

How can we explain the congressional death toll? In stark contrast to political scientists, who have been deathly silent about this issue, members of Congress have been fascinated by it.[4] Their obsession stems in large measure from the conviction that their own days are numbered. Senator Hiram Bingham (R-CT) sounded the death knell in 1931—the very year when House members were dropping like flies, costing Republicans control of the chamber:

> It is a very striking fact and one which cannot be too often called to the attention of Senators that there is no other body of this size in the world which has as high a death rate as this body. Out of the 96 Senators, during the past 7 or 8 years at least three have died each year, and if there is anything that can be done to cause members of this body to enjoy greater health and to prolong their lives, it seems to me that no one should object to it (*Congressional Record*, 71st Congress, 3rd session, p. 4921, February 14, 1931).[5]

By 1945, anxiety on Capitol Hill ran so high that the House convened a special closed-door hearing at which Dr. George Calver, the Capitol Physician, was the star witness. Dr. Calver did little to assuage members' intimations of mortality. "When I first came to the Capitol," he testified, "it was not uncommon to pick up a Member of Congress who had died in his office at the rate of about one a month" (1945, 64).

Job Stress

To account for the carnage, Dr. Calver pointed to the "environmental conditions" under which members of Congress operate, referring specifically to the high levels of stress they experience on a daily basis:

> Taking a day's work, starting on an average [at] 9, and running until 7 in evening is a 10-hour day of very considerable stress and strain. . . . If, however, a man has to attend some social gathering at night, or some particular committee meeting at night, when he arrives at home and goes to bed, he is too tired to feel like getting up in the morning. . . . With all the irons which a Member of Congress has in the fire, it is difficult to see, under the present situation . . . how he gets along as well as he does (Calver 1945, 65).

Because most physical disorders, from the common cold to cancer, can be psycho-physiological (Bootzin and Acocella 1988, 199), sooner or later the high level of stress that members experience is certain to exact a physical toll. Of course, not all sessions of Congress are equally stressful. Some are frenzied, while others are dull, though presumably not deadly so. If members are keeling over due to job stress, they should be especially likely to do so when the pressure is on and more likely to survive when the pace of legislative life is relatively relaxed.

Air Pollution

For many years, an altogether different environmental hazard—the poor quality of the air in the Capitol—posed a palpable threat to physical well-being. In 1859, within weeks after moving into a chamber fitted with a ventilation system that the *New York Herald* hailed as "the largest in the world," senators began complaining. Senator John Parker Hale (Free Soil-NH) denounced the ventilation for turning the chamber into "the most unhealthful, uncomfortable, ill-contrived place I was ever in my life; and my health is suffering daily from the atmosphere" (*Congressional Globe*, 21 January 1859: p. 507). A decade later, Rep. John Covode (R-PA), chair of the Committee on Public Buildings and Grounds, introduced a resolution that began, "Whereas the confined and poisonous air of the Hall and the corridors of the Representatives' wing of the Capitol has caused much sickness and even death among the members of the House" (Brown 1970, 152).[6] Smoking was banned in the House during the nineteenth century, but the prohibition did not filter through to the Senate until 1914, and then only after Senator Benjamin "Pitchfork Ben" Tillman (D-SC) heaped scorn on his colleagues for their slavish adherence to "the pernicious habit," which had so mastered them "that they are nervous and miserable when they cannot get the nicotine poison that soothes their nerves" (*Congressional Record*, 9 March 1914: p. 4531):

> The ventilation of this chamber *is* poor, as everyone knows: and when we increase its impurities by tobacco smoke, as is being done all the while, the air is

never cleansed and is very unwholesome and unhealthy. Let us stop smoking in the Senate Chamber, and have the attendants open the gallery doors every night . . . and have the windows leading to the open air outside opened all night so that pure air can come into the Chamber and wash it out and make it habitable and more healthy, and there will be fewer deaths among us (*Congressional Record*, 9 March 1914: p. 4532).

In a rhetorical coup *de grace*, Tillman prophesied that a no-smoking rule would add "six to 15 years to their lives" and read aloud the names of 25 current and former senators who had died during the preceding four years.[7]

Tragically, though, the expulsion of the evil weed did not purify the Capitol air, as becomes clear in the following exchange during a 1924 Senate debate over whether to spend $10,000 on a new ventilation system:

> Senator Overman (D-NC): I know perfectly well that we ought to have better air in this Chamber, but if what is proposed in the resolution shall be done as I understand, this beautiful Chamber will be torn to pieces. Senator Copeland (D-NY): I wish to say the chief object of the resolution, if passed, is to prolong the life of the Senator from North Carolina. Senator Overman (D-NC): I do not desire that my life be prolonged at an expense of $10,000 of the taxpayers' money (*Congressional Record*, 3 June 1924: p. 10272).[8]

Others apparently valued their lives more highly than did Overman, and in 1932 the installation of a modern ventilation system, complete with air-conditioning, brought an end to a century of congressional wailing.[9] Before then, though, there seems little question that, had members been asked to account for the high congressional body count, most would have pointed to air pollution as a primary cause.

Demography Is Destiny

Though members of Congress—especially senators—may not perceive themselves as mere mortals, they cannot repeal the laws of nature. Older people are at greater risk of dying than younger people are, and women live longer than men. Moreover, during this century, advances in medical science and changes in lifestyle have extended life expectancy. Accordingly, long-term trends in the congressional death toll can hardly be considered apart from changes in mortality rates and in the age and gender composition of Congress.

Findings

To assess the vitality of these explanations, we fitted a model of deaths in the House and Senate during the twentieth century, beginning with the 57th Congress (1901–1903) and extending through the 103rd (1993–1994). We used the congressional workload, as measured by the mean number of bills introduced per day in a Congress, as an indicator of job stress, anticipating that the Capitol Physician's 1945 testimony would be borne out by a positive coefficient. On the other hand, if toxic air killed members for the first third of the century, deaths should have declined significantly after the installation of the new ventilation system in 1932. Accordingly, we also included in the model a mummy variable, coded 1 to denote the improved air quality of the 73rd (1933–1935) through 103rd congresses, or 0 for earlier congresses; we expected the coefficient for this variable to be negative. Finally, to represent broader societal trends, we calculated the "expected" number of deaths in Congress based on official estimates of age- and gender-specific mortality rates in the general population (Bureau of the Census 1960; Department of Health, Education and Welfare [Department of Health and Human Services] annual), the age and gender profile of members of Congress, and the number of members. For example, nationwide in 1990 there were 35.7 deaths per 1,000 males between the ages of 55 and 65, and 20.1 per 1.000 females in the same age bracket; that year, 10.6% of the male members of Congress and 9.4% of the women were between 55 and 65; and 5.6% of all the members were women. By combining age- and gender-specific mortality data for the general population with data on the age and gender composition of Congress, then correcting for changes in the size of Congress, we derived an estimate of the number of congressional deaths expected if, controlling for gender and age differences, members died at the same rate as their constituents.

The fears that members so often expressed during the first half of the century were well-grounded. With only one exception, in each Congress from the 57th through the 83rd, more members—often many more members—died than would have been forecast from actuarial tables. For example, the 29 members of the 76th Congress who fell into the sleep which knows no waking greatly outnumbered the expected 12. More generally, during those years a stiff toll of 18.9 members died per Congress, far in excess of the expected 11.7. Thereafter, congressional mortality declined sharply, both in absolute terms and relative to expectations. Indeed, in recent years the actual count has been about three corpses (hence six feet) below the expected number.

There has also been a broad correspondence between deaths in Congress and in the body politic, for actual deaths have followed the same general course as expected deaths—albeit with more extreme swings and fluctuations. The number of members who breathed their last during a given Congress has been closely tied to the expected number ($r = .792$).

To test the three explanations advanced earlier—and possibly lay them to rest—we estimated a Poisson regression model of the number of deaths per Congress (King 1989). As Table 1 indicates, the number of deaths expected on the basis of the age-gender profile of Congress dominates the model. This simply means that if we know how many men and women in each age cohort of the general public went the way of all flesh during a given period, we will have a very good idea of how many members of Congress began their eternal rest during the same period.

Contrary to the testimony of the Capitol Physician, job stress (at least as measured by the number of bills introduced per day in a given Congress) has not significantly affected the congressional death toll.[10] However, the significant negative coefficient for the ventilation/air-conditioning system dummy variable establishes the installation of the new ventilation and air-conditioning system as a real life-saver. How many members have been spared by this marvel of modern engineering? A reasonable estimate is approximately three members per Congress.[11] Unfortunately, we cannot say *which* three.

Post-Mortem

The data we have dug up, even in skeletal overview, promise to breathe new life into a field long moribund. What remains, so to speak, is to provide some grounding for this body of evidence.

Members of Congress are well insulated from the rigors of real life. Staffers cater to their every need. The members are showered with bountiful perquisites of office. However, these perquisites do not include immunity to the maladies that annually dispatch hundreds of thousands of Americans to the Great Beyond. To be sure, when a member of Congress dies in office, it is news.[12] But even though a particular death may be unexpected, death in the aggregate is routine. Congress is composed disproportionately of older men, and when older men lie down to take a nap, they sometimes remain horizontal. What warrants special note, however, is not that so many members of Congress die, but rather that for the last three decades congressional deaths have consistently fallen below actuarial expectations. Whereas members once bemoaned that the job was killing them, it now seems more appropriate to point to congressional pampering as the main reason why members live longer than expected.

For the most part, death in Congress reflects forces beyond the control of the members—but not entirely. After decades of deadlock about whether to install a new ventilation system, the 72nd Congress finally acted. The effects were not instantaneous, for the deadliest Congress of all was the 76th; but this delayed reaction simply means that it took a few years for those enfeebled by the malignant Capitol air to die off. As they were replaced by hardy new members working in a purified atmosphere, the body count plummeted. Accordingly, we think there is at least a ghost of a chance that Polsby (1981, 30) is correct when he argues that the advent of air-conditioning in the 1930s and 1940s may have had no less momentous an impact on political life (and death) in the nation's capital than the massive changes the city underwent during the 1960s and 1970s— racial desegregation, home rule, and rapid population growth.

More generally, we have established that it is possible to forecast with considerable accuracy how many members of Congress will die in office. Although it may strike some as ghoulish, the next logical step is to begin developing and testing predictive models of which members will die. An answer to this grave question will require much digging.

Table 1. Summary of Poisson Regression Model of Congressional Deaths

Predictor	Estimate	Std. error	t-statistic
Constant	.296	.329	.899
Expected death based on the gender composition of Congress	.233	.026	9.040**
Ventilation/air-conditioning system (0=pre-installation, 1=post installation)	-.209	.107	-1.960*
Bills considered per day	-.002	.002	-.962

p < .05 (one-tailed). p < .001 (one-tailed). Poisson log-likelihood = -129.8. X2 = 55.1. N=47.

Notes

1. According to the most reliable estimate available, eight members of Congress have committed suicide (Eisele 1995). Amer (1989) reported only seven, but the 1925 suicide of Senator Joseph McCormick (R-IL), who overdosed on barbiturates, was subsequently made public (Miller 1992). Senator Lester Hunt (D-WY) is the only member to have killed himself in the Russell Office Building. He did so after supporters of Senator Joseph McCarthy (R-WI) threatened to publicize the arrest of Hunt's son for committing homosexual acts in a Washington park unless Hunt withdrew from his 1954 re-election campaign—an incident that provided the inspiration for Allen Drury's (1959) novel *Advise and Consent*.

2. These figures and those reported below are from ICPSR and McKibbin (1993), the main data source for the present study. We alone are responsible for the findings and interpretations presented here.

3. Those two members were Representative George Heinke (R-NE), who was killed in an auto accident, and Senator Ernest Lundeen (R-SD), who died in an airplane crash. Heinke and Lundeen were two of many members to die in transportation-related accidents: by 1994, 17 died in airplane accidents, 11 in auto accidents, two in train mishaps, and two in steamboat explosions. Of the rest, many were assassinated, but only one (Rep. Jonathan Cilley, D-ME) died at the hands of a fellow member (William Graves, Whig-KY). Inter-branch relations have not always been so serene. For example, Senator David Broderick (D-CA) was mortally wounded in a duel with David Terry, Chief Justice of the California Supreme Court. For an extensive listing of members felled by unnatural causes, see Amer (1989); for more detailed discussions, see Kahn (1995) and Eisele (1995).

4. Elaborate rules cover virtually every conceivable legislative aspect of the death of a sitting or former member, including the form and timing of the resolution of regret, the suspension of business for memorial services, and even the placement of floral arrangements on the desk of the recently departed member (Riddick and Frumin 1992). The cemetery founded by Congress bears living testimony to this obsession, although one need not be a member of Congress to be buried there and only 70 of the 60,000 interred in the cemetery are former members. Many other members, including former Majority Leader Hale Boggs (D-LA), Speaker Tip O'Neill (D-MA), and almost every member who died before 1870, are memorialized, but not buried, there (Burger 1995). Congress no longer contributes to the maintenance of the cemetery, which now relies on funds from

the sale of the remaining plots and from fees area dog owners pay to walk their dogs on cemetery grounds ($100 for the first dog and $5 for every dog thereafter). Currently about 125 dogs are enrolled.

5. Senator James Thomas Heflin (D-AL) exclaimed in exasperation, "If this is such an unhealthy place, so dangerous to the physical well-being of senators, is it not exceedingly strange that in generation after generation so many men will exert themselves to get elected to a place where ... death stands threatening them all the time?" (*Congressional Record*, 71st Congress, 3rd session, February 14, 1931: 4923–4924). Heflin's "generation after generation" reference proved prescient: Senator Howell Heflin (D-AL) is his nephew.

6. Covode's mortal fears were well grounded. He died in office on January 11, 1871.

7. It is perhaps not unduly cynical to question the sincerity of Tillman's concern for the well-being of his colleagues. In 1902, he was censured by the Senate for physically assaulting another senator on the floor. He died in office on July 3, 1918, and is interred in the Ebenezer Cemetery in Trenton, SC.

8. Copeland knew whereof he spoke: a physician, he was the author of *Dr. Copeland's Home Medical Book* (U.S. Senate 1945). Unfortunately, he was living proof that members of Congress do not live by air quality alone, for he died in office in 1938, six years after a new ventilation system, with air-conditioning, was installed.

9. The new system also reduced the need for periodic testing of air quality in the Capitol; on this point, the classic reference is, of course, "Air Tests in the Capitol" (1914).

10. The poor performance of this variable may reflect strategic behavior by members who, late in a session, recognize that if they file another bill, someone will have to make the supreme sacrifice. The Capitol Physician pointed to two other aspects of serving in Congress as stress-inducing: "glad-handing," or "the attention [a member] receives from well-wishers, which really is a handicap"; and concern about financial well-being (Calver 1945, 63). "Glad-handing" was a euphemism for overindulgence in rich foods and alcoholic libations:

> Perhaps the greatest physical handicap under which a Congressman is placed is the necessity of entertaining and being entertained by political well-wishers. The old expression that the way to a man's heart is through his stomach is practiced by many of these persons who think that by serving a particularly rich and over-delicious meal, they are doing the Congressman a great favor. Actually, all they are doing is loading up his metabolic furnace with fuel which he is not able to consume, and because of that he develops what we call a high blood fat which is a predisposing cause in the opinion of great many physicians of the condition which we call arteriosclerosis (Calver 1945, 64).

Lacking time-series data on congressional gluttony and drunkenness, we could not incorporate this factor in the model. In preliminary statistical spadework, we did include a measure of congressional salaries, expressed in constant dollars, as a rough index of financial pressure. After determining that this variable added nothing to the predictive power of the model, we dropped it from consideration.

11. This estimate follows from the standard method of interpreting coefficients in a Poisson regression model, which involves multiplying the coefficient by the mean of the dependent variable (King 1989). In this instance, -.209 x 13.8 = -2.88.

12. It is also an occasion for the bipartisan "Flower Fund" to spring into action. If the deceased served on the House Appropriations Committee, the Flower Fund is used to buy flowers to honor the member—assuming that the fund is solvent. At the start of 1996, even though no member had died in the previous year, the fund was broke (Winneker 1996).

References

"Air Tests in the Capitol: Results Obtained With and Without Humidity Apparatus." 1914. *Heating and Ventilating Magazine* 11: 20–22.

Amer, Mildred. 1989. "Members of the U.S. Congress Who Have Died of Other Than a Natural Death While Still in Office: A Selected List." Washington: Congressional Research Service.

Bootzin, Richard R., and Joan Ross Acocella. 1988. *Abnormal Psychology: Current Perspectives* (5th edition). New York: Random House.

Brown, Glenn. 1970. *History of the United States Capitol*. New York: Da Capo Press.

Bureau of the Census. 1960. *Historical Statistics of the U.S., Colonial Times to 1957*. Washington, DC: Government Printing Office.

Burger, Timothy J. 1995. "For a Scare, Parker Digs Congressional Cemetery." *Roll Call* (October 30).

Calver, George W. 1945. *Testimony before the Joint Committee on the Organization of Congress, Executive Session* (June 12).

Collie, Melissa. 1981. "Incumbency, Electoral Safety, and Turnover in the U.S. House of Representatives, 1952–1976." *American Political Science Review* 75: 119–131.

Congressional Globe. 1859. 35th Congress, 2nd Session. 21 January: 507.

Congressional Record. 1914. 63rd Congress, 2nd Session. 9 March: 4531.

Congressional Record. 1924. 68th Congress, 1st Session. 3 June: 10272.

Congressional Record. 1931. 71st Congress, 3rd Session. 14 February: 4921.

Department of Health, Education, and Welfare [Department of Health and Human Services]. Annual. *Vital Statistics of the United States*. Washington: Government Printing Office.

Drury, Allen. 1959. *Advise and Consent*. New York: Doubleday.

Eisle, Albert. 1995. "Members of Congress No Strangers to Violent Deaths." *The Hill* (September 6).

Ferejohn, John. 1977. "On the Decline of Competition in Congressional Elections." *American Political Science Review* 71: 166–176.

Gerhart, Anne, and Annie Groer. 1995. "The Reliable Source: Charlie Wilson, Kissing Congress Goodbye." *Washington Post* (October 26).

Gilmour, John B., and Paul Rothstein. 1996. "A Dynamic Model of Loss, Retirement, and Tenure in the U.S. House of Representatives." *Journal of Politics* 58: 54–68.

Groseclose, Timothy, and Keith Krehbiel. 1994. "Golden Parachutes, Rubber Checks, and Strategic Retirements from the 102nd House." *American Journal of Political Science* 38: 75–99.

Hall, Richard L., and Robert P. Van Houweling. 1995. "Avarice and Ambition in Congress: Representatives' Decisions to Run or Retire from the U.S. House." *American Political Science Review* 89: 121–136.

Hibbing, John. 1982. *Choosing to Leave: Voluntary Retirements from the U.S. House of Representatives*. Washington: University Press of America.

Inter-university Consortium for Political and Social Research, and Carroll McKibbin. 1993. *Roster of United States Congressional Officeholders and Biographical Characteristics of Members of the United States Congress, 1789–1992 Merged Data*. Computer file. 9th ICPSR ed. Ann Arbor, MI: Inter-university Consortium for Political and Social Research, producer and distributor.

Jacobson, Gary C. 1992. *The Politics of Congressional Elections*, 3d ed. New York: HarperCollins.

Kahn, Gabriel. 1995. "Ultimate Term Limit. Member Deaths Down." *Roll Call* (March 27).

Kiewiet, D. Roderick, and Langche Zeng. 1993. "An Analysis of Congressional Career Decisions, 1947–1986." *American Political Science Review* 87: 928–941.

Kincaid, Diane D. 1978. "Over His Dead Body: A Positive Perspective on Widows in the U.S. Congress." *Western Political Quarterly* 31: 96–104.

King, Gary. 1989. *Unifying Political Methodology: The Likelihood Theory of Statistical Inference*. New York: Cambridge University Press.

Mann, Thomas E, 1978. *Unsafe at Any Margin: Interpreting Congressional Elections*. Washington: American Enterprise Institute.

Miller, Kristie. 1992. *Ruth Hanna McCormick: A Life in Politics 1880–1944*. Albuquerque: University of New Mexico Press.

Polsby, Nelson W. 1981. "The Washington Community 1960–1980." In *The New Congress*, eds. Thomas E. Mann and Norman J. Ornstein. Washington: American Enterprise Institute for Public Policy Research, 7–31.

Riddick, Floyd M., and Alan S. Frumin. 1992. *Riddick's Senate Procedure: Precedents and Practices.* Washington: Government Printing Office.

Schansberg. Eric D. 1994. "Moving Out of the House: An Analysis of Congressional Quits." *Economic Inquiry* 32: 445–456.

U.S. Senate. 1995. *Senators of the United States: A Historical Bibliography, 103rd Congress.* S. Doc 103–34. Washington: Government Printing Office.

Winneker, Craig. 1996. "Heard on the Hill: Power Flowers." *Roll Call* (May 27).

Death, Where Is Thy Sting? The Senate as a Ponce (de Leon) Scheme[1]

A Wuffle, Thomas Brunell, and William Koetzle

Maltzman, Sigelman and Binder (1996), in what we regard as monumental work, have reinvigorated the study of death in office. But their data analysis is incomplete. First, they fail to project realistically the trends in actual and expected congressional deaths. Second, like many congressional scholars, they do not pay sufficient attention to the Senate. We provide new evidence that the U.S. Senate may offer the solution to mankind's oldest quest, the fountain of youth (Gilgamesh n.d.; de Leon 1460–1521).[2]

Table 1 presents data on the proportion of U.S. Senators who died in office, by decade, from 1910 to 1990 (CQ 1995).

The r^2 for the regression of mortality rates on time is an astonishingly large .87.[3] Rarely have we seen such a clear time trend. Senators are increasingly not dying in office.

We plotted the senatorial mortality rate data reported in Table 1 versus year (for data grouped by decade) as shown in Figure 1. However, as our colleague, Bernard Grofman, pointed out to us (personal communication, April 2, 1995), projecting this equation past 1990 would give us negative estimates of mortality rates as early as the year 2000. Given the strength of our empirical results and the scholarly commitment we share with Gelman and King (1990) to investigating incumbency effects without *a priori* bias, we do not reject the idea of revenants out of hand.[4] Nonetheless, to obtain a mortality function with the more commonly accepted

Table 1. Mortality of Sitting Senators by Decade

Decade	Proportion of Senators Who Die While in Office
1910-1919	.30
1920-1929	.25
1930-1939	.24
1940-1949	.28
1950-1959	.20
1960-1969	.15
1970-1979	.08
1980-1989	.03

lower bound of zero, we have re-estimated the data with a logarithmic specification, by regressing the log odds of senatorial mortality versus time.[5]

Here we obtain

(1) log odds MORTALITY RATE
 = 61.78 - .033 YEAR

The r^2 value for this logarithmic regression is .78 (with an adjusted r2 of .74.) While not quite as good as the previous linear fit, the fit of the logarithmic estimate is still impressive.

We may reexpress Equation (1) in more convenient form as

(2) MORTALITY RATE
$$= \frac{e^{61.78 - .033 \text{ YEAR}}}{1 + e^{6178 - .033 \text{ YEAR}}}$$

Substituting in the value 2000 for YEAR, we find that senatorial mortality rate for that year is estimated to be about 2 percent. By 2050, estimated Senate mortality will be under 1 percent. By the year 3000, it will be virtually indistinguishable from zero.

Figure 1. Plot of Mortality of Sitting Senators versus Year

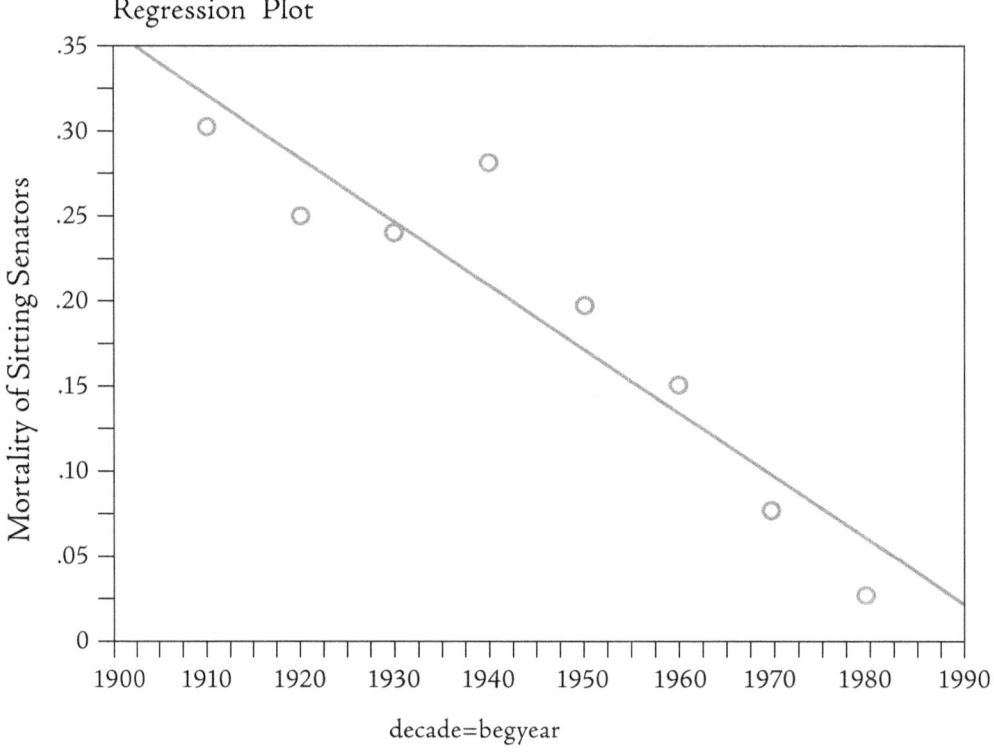

Y = 7.38 - 3.70E-3*X; R^2 = .87

Discussion

The sophisticated logarithmic regression above provides clear and compelling evidence that, in the modern era, Senators who manage to retain office will be nearly immortal.[6] Moreover, we may rule out a selection bias effect as the explanation for this phenomenon in that there is equally clear and compelling evidence that Senators who leave office do die.[7]

Senator Strom Thurmond

Our work provides a new and powerful substantive underpinning to Anthony Downs' oft-repeated yet sometimes disputed assertion that politicians have one motivation only—to retain office (Downs 1957; cf. Mayhew 1974). We learn from our findings that all previous work on incumbency advantage (e.g., Fiorina 1989; Gelman and King 1990; King and Gelman 1991) has completely missed the *real* nature of incumbency advantage, at least for the Senate. Thus, once our findings have been disseminated and their implications digested, we should see a drastic change in the willingness of Senators to seek the presidency. Our work also has clear implications for public policy in that it leads us to predict that the imposition of federal term limits will raise the national death toll.[8]

Although our empirical contribution is resolutely pre-mortem in spirit, it makes a valuable contribution to post-rationalist theory in the Wuffeauldian tradition.[9] Of course, our findings need to be replicated for House members and for other bodies.[10] Moreover, just exactly what it is about serving in the Senate (or being re-elected thereto) that keeps one from dying is a topic that must be left to future research.[11]

Notes

1. This paper was not prepared for delivery in Barbara Sinclair's class on the "U.S. Congress," UC Riverside, Winter Quarter, 1995. Nonetheless it was handed out there. The listing of authors is alphabetical by first name.

2. Our own work on this topic was written before we had the benefit of Maltzman, Sigelman, and Binder's (1996) remarkable insights, but we have found no reason to change anything we had previously written.

3. Even the adjusted r^2 is still a whopping .84.

4. Cf. Kubrick and Clarke (1968).

5. If we let M denote mortality rate, what we have done is to regress log odds MORTALITY RATE (= ln(M/1-M)) versus YEAR, for data grouped by decade.

6. See e.g., Strom Thurmond.

7. Witness Hubert Humphrey or Lyndon Johnson, for example. Thus, we may reject the selection-bias inspired hypothesis that Senators do not die in office because only immortals (or near immortals) are elected to that office.

8. Even Cain's mind-boggling review of 666 (mutually contradictory) hypotheses about the effects of term limits (Cain 1996) omits this one.

9. Stone (1995) compares and contrasts the Wuffeauldian paradigm (see e.g., Wuffle, 1979, 1982, 1984, 1988, 1989, 1992, 1993, 1997 forthcoming) to other work in the continental tradition. Stone's one sentence summary of the Wuffeauldian approach to the scientificistic method—"Truth is like a truffle; to find it we must dig around a lot—and then somehow get rid of all the dirt"—has not yet been improved upon.

10. Christopher Zorn, Ohio State University (personal communication, March 26, 1995) has suggested a similar pattern obtains for the U.S. Supreme Court.

11. In this context, consider the joke about the scorpion and the lawyer, the punchline to which is: "professional courtesy."

References

Cain, Bruce. 1996. "The Varying Impact of Legislative Term Limits." In Bernard Grofman (ed.) *Term Limits: Public Choice Perspectives*. Boston, MA: Kluwer Publishers.

Congressional Quarterly Guide to U.S. Elections. 1995. Washington: Congressional Quarterly Press.

Downs, Anthony. 1957. *An Economic Theory of Democracy*. New York: Harper and Row.

Fiorina, Morris. 1989. *Congress: Keystone of the Federal Establishment*, 2d Edition. New Haven, CT: Yale University Press.

Gelman, Andrew, and Gary King. 1990. "Estimating Incumbency Advantage Without Bias." *American Journal of Political Science* 34: 1142–1164.

King, Gary, and Andrew Gelman. 1991. "Systematic Consequences of Incumbency Advantage in U.S. House Elections." *American Journal of Political Science* 35: 110–138.

Kubrick, Stanley, and Arthur C. Clarke. 1968. "2001: A Space Odyssey."

Maltzman, Forrest, Lee Sigelman, and Sarah Binder. 1996. "Leaving Office Feet First: Death in Congress." *PS* 29: 664–71.

Mayhew, David. 1974. *Congress: The Electoral Connection*. New Haven, CT: Yale University Press.

Stone, Alec. 1995. "Of Wuffle and Truffles: Gastronomic Investigations in the Neighborhood of the 1995 ECPR Meeting in Bordeaux." Unwritten manuscript, School of Social Sciences, UCI, April 30.

Wuffle, A. 1979. "Mo Fiorina's Advice to Children and Other Subordinates." *Mathematics Magazine* 52: 292–297.

Wuffle, A. 1982. "The Pure Theory of Elevators." *Mathematics Magazine* 55: 30–37.

Wuffle, A. 1984. "Should You Brush Your Teeth on November 6, 1984? A Rational Choice Perspective." *PS* 17: 577–580.

Wuffle, A. 1988. "The 'Minimax Blame' Model for Voter Choice: A Guide to the Perplexed." *PS* 21: 85–88.

Wuffle, A. 1989. "Finagle's Law and the Finagle Point, a New Solution Concept for Two-Candidate Competition in Spatial Voting Games Without a Core." *American Journal of Political Science* 33 (2), 427–454 (with Scott Feld, Guillermo Owen, and Bernard Grofman).

Wuffle, A. 1992. "A Corollary to the Third Axiom of General Semantics." *Journal of Theoretical Politics* 4: 238–240.

Wuffle, A. 1993: "The Political Economy of the Automobile: Four Approaches." *Journal of Theoretical Politics* 5: 409–412.

Wuffle, A. 1997. "Why Democrats Shouldn't Vote and Probably Shouldn't Register Either (with acknowledgements to R. Erikson)," *Journal of Theoretical Politics*, Forthcoming (with Christian Collet).

The Dakota Effect

Garry Young and Lee Sigelman

> Just a ragged kid in overalls, he thumbed a ride one day
>
> He told me, "anywhere you're going's on my way."
>
> But as we passed by Big Al's drive-in his eyes began to flash
>
> He was leavin' Rapid City mighty fast.
>
> He said, "I hope to God she finds the good-bye letter that I wrote her,
>
> But the mail don't move so fast in Rapid City, South Dakota."
>
> —Kinky Friedman, "Rapid City, South Dakota"

If challenged to do so, relatively few Americans could probably find North and South Dakota on a map, let alone correctly name, spell, and pronounce the capitals of the two states. Nor would they be able to recall anything interesting about the Dakotas, whose main tourist attractions, besides Mount Rushmore, are a drug store, a civic arena festooned in corn, and a peace garden. Although one of the Dakotas bills itself as "The Land of Infinite Variety," its sociocultural diversity consists primarily of different synods of Lutherans who engage in endless disputation with one another because they are so similar. Dakotans prefer their food bland—they consider ketchup daringly spicy—and their politicians low-key. When they encounter something new, they call it "different," which they rarely mean as a compliment, and they wait for it to go away—which, because there is so little to hold it in the Dakotas, it probably will do. They keep their opinions to themselves (a typical Dakotan being the fellow from Sioux Falls who loved his wife so much that he almost told her), and they do not like it when people make a fuss about themselves or anything else. Thus, when South Dakotans perceived the previously popular Senator George McGovern as having gotten too big for his britches by seeking the presidency in 1972, they saw to it that he would fail to carry his home state, and three decades later they voted long-time Senator Tom Daschle out of office as soon as he repeated McGovern's mistake of seeing a president whenever he gazed into a mirror.

As veritable Rodney Dangerfields of the American states, the Dakotas get little respect from the rest of the country. Tellingly, *Fargo*, the only major motion picture ever named after a city in the Dakotas, was actually set in Minnesota (Coen and

Coen 1996). This disrespect tends to irk Dakotans, who are a proud but humble people. (A cynic would say they are humble because they have so much to be humble about.) The most illustrious Dakotans have themselves been a humble lot, to judge by those depicted in Statuary Hall; the fame of these Dakota luminaries—John Burke, Sakakawea, William Beadle, and Joseph Ward—pales in comparison to that of many others—Tom Brokaw, Peggy Lee, Lawrence Welk, and Roger Maris, for example—who got out of the Dakotas as soon as they could.

This tendency to leave the Dakotas is the very phenomenon under consideration here. As a starting point, we note that these two states, which rank seventeenth and nineteenth among the 50 states in land mass, are virtually empty, ranking forty-sixth and forty-seventh in both total population and population density. The prairie dogs and coyotes with which Dakotas' human residents share the frigid tundra easily outnumber them. At first blush, the political implication seems obvious: a lack of clout on the political scene. After all, the Dakotas' combined congressional delegations, which number only six in all, could caucus in an ice-fishing shack. Commanding so few electoral votes and having been safely ensconced in the Republican column in the last 10 presidential elections in any event, the Dakotas are routinely ignored by presidential candidates, who fly over but rarely drop in.

A lack of political clout, at any rate, is the consequence that one might logically have expected based on the sheer dearth of people living in the Dakotas. Yet, while the rest of the country was paying them little heed[1] the Dakotas have been successfully pursuing an extra-constitutional strategy for advancing their interests—a strategy of selective out-migration. In addition to sending their own duly allotted congressional delegations to Washington, they have been quietly slotting their native sons and daughters into Congress as members from other states. In what follows, we show that this Dakota Effect is not simply an artifact of the eagerness of those born in the Dakotas to seek greener pastures elsewhere, and that it has policy consequences not just for the Dakotas, but for the nation as well.

The 107th Congress, for which the *Congressional Quarterly* noted what it called the "Dakota Connection," contained 15 natives of the Dakotas, including the entire six-person contingent representing the Dakotas themselves, three representing neighboring Minnesota, and six who had fanned out to more distant venues (one each from Florida, Kansas, Oregon, and Virginia, and two from Texas).[2] Table 1 establishes that on a per capita basis the Dakota Connection far exceeds its counterpart in any other state. No other state even comes close to North Dakota's 3.7 exported members of Congress for every 400,000 current residents, nor, for that matter, does any other state even come close to South Dakota's 1.6 exported members per 400,000 current residents. Moreover, as just noted, in both North and South Dakota representation begins at home: every member of the two Dakota delegations was homegrown. Thus, in terms of *all* members of Congress (that is, natives of a state plus exports to other states) rather than just exports, the very same pattern holds: North Dakota, with 5.6 members of Congress per 400,000 residents,

Table 1. Members of Congress Born in the State per 400,000 Citizens of the State

State	Represent Other States	State	Total in Congress
North Dakota	3.737	North Dakota	5.606
South Dakota	1.590	South Dakota	3.179
West Virginia	0.885	West Virginia	1.770
Massachusetts	0.756	Idaho	1.546
Alabama	0.450	Rhode Island	1.526
Arkansas	0.449	Nebraska	1.402
New Mexico	0.440	Massachusetts	1.323
Iowa	0.410	Vermont	1.314
Kentucky	0.396	Alabama	1.259
Rhode Island	0.382	Maine	1.255
New York	0.358	Iowa	1.230
Washington	0.339	Arkansas	1.197
Pennsylvania	0.326	Kentucky	1.089
New Hampshire	0.324	Hawaii	0.990
Idaho	0.309	Ohio	0.916
North Carolina	0.298	Pennsylvania	0.912
Georgia	0.293	South Carolina	0.897
Missouri	0.286	Wisconsin	0.895
Connecticut	0.235	Montana	0.887
Nebraska	0.234	New Mexico	0.880
Oklahoma	0.232	New York	0.864
Maryland	0.227	Indiana	0.855
Illinois	0.225	Mississippi	0.844
Wisconsin	0.224	Illinois	0.837
Tennessee	0.211	Connecticut	0.822
Ohio	0.211	Washington	0.814
South Carolina	0.199	Wyoming	0.810
New Jersey	0.190	Louisiana	0.806
Colorado	0.186	Montana	0.786
Virginia	0.170	Tennessee	0.773
Arizona	0.156	North Carolina	0.745
Kansas	0.149	Utah	0.716

Table 1, continued			
State	Represent Other States	State	Total in Congress
Indiana	0.132	Oklahoma	0.696
Oregon	0.117	New Jersey	0.666
Texas	0.096	Minnesota	0.650
Louisiana	0.090	New Hampshire	0.647
Michigan	0.080	Georgia	0.635
California	0.071	Maryland	0.604
Alaska	0.000	Michigan	0.604
Florida	0.000	Oregon	0.585
Nevada	0.000	Colorado	0.558
Delaware	0.000	Texas	0.556
Utah	0.000	Delaware	0.510
Wyoming	0.000	Arizona	0.468
Mississippi	0.000	California	0.413
Montana	0.000	Nevada	0.400
Hawaii	0.000	Virginia	0.396
Maine	0.000	Florida	0.275
Vermont	0.000	Alaska	0.000

and South Dakota, with 3.2, stand out far above the rest.[3] Notably, the profusion of Dakotans in Congress is nothing new, as evidenced by the long careers of senators like Hubert Humphrey of Minnesota (born in Wallace, SD) and J.J. Exon of Nebraska (a native of Geddes, SD).

The abundance of congressional Dakotans raises two fundamental questions: Why? And so what?

Accounting for the Dakota Effect

As to the first question, one possibility that may come to mind is that this is a more general characteristic of small states rather than a Dakota Effect per se. It has long been recognized that members of Congress are disproportionately likely to hail from rural, small-town America (Matthews 1968; Rieselbach 1970; Spillman 1909). However, Table 1 shows that we can dismiss this notion. Of the five states other than the Dakotas—Alaska, Delaware, Montana, Vermont, and Wyoming—with populations of less than a million, none has exported even a single member of recent sessions of Congress to any other state. Indeed, more often than not these five states have outsourced their own congressional delegations; none of Alaska's three members of Congress was born in Alaska, while only one of Delaware's and Wyoming's and only two of Montana's and Vermont's were born in the states they represent.

Having laid that possibility to rest, we must consider another skeptical claim, namely that the Dakota Effect is probably an artifact of the broader outflow of the Dakota-born that began during the 1930s and has continued ever since. When as many people leave a state as have ditched the Dakotas, some of them are bound to become active in public life in their adopted state and some may therefore end up in Congress. Thus, by the sheer luck of the draw the odds are that some other states' congressional delegations will contain former Dakotans. By contrast, because virtually no one moves to the Dakotas, the Dakota delegations should be composed solely of native Dakotans. It follows that if we control statistically for aggregate population trends, the Dakota Effect should vanish.

That sounds fairly convincing, but there are other possibilities as well. One possibility goes a step farther by focusing on the characteristics of those who leave. In recent decades the Dakotas have experienced a brain drain, with many of their best high school students matriculating out of state and many of their college degree–holders seeking career opportunities elsewhere. Importantly, as Dakotans themselves would be too humble (or perhaps too wily) to mention, and as those in the rest of the country would be dumbfounded to learn, students from the Dakotas are the creme de la creme nationally: year in and year out the Dakotas, along with Iowa, lead the nation in mean state-by-state SAT college entrance exam scores. In combination with the high rates of out-migration from the Dakotas, this suggests another plausible explanation of the Dakota Effect. This explanation is that it is not simply by the luck of the draw that some of the numerous Dakotans who emigrate end up representing other states in Congress. Rather, because many of the departing Dakotans are smarter than the residents of their adopted states (especially Minnesota), they rise in Darwinian fashion to the top in their chosen fields. It may, then, be competence rather than randomness that accounts for the Dakota Effect.

Nor does this exhaust the range of reasons for supposing that the Dakota Effect may be more apparent than real. Beyond the ideas that it is simply a product of the luck of the draw, given the high rate of out-migration from the Dakotas, or that it reflects the fact that Dakotans are smart enough not only to leave but also to end up in Congress after they do, we should note that the Dakotas offer remarkably few distractions for those who grow up there. There is virtually nothing for them to do. After all, it is too cold for them to go outside and play, and there are no high-profile local sports teams for them to spend time following. Youngsters in the Dakotas, more or less by process of elimination, are likely to devote unusual amounts of time and energy to pursuits that elsewhere would get them labelled as hopeless nerds— pursuits like student government and civic involvement.[4] Thus, it may not be just their intelligence but also the activist orientations that they acquire early in life that turn young Dakotans into members-of-Congress-in-the-making.

We put these possibilities to the test in Table 2, which summarizes a 50-state regression analysis in which the dependent variable is the total number of natives of a state in the 107th Congress per 400,000 residents (as based on the 2000 census). Reflecting the preceding discussion, the predictors in the model are the 1970–2000 net population change for the state, the 1999 mean SAT score for students from the state, the mean annual temperature in the state, a dummy variable denoting the presence (1) or absence (0) in the state of teams in any of the four major professional sports (baseball, basketball, football, and hockey), and another dummy variable indicating whether the state is one of the two Dakotas (1) or not (0).

The fit of this model is excellent, with the five predictors jointly accounting for 80% of the variance in the number of state natives serving in Congress per 400,000 current state residents. This explanatory power is attributable to the performance of three predictors. As expected, high-growth states like Florida and Texas are less likely to export members of Congress to other states and are more likely to be represented by immigrants from other states. By contrast, low-growth states like the Dakotas are both more likely to be represented by their own natives and to have exported members of Congress to other states. Also as expected, states with no professional sports teams, like the Dakotas, tend to be represented in Congress by their own natives while they are also supplying representatives and senators to other states.

What stands out in Table 2, though, is the persistence of the Dakota Effect even when these factors, along with mean state SAT scores and temperatures, are held constant. Thus, the Dakota Effect is not a mere artifact of the tendencies for the Dakotas to leak population to the rest of the country, or for Dakotans to be smarter than residents of other states, or for there to be so little to do in the Dakotas. Moreover, the magnitude of the Dakota Effect is absolutely gargantuan.[5] Independent of all the other factors we have just been considering, the Dakota Effect is worth more than three extra seats in Congress for every 400,000 state residents. For the Dakotas, with a combined population of approximately 1.4 million, that works

Table 2. Number of Natives from State Serving in Congress (per 400,000 citizens)

Variable	OLS Estimate (Standard Error)
Net Population Change	-.003 (0.001)
Mean SAT Score	0.001 (.001)
Average Temperature	0.001 (0.007)
Professional Sports Team	-0.243* (0.112)
Dakota	3.250** (0.308)
Intercept	0.454 (1.120)
R2	80
N	50

out to 11 seats without even taking into account the extra seats attributable to the significant effects of low population growth and the absence of professional sports teams, both of which work to the Dakotas' advantage.

The Effect of the Dakota Effect

To say that the Dakota Effect is real—as it unquestionably is—is one thing, but whether it matters is a different question altogether. Perhaps it is simply an obscure, inconsequential factoid, like the observations that rodeo is the state sport of South Dakota and western wheatgrass is the state grass of North Dakota. The question is whether the extra representation that the Dakotas enjoy in Congress by virtue of providing members to other states, as well as to themselves, pays off in concrete ways. Because they supply far more than their constitutionally prescribed allotment of members of Congress, do they reap disproportionate benefits from Congress?

Congress's provision of pork barrel projects constitutes a clear window through which to watch the Dakota Effect in action. To peer through that window, we replicate and extend a previous analysis of pork barrel legislation, Balla *et al.*'s (2002) study of congressionally earmarked grants to institutions of higher education during the 100th through 106th Congresses (1995–2001). They modeled the allocation process via a selection equation for whether a given congressional district received an earmark or not and an outcome equation for the dollar amount allocated to each district that received any earmarks. (See Balla *et al.* 2002 for a full description of theory, data, and methods.) To probe the Dakota Effect, we have simply re-run the Balla *et al.* model with one modification: the addition of a dummy variable designating the Dakotas.

Table 3 shows the results. The crucial result is at the bottom of the outcome equation estimates. Despite Balla *et al.*'s elaborate set of statistical controls, the Dakota Effect is statistically significant, and because the dependent variable is expressed in dollars, its magnitude is easy to gauge. During the period in question, the coefficient for the Dakota Effect was approximately $2.6 million per congressional district. This means that, with all the other factors that affected earmarks for higher education held constant, an extra $2.6 million was earmarked for each of the Dakotas' two congressional districts—a tidy $5.2 million bonus for the Dakotas in all. And of course these were only the funds that Congress earmarked for institutions of higher education—a small slice of Congress' overall discretionary spending pie.

Conclusion

Having considered and rejected other plausible sources of the overrepresentation of the Dakotas in Congress, we can only speculate about its causal mechanisms. We suspect that the key lies in the distinction between sheer intelligence, on the one hand, and political guile, on the other. Earlier we acknowledged the unpublicized

Table 3. The Dakota Effect on Academic Earmarks

Variable	Selection Estimate (Robust Std. Error)	Outcome ($) Estimate (Robust St. Error)
House Majority Party	-.045 ((0.106)	-278637 (330858)
House Majority x Lagged $	0.047 (0.230)	0.555** (0.214)
Senate Majority Party	-0.0001 (0.071)	115727.8 (237009.1)
House Appropriations Committee	0.096 (0.131)	675178.7 (639794.4)
Senate Appropriations Committee	0.082 (0.097)	990640.5* (421096.4)
House Appropriations Cardinal	0.781** (0.266)	757610.5 (1456249)
Senate Appropriations Cardinal	0.228 (0.152)	-123407 (589512.9)
House Party Leader	-0.297 (0.335)	221297 (896002.5)
Senate Party Leader	0.349 (0.191)	1108097 (651420.9)
House Seniority	-0.013* (0.006)	40266.98 (26312.0)
Senate Seniority	0.019** (0.007)	75839.09 (39931.7)
Size of State	-0.006 (0.003)	———
District Density	0.000002 (0.000002)	———
Ideology	-0.004 (0.003)	-8032.82 (10369.9)
Margin	-0.163 (0.163)	-20224.87 (631591.3)
Research	0.581** (0.123)	———
Students	12.850** (1.944)	———
Refuse	0.734 (0.530)	———
Lagged $	1.157** (0.168)	0.3698029* (0.1657826)
104th Congress	-1.530** (0.116)	-2406879 (574258.1)
105th Congress	-0.430** (0.122)	-977648.8 (342815.1)
Dakota	-0.195 (0.676)	2592068** (670958)
Constant	-0.386 (0.216)	2000848 (751918.5)
Number of Observations	1,293 527 Uncensored	
Arctangent of Rho	-0.321 (.104)**	

**p < .01, *p < .05. NOTE: This table replicates Table 1 from Balla *et al.* (2002, 522) with the addition of the Dakota Effect. See Balla *et al.* (2002) for theory, methods, and data analysis.

but undeniable superior intelligence of Dakotans. Being smart does not necessarily translate into being politically astute, but in the case of Dakotans the two traits seem to have been conjoined. Notwithstanding their image as humble rustics, untutored in the sophisticated ways of the world east of the Red and Sioux Rivers, the historical record unequivocally establishes that Dakotans are amply endowed with the political virtues of cunning and guile. After all, the "uneducated" Lakota schooled West Point graduate George Custer in military tactics, and New Yorker Theodore Roosevelt returned from his sojourn in the Dakotas a far sturdier form of presidential timber (Mortis 1979). Indeed, the very fact that the erstwhile Dakota Territory entered the Union as two states rather than just one testifies to the political acumen of the wily Dakotans, who instinctively grasped the nuances of the Electoral College and the U.S. Senate.[6] Consider, too, as clear evidence of the political wiles and clout of the Greater Dakota Delegation (that is, members of Congress from the Dakotas themselves and their outposts in other states), that when Francophobes raised a hue and cry in the House of Representatives to change the name of french fries to "freedom fries," no member dared to suggest that South Dakota's capital be renamed "Peter."

The Dakota Effect has obvious policy implications. To cite just one example, taking their cue from the results reported here, states should begin providing college tuition support for promising high school seniors who vow to become political

science majors at out-of-state schools. To be sure, this could prove costly in the short term, but these costs should be recouped in the medium to long run when the awardees get themselves elected to Congress while retaining their gratitude and deeply ingrained allegiance to their state of origin. To be sure, some states may not boast a critical mass of the wily stock capable of getting elected to Congress as outsiders—but many such states, e.g., Iowa, seem bent in any event on the ill-considered opposite strategy of encouraging their residents to stay at home (Glover and Pitt 2005).

Finally, our results suggest a broad new avenue for future research and theory. A narrow path opening into this avenue involves reconsiderations of findings reported in prior studies. For example, Lee and Oppenheimer's (1999) argument that small states benefit greatly from Senate malapportionment, upon re-examination, seems likely to turn out to be an artifact of the Dakota Effect. More ambitiously, by taking the present study as their starting point, political scientists may find it possible to reconcile previously antagonistic approaches like area studies and rational choice theory. Accordingly, it seems entirely appropriate to establish an entirely new subdiscipline of Dakota Studies, which should be generously underwritten by federal grants earmarked for institutions in the Dakotas themselves and in states that have the good sense to let themselves be represented in Congress by agents of the Dakota Diaspora.

Notes

1. Actually, staffers at Congressional Quarterly (Nutting and Stern 2001, 1, 130) have been paying attention. However, political scientists seem to have ignored this phenomenon until now. Or, more conspiratorially, we might speculate that news of its existence has been suppressed by the small but immensely powerful band of Dakotans who have controlled the discipline of political science for the past several decades; in the last quarter-century South Dakota alone has been the birthplace of two APSA presidents, four editors of the top two general-readership political science journals, and many other leading lights of the political science profession.

2. By the end of the recently completed 109th Congress, this number had declined slightly with the departures of Reps. Dick Armey (R-TX, born in Cando, ND) and Karen Thurman of Florida (D-FL, born in Rapid City, SD).

3. In addition, Dakota natives held major institutional positions in recent congresses. Both Dick Armey and Tom Daschle (D-SD, born in Aberdeen, SD) served as majority leader in their respective chambers. Martin Olav Sabo (D-MN, born in Crosby, ND) and Tom Davis (R-VA, born in Minot, ND) have been standing committee chairs in the House.

4. Perhaps as an extreme form of overcompensation for their nerdiness, a clear sign that they watch too much television and film, or both, Dakota youths have taken to brawling in cages (Wilson 2005).

5. On the underutilization of the word "gargantuan" in discourse, see especially Tarantino (2004). Unfortunately, this is often confused with "Fargantuan," which refers to a resident of Fargo.

6. Or it was simply because Dakota Territory's southern residents could not stand the northerners and vice versa? The rivalry between the two states lives on. A few years ago, the Greater North Dakota Association hatched a plan to rename their state "Dakota" in an attempt to purvey a more pastoral image and avoid images of the frozen north country. Bemused South Dakotans countered with a proposal, equally unsuccessful, to shorten

the name of North Dakota to "North," which they argued was appropriate because the two states are usually referred to as "North and South Dakota."

References

Balla, Steven, Eric Lawrence, Forrest Maltzman, and Lee Sigelman. 2002. "Partisanship, Blame Avoidance, and the Distribution of` Legislative Pork." *American Journal of Political Science* 46: 515–25.

Coen, Joel, and Ethan Coen. 1996. *Fargo*. Gramercy Pictures.

Glover, Mike, and David Pitt. 2005. "Broad Skepticism About Under-30 Tax Break." The Associated Press State & Local Wire (January 25).

Lee, Frances, and Bruce Oppenheimer. 1999. *Sizing Up the Senate*. Chicago: University of Chicago Press.

Matthews, Donald R. 1968. "United States Senators: A Collective Portrait." In *American Legislative Behavior: A Reader*, ed. Samuel C. Patterson. Princeton, NJ: Van Nostrand, 620–34.

Morris, Edmund. 1979. *The Rise of Theodore Roosevelt*. New York: Coward, McCann & Geoghegan,

Nutting, Brian, and H. Amy Stern, eds. 2001. *Politics in America*. Washington: CQ Press.

Rieselbach, Leroy N. 1970. "Congressmen as 'Small Town Boys': A Research Note." *Midwest Journal of Political Science* 14: 321–30.

Spillman, W.J. 1909. "The Country Boy Again." *Science* 29: 739–41.

Tarantino, Quentin. 2004. *Kill Bill: Vol. 2*. Miramax Films.

Wilson, Michael. 2005. "Alive and Thriving in the Midwest: Brawling in Cages." *New York Times* (July 28).

A Rational Choice Model for the Dakota Effect
Jac C. Heckelman

In a recent issue, Young and Sigelman (2008) present evidence of a "Dakota effect" in which persons born in the Dakotas are disproportionately likely to represent their home state, other states, and also generate government spending directed toward the Dakotas. These authors are unable to explain the causal underpinnings for overrepresentation in Congress or the Dakotan natives' keen ability to direct pork back to these two states.

As is now well established, rational choice modeling can be successfully employed to explain every political phenomenon under the sun, as well as some over the sun. Even the harshest critics of rational choice analysis, such as Green and Shapiro (1994), have recently admitted this.[1] As such, a rational choice model will be employed here, and using fictitious data, empirical analysis will be shown to corroborate the model. We believe this to be a major breakthrough.[2]

The Rational Choice Model

As with most rational choice models, the equations are too complex to be understood by mere rank-and-file political scientists. Thus, the model will not be presented but merely summarized. In sum, the model predicts the Dakota effect.

Empirical Support

Having stated the model is correct, no empirical evidence should be needed. But we recognize some of the readers of this journal may not be convinced by the theoretical model alone. To placate such luddites, we now present direct evidence of the model's veracity.

We supplement Young and Sigelman's (2008) specification, which supplemented Balla *et al.*'s (2002) original specification with a Dakota dummy variable, by introducing a New Variable. Data for the New Variable is generated internally from a non-existent source[3] and the regression is estimated using the Heckelman Non-Parametric Inference Procedure (HNPIP).[4]

As clearly shown in the first column of Table 1, the New Variable is statistically significant, within a 45% error bound. None of the other variables, including the Dakota variable, comes close to this, as predicted by the model. Additional estimations do not support the model and are therefore not reported.[5]

To further show the power of the model, the New Variable is also used in the final column to explain a totally unrelated result, namely the heretofore previously undescribed "Dragonfly effect."[6] Because there is no dependent variable to relate

Table 1. Importance of the New Variable (HNPIP estimates)

Variable	Dependent Var. Academic Earmarks	Dep. Var. unknown
House Majority Party	0.00	—
House Majority Party x Lagged $	0.00	—
Senate Majority Party	0.00	—
House Appropriations Committee	0.00	—
Senate Appropriations Committee	0.00	—
House Appropriations Cardinal	0.00	—
Senate Appropriations Cardinal	0.00	—
House Seniority	0.00	—
Senate Seniority	0.00	—
Size of State	0.00	—
District Density	0.00	—
Ideology	0.00	—
Margin	0.00	—
Research	0.00	—
Students	0.00	—
Refuse	0.00	—
Lagged $	0.00	—
104th Congress	0.00	—
105th Congress	0.00	—
Dakota	0.00	—
New Variable	0.01*	16.37**
Number of Observations	A lot	One

*Significant at p < .45; **significant at p < .00.

this to, the estimated coefficient is difficult to interpret. However, the New Variable alone explains 137% of the variation.[7]

Conclusion

Once again, rational choice analysis has been used to explain an effect that traditional political science methods could not. Because the model was not presented and the New Variable was not identified, such flexibility will be exploited in future work to explain other important findings in the field of political science. One example is why the two major party labels in the United States, Democratic and Republican, both contain 10 letters. In support of the model, it is found in preliminary analysis that the number of letters in the candidate's party label perfectly explains the winner of each of the last 20 presidential elections. Future work in this area appears promising.

We conclude by quoting Adam Smith: "I'm right because I'm bigger than you."[8]

Notes

1. Actually, they have done no such thing.
2. Following convention of the literature, the term *we* will be used throughout the text, in an effort to fool the reader into believing the perspective presented here represents the views of more than just one person.
3. On the use of fictitious data from non-existent sources, see the following fictitious studies that appeared in non-existent journals. These sources are not presented below.
4. HNPIP estimates represent the researcher's estimates of how an estimated equation should look in order to support the hypotheses in question. For additional details, reread the previous sentence.
5. These additional results are not available, even upon request.
6. For a completely unrelated paper, see Heckelman (2007). This note serves as the obligatory self-reference.
7. Without any dependent variable, the R-square measure does not retain its normal interpretation.
8. Spoken by Smith to the author during fourth-grade recess, Thursday, April 15, 1976.

References

Balla, Steven, Eric Lawrence, Forrest Maltzman, and Lee Sigelman. 2002. "Partisanship, Blame Avoidance, and the Distribution of Legislative Pork." *American Journal of Political Science* 46: 515–25.

Green, Donald P., and Ian Shapiro. 1994. *Pathologies of Rational Choice Theory: A Critique of Applications in Political Science*. New Haven: Yale University Press.

Heckelman, Jac C. 2007. "Explaining the Rain: *The Rise and Decline of Nations* after 25 Years." *Southern Economic Journal* 74: 18–33.

Smith, Adam K. 1976. Personal correspondence to author.

Young, Garry, and Lee Sigelman. 2008. "The Dakota Effect." *PS: Political Science & Politics* 41: 349–53.

Executives

Presidents, Extramarital Sex, and the Public: Testing a Rational Theory

Lee Sigelman

One need not be a deep thinker to grasp the intimate linkage between sex and politics, enshrined in the hoary adage that "Politics makes strange bedfellows" and more recently in the confession of Henry Kissinger—surely one of history's most unlikely Casanovas—that "Power is the greatest aphrodisiac." Still, pundits and political scientists alike were left groping for an explanation in early 1998 when, with allegations of sexual improprieties involving White House intern Monica Lewinsky surging rampantly around him, President Clinton's public standing rose higher and higher instead of going down. Why wasn't the normally puritanical American public condemning the president rather than getting behind him? Perhaps, some opined, Americans were ceding a "zone of privacy" to the president. Or perhaps, having grown accustomed to Clinton's recurrent "bimbo eruptions," they considered the latest allegations simply more of the same. Or perhaps half of the public—the male half—was engaging in projection.

These speculations are wrong, of course, but an even more grievous failing is that they cannot be derived from the theory of rational choice, which holds the key to understanding all of politics, economics, and, indeed, life. Thus, in what follows I outline and then provide empirical validation of a rational theory of the American public's fluid reaction to the Lewinsky sex scandal. The statistical results demonstrate that I have indeed hit on the key to understanding presidential performance.

The Interpretation in a Nutshell

Underlying my interpretation is the assumption that the American public behaves rationally. This penetrating insight simply means that, given a modicum of information, the public is capable of reaching a satisfying conclusion. Once this seminal assumption has been laid out, the rest of the interpretation flows:

(1) The public wants presidents to succeed.

(2) The most successful presidents are those who are sexually active outside the marital bed.

(3) Therefore, the public wants presidents to engage in extramarital sex, and welcomes signs that they are doing so.

Of the three components of the model, (1) is noncontroversial, and (3), when combined with the rationality assumption, is simply the logical climax of (1) and (2). My task, then, is to establish the correctness of (2).

Validating the Interpretation

Anecdotal evidence on behalf of my interpretation is easy to find: for example, the public is most supportive of presidents during their "honeymoon" period, and turns against them after they have become "lame ducks" (that is, once their potency is spent). As a scientist, however, I need hard evidence. To validate my interpretation, what is required, first, is a measure of presidential success. Fortunately, historians aroused by presidential performance have produced several ratings of the presidents, four of which I have merged into a composite score.[1] Of course, I also need for some presidents to have strayed from the fold as well as a means of identifying those who have done so. Fortunately for science, many presidents have looked upon sex as "just a perk of public office" (Uhlenhuth 1998), and, bearing out the wisdom of Henry Kissinger, they have often triumphed in their amorous conquests. In the words of Gil Troy, author of *Affairs of State*, "The President in the modern world is like a rock star. He walks in a room and people's hearts go aflutter. . . . Add to that the fact that in some way, the entire executive branch of government works 24 hours a day, seven days a week to serve the president's needs, all the president's needs" (Uhlenhuth 1998).

Nor does identifying presidents who have had affairs pose any problem, for Wesley Hagood (1995), in a volume propitiously titled *Presidential Sex: From the Founding Fathers to Bill Clinton*, has provided a blow-by-blow account of such affairs, based on oral histories and undercover reports. In all, thirteen presidents (Washington, Jefferson, Jackson, Buchanan, Garfield, Cleveland, Wilson, Harding, Franklin Roosevelt, Eisenhower, Kennedy, Johnson, and Clinton) are classified as philanderers.

Finally, because not even the most hard-core Freudian would argue that sex is the sole determinant of presidential greatness, I bring four other distinguishing presidential characteristics into play. First, some presidents have been better endowed than others, intellectually. Second, while some presidents have pushed hard to succeed, others have been content to lie back. To take these factors into account, I have included in the model the brilliance and need-achievement factor scores from Simonton's (1986) presidential personality inventory. Third, presidential performance also depends on the partisan makeup of Congress (Edwards, 1989). In recognition thereof, I erect a variable coded 1 for presidents whose party was in full control of Congress for at least half of their time in office and 0 for others (Ragsdale 1996). Fourth, I recognize that historians' ratings may be inflated for presidents who were assassinated; to correct for any halo effect, the model contains a term distinguishing the four slain presidents (Lincoln, Garfield, McKinley, and Kennedy) from the rest.

The estimated model is:

Performance rating = -.28 (-.95) + .37*Brilliance (2.50)** + .26*Need for achievement (1.90)

+ .15*Unified government (.46) - .44*Assassination victim (.86) +
   .50* Extramarital sex (1.66)*

where R²=.44, the number in parentheses following each predictor is the t-ratio, and the asterisks denote effects that are significant at the .05 level (one-tailed). (Although a multi-tailed test initially seemed more appropriate, the prediction was that the president's popularity would surge upward rather than shriveling to nothing.) These results indicate, reassuringly, that presidents who try harder and are smarter are significantly more successful, but neither unified versus divided government nor assassination significantly affects success. The thrust of the results, however, is conveyed by the significant positive coefficient for extramarital sex. As anticipated in the key second component of my rational choice-based interpretation, the most successful presidents are indeed those who are sexually active outside the marital bed. Thus, whereas "enlightened" political observers contend that "Greatness in leadership does not depend on sexual purity" (Lewis 1998), the rational public carries the analysis a step further to the recognition that greatness in leadership depends on sexual impurity.

Of course, size matters, and the impressive magnitude of the coefficient for extramarital sex means that this effect cannot be pooh-poohed. Even if it were assumed, for example, that a president is both uncommonly stupid (i.e., a full standard deviation below the mean on the intelligence dimension) and unusually unmotivated (i.e., a full standard deviation below the mean on the need-achievement dimension), extramarital presidential sex can still be the saving grace for the nation, offsetting these shortcomings. On the other hand, even an unusually bright, highly motivated chief executive can be plunged into mediocrity by a failure to do what seems to have come naturally for so many of our most illustrious presidents. It follows that the best of all possible presidents is one who is highly energetic, very smart, and dates, which is exactly what the American public, being rational, got when it elected Bill Clinton.

Notes

1. The ratings are those of McDougall (1997), Murray and Blessing (1988), Ridings and McIver (1997), and Schlesinger (1997). A single factor accounts for 84% of the variance in the four scales, and coefficient alpha for the composite scale is .93.

References

Edwards, George C., III. 1989. *At the Margins: Presidential Leadership of Congress*. New Haven: Yale University Press.

Hagood, Wesley O. 1995. *Presidential Sex: From the Founding Fathers to Bill Clinton*. New York: Birch Lane Press.

Lewis, Anthony. 1998. "Sex and Leadership." *New York Times* (February 23).

McDougall, Walter A. 1997. "Rating the Presidents." *National Review* (October 27): 32–36.

Murray, Robert K., and Tim H. Blessing. 1988. *Greatness in the White House: Rating the Presidents, Washington through Carter.* University Park: Pennsylvania State University Press.

Ragsdale, Lyn. 1996. *Vital Statistics on the Presidency: Washington to Clinton.* Washington: CQ Press.

Ridings, William J., Jr., and Stuart B. McIver. 1997. *Rating the Presidents: A Ranking of U.S. Leaders, From the Great and Honorable to the Dishonest and Incompetent.* Secaucus, NJ: Citadel Press.

Schlesinger, Arthur M., Jr. 1997. "Rating the Presidents: Washington to Clinton." *Political Science Quarterly* 112: 179–190.

Simonton, Dean K. 1986. "Presidential Personality: Biographical Use of the Gough Adjective Check List." *Journal of Personality and Social Psychology* 51: 149–160.

Uhlenhuth, Karen. 1998. "Philanderer-in-Chief? Power as an Aphrodisiac—It Has Marked Presidencies Since the Nation's Beginning." *Kansas City Star* (January 24).

The Presidential Horoscope: Predicting Performance in the White House

Lee Sigelman

Each new President is swept into office amidst a wave of great expectations. That he will eventually disappoint most people is virtually inevitable: according to John Mueller (1973: 233), the only way a President can leave office with his popularity intact is to be named Dwight Eisenhower or to resign the day after inauguration. Despite this near-inevitablity, it is notoriously difficult to predict what a President will do after he assumes office—how and how well he will play his role. One is reminded of a bittersweet joke that circulated during the late 1960s: "They told me in '64 that if I voted for Goldwater we'd get into a major land war in Southeast Asia. I did, and we are."

Predicting performance in the White House is a challenge of the highest order. It is complex and important, because the presidency is complex and important. It is a task toward which political scientists, in performance of their civic duty, ought to be oriented. It is also a task so formidable that few have been willing to try.

Barber's Analysis of Presidential Performance

One who has tried is James David Barber. At the outset, let me make it perfectly clear that I have the utmost regard for Barber's work.[1] He boldly addresses a question to which his fellow political scientists should be paying far greater attention, in order "to help citizens and those who advise them cut through the confusion and get at some clear criteria for choosing Presidents" (Barber, 1977a: 3). His approach is psychological, verging on psychiatric; it emphasizes the President's "personality," "character," "world view," and "style." His approach is also controversial: political scientists consider it terribly un-politically-scientific but psychoanalytically engaging, while psychologists think it psychologically primitive but politically revealing.

The present study attacks Barber's analysis from an entirely different direction. Some may accuse him of forging overly simplistic links between presidential performance and early childhood experiences, but from my perspective Barber's analysis, far from being simplistic, is far too complex. Therefore, I intend to outline and test a much more parsimonious approach to predicting presidential performance than Barber, or anyone else, has ever considered.

In Barber's view, the key to understanding and predicting presidential performance lies in personality: "The burden of this book is that the crucial differences can be anticipated by an understanding of a potential President's character, his world view, and his style" (Barber, 1977a: 6). This, in turn, directs attention toward early life experiences: "The best way to predict a President's character, world view, and- style is to see how they were put together in the first place. What happened in his early life . . ." (Barber, 1977a: 6). In short, Barber believes that to know the President, one must know the inner man. This premise may seem routine to psychologists, but it strikes many hide-bound institutionalist political scientists as extremely exotic. My disagreement with Barber is over the manner in which he tries to understand the inner man—by quasi-Freudian vaporings about personality, based on long-distance psychoanalysis of behavior somewhere between the womb and the Oval Office. This I consider a fundamental error, for it will never reveal the true inner man; psychoanalysis is about as scientific as the reading of a sheep's entrails. Still, looking at the President, Barber agrees with Shakespeare's Cassius that "The fault, dear Brutus, is not in our stars but in ourselves." That, in a nutshell, is where Barber goes wrong.

A New Approach to Predicting Presidential Performance

Before I present my new approach to predicting presidential performance, a brief comment is in order about what should be expected of such an approach, whether it be mine, Barber's, or anyone else's. It seems to me that such an approach should offer predictions that are clear and accurate. Barber has come in for some criticism in this respect (see, e.g., George, 1974), for he often seems to be arguing that, for example, the presidents he has classified as active-positive tend to behave like active-positives—which, after all, is why he classified them as active-positive in the first place. He makes much of what he calls his "Nixon prediction," but I for one confess that in reading the 1973 edition of *The Presidential Character* I never even recognized that there was a Nixon prediction somewhere in there. If a prediction is either true by definition or so vague that its meaning or its very existence is questionable, then its accuracy becomes a moot point.

My new approach offers clear-cut predictions about presidential performance. I will demonstrate that these predictions point in the right direction empirically. I have already indicated that the approach is parsimonious. Let me now present this approach, so that readers can admire for themselves its clarity, accuracy, and parsimony.

My approach begins with a premise that may seem self-contradictory: If the key to understanding the President lies in knowing the inner man, then we must look outside rather than inside the man. "Character," "personality," "style," "world view," and other such psychological mumbo-jumbo can only deflect a true understanding of the forces that impel the inner man. Let us, then, look not inside the man, which will not reveal these vital forces. Let us look higher. Let us follow the lead of the ancients, raise our eyes to the heavens, and take our counsel there. Let us, in short, look to the stars.

It was the Babylonians who first linked the movements of the stars with the concept of fate. When Alexander the Great conquered Mesopotamia, he found a highly developed theology based on astronomical observation and a system of divination in which the stars revealed the secrets of the future and the destinies of man (Linton and Linton, 1952: 54–55). Astrology spread through the world, finally reaching its fullest flowering in sixteenth-century Europe and twentieth-century Los Angeles.

Astrology involves the casting of horoscopes. If one demands extreme precision, a horoscope must be based on the exact moment a person was born, the exact place of birth, and many other situational factors. For most purposes, though, it is sufficient to know which of the twelve periods of the zodiac a person was born into. Knowing a person's zodiacal sign reveals a great deal about him. As the respected anthropologist Ralph Linton has written, "The character readings assigned to the natives of each zodiacal period have remained consistent for many centuries. Since so many generations of men have followed and put credence in this, it seems that perhaps the conjunction of the planets at the time we were born does influence our nature in some way" (Linton and Linton, 1952: 66).

Exactly what characteristics are associated with each of the twelve signs of the zodiac? The Lintons (1952: 69–116) conveniently summarize what have come down through the ages as the attributes of natives of each zodiacal period, and from their summaries I have distilled the profiles that are presented in Table 1.

Data and Methods

How accurately do these zodiacal profiles predict performance in the White House? Rather than using my own possibly biased judgment to answer this question, I propose to rely on the results of a survey of American historians conducted by Maranell (1970) in 1968.[2] Maranell asked a panel of historians, 571 of whom responded to his request, to rate American presidents from Washington through Lyndon Johnson on six dimensions: the strength or weakness each President displayed in directing government and shaping events; the activity or passivity of each President's approach; the idealism or pragmatism of each President's official actions; the flexibility or rigidity of each President's style of policy implementation; the significance, great or small, of each President's accomplishments; and each President's overall prestige. All these ratings were made on eleven-point scales, and Maranell subsequently converted them into standard-score format.[3]

With these evaluative dimensions in mind, the next step is to use the profiles in Table 1 to generate a specific set of predictions. One initial problem is that not all the birth signs can be associated with such a prediction for each dimension. It is easy enough to predict, for example, that a President who is a child of Aries should score higher on the activity scale than a Gemini. But what about a Sagittarian, for whom the profile gives no indication of activity levels one way or the

Table 1. Astrological Signs and Descriptions

Sign	Description
Aries (March 21 to April 20)	Strong, vital, a leader, aggressive, independent, venturesome, arrogant, restless
Taurus (April 21 to May 21)	Headstrong, vehement, extravagant, vengeful, brooks no opposition
Gemini (May 22 to June 21)	Intellectual, unenergetic, impractical, restless
Cancer (June 22 to July 23)	Sociable, dependent, needs to be liked, practical, economical
Leo (July 24 to August 23)	Born to rule, dominant, high-minded, tireless, energetic, driven for power, generous
Virgo (August 24 to September 23)	Industrious, systematic, pragmatic, controlled
Libra (September 24 to October 23)	Idealistic, lover of beauty and justice, indecisive and hesitant, not a go-getter
Scorpio (October 24 to November 22)	Energetic, obstinate, extreme, vindictive, dominant
Sagittarius (November 23 to December 22)	Idealistic, charming, jovial, high-strung, optimistic, a fine speaker
Capricorn (December 23 to January 20)	A plodder, economical, pragmatic, not brilliant
Aquarius (January 21 to February 19)	Socially aware, humanitarian, charismatic, innovative
Pisces (February 20 to March 20)	Impractical, intelligent, avoids competition and hurting anyone

other? I have followed the very conservative course of treating such instances as missing data for purposes of comparison. This decision has the effect of depressing the number of presidents who are involved in any particular comparison, but because it also restricts comparisons to presidents for whom clear, unambiguous predictions can be formulated, it should enhance the validity of the analysis.

This methodological issue having been resolved, I derived the following predictions from the zodiacal profiles:

> (1) Presidents born under the signs of Aries, Leo, or Scorpio should score higher on the *strength* and *activity* dimensions than Gemini, Cancer, or Libra presidents.
>
> (2) Geminis, Leos, Libras, Sagittarians, Aquarians, and Pisceans should display greater *idealism* than the pragmatic Cancers, Virgos, and Capricorns.

(3) Aries, Tauran, and Aquarian presidents should have made greater *accomplishments*, and thus have been accorded greater prestige, than Geminis, Cancers, Libras, Capricorns, or Pisceans.

Unfortunately, no comparisons can be made on the *flexibility* dimension, for although the profiles of four of the zodiacal groups (Aries, Taurus, Leo, and Scorpio) suggest rigidity, none suggests high flexibility.

The birthdates of the first 35 presidents were ascertained from standard biographical sources. Three different binary or dummy variables were then coded for each President. For example, Aries, Leo, and Scorpio natives were assigned scores of 1, and Geminis, Cancers, and Libras scores of 0, on the first dummy, which could then be used to test the predictions concerning strength and activity. Parallel dummies were coded for testing the two other sets of predictions, and simple correlations were calculated between scores on the dummy variables and on the corresponding Maranell scales; in each case, of course, a positive correlation was anticipated.

Findings

Table 2 presents the correlations between presidential birth signs, as summarized by the three zodiac dummy variables, and five different dimensions of presidential performance, as measured in the Maranell survey. Four of the five correlations are, as predicted, positive, indicating that *individuals who are born under more auspicious signs do in fact turn into presidents who are stronger and more active, accomplish more, and enjoy greater prestige because of it.*

Two aspects of these correlational findings merit special attention. First, there is the fact that the strongest correlation, the one between birth sign and presidential idealism, runs in the direction opposite from the prediction. How can this seeming anomaly be explained? To a considerable degree, this finding strikes me as nothing more than a methodological artifact. Maranell's panel gave Aquarians Abraham ("Government of, by, and for the People") Lincoln and Franklin ("The Four Freedoms") Roosevelt and Piscean George ("I cannot tell a lie") Washington

Table 2. *Statistical Results*

Independent variable	Dependent variable	Pearson's r	n
Zodiac dummy #1	Strength	.233	14
Zodiac dummy #1	Activity	.217	14
Zodiac dummy #2	Idealism	-.309	22
Zodiac dummy #3	Accomplishment	.142	23
Zodiac dummy #3	Prestige	.070	23

idealism scores that I consider unconscionably low—well below the mean for all presidents. The panel also awarded Capricorn native Woodrow Wilson an idealism rating that was almost off the charts—more than four standard deviations above the mean, immensely higher than any other President has ever received on any dimension. Moreover, the Maranell poll stopped with Lyndon Johnson; had it been extended to Johnson's successor, Richard Nixon, the depressing effect on the idealism scores of the Cancer-Virgo-Capricorn natives would doubtless have been profound. In order to try to offset these methodological problems, I (1) took a square-root transformation on Wilson's idealism score to make him less of an outlier; (2) assigned the converse of Wilson's transformed score to Nixon, assuming that Nixon was about as unidealistic as Wilson was idealistic; and (3) moved Washington, Lincoln, and Roosevelt up the idealism scale into a tie with Millard Fillmore—a procedure that seemed quite conservative in that Fillmore was hardly the world's best-known idealist. Once these changes had been made, the correlation between birth signs and idealism changed from -.309 to +.030, indicating a very slight positive association.

This leads to a second aspect of the correlational findings: the fact that all are of a modest magnitude. Just as Barber (1977a: 7) cautions that he is "not about to argue that once you know a President's personality you know everything," let me make it perfectly clear that the stars do not tell us *everything* we need to know in order to predict presidential performance. They do, however, point us in the right direction, and thus provide a more rigorously empirical basis for prediction than has previously been available.

Notes

1. Barberian instincts often come to the fore in response to unfriendly criticism (see Barber's [1977b] rejoinder to a critique by Qualls). Therefore, readers will appreciate why I am trying to keep my fences well mended.
2. The Maranell ratings are also employed in a recent nonscientific (i.e., non-zodiacal) analysis by Simonton (1981); see also Taylor and Perthel (1980).
3. I pondered long and hard on the difficult issue of whether to count Grover Cleveland once or twice. Counting Cleveland twice would have had a very salutary effect on the statistical results, as for that matter would counting Franklin Delano Roosevelt four times. But, ultimately, I decided to count Cleveland only once, for there was, after all, only one Grover Cleveland.

References

Barber, James David. 1977a. *The Presidential Character: Predicting Performance in the White House*, 2d ed. Englewood Cliffs, N.J.: Prentice-Hall.

Barber, James David. 1977b. "Qualls' Nonsensical Analysis of Nonexistent Works." *American Political Science Review* 71: 212–225.

George, Alexander. 1974. "Strategies for Understanding Politicians." *American Journal of Political Science* 18: 443–467.

Linton, Ralph, and Adelin Linton. 1952. *The Lore of Birthdays.* New York: Henry Schuman.

Maranell, Gary, 1970. "The Evaluation of Presidents: An Extension of the Schlesinger Polls." *Journal of American History* 52: 104–113.

Mueller, John E. 1973. *War Presidents and Public Opinion.* New York: Wiley.

Simonton, Dean K. 1981. "Presidential Greatness and Performance: Can We Predict Leadership in the White House?" *Journal of Personality* 49: 306–323.

Taylor, Marcia W., and Carl Perthel. 1980. "Correlates of Presidential Character." Paper prepared for delivery at the annual meeting of the Southern Political Science Association.

Zog for Albania, Edward for Estonia, and Monarchs for All the Rest? The Royal Road to Prosperity, Democracy, and World Peace

Jeremy D. Mayer and Lee Sigelman

Down with Communists, we want a king!
—Albanian demonstrators in Tirana's central square, rioting for the return of King Zog

Monarchy has been the predominant form of governance throughout recorded history, and its hegemony extended well into the twentieth century. On the eve of World War I, only four nations in Europe, and none of any consequence (France, Portugal, San Marino, and Switzerland), were not monarchies. Today, however, democracy reigns, and monarchs are widely seen, in the words of the American writer Austin O'Malley, as "a vermiform appendix: useless when quiet; when obtrusive, in danger of removal" (quoted in Esar 1962, 140), or even as the capstone of a sinister conspiracy. "The Royal Family stands at the pinnacle of the class system, and its wealth is linked to the creation of poverty and need," charges British Marxist Mark Kirby (1998, 37). For antimonarchists, the crown is not only a symbol but also a source of centuries-old class domination, social injustice, and imperialism, a wasteful frippery at best (Came 1998) and a malignant atavism at worst (Nairn 1994). Thus, the forces of blond egalitarianism have humbled the Nordic royalty by replacing their horse-drawn carriages with bicycles, and the British have reduced their nobility to guiding hordes of T-shirted, gum-snapping American tourists through their ancestral homes in order to make ends meet. In Australia, "progressive" forces succeeded in scheduling a referendum in 1999 on whether the current head of state, Queen Elizabeth, should be replaced by an illustrious Australian—if one could be found.

Though an endangered species, monarchs are by no means extinct. On five of the world's six inhabited continents, monarchs (emirs and emiras, emperors and empresses, grand dukes and duchesses, kings and queens, princes and princesses, sultans and sultanas) still preside over nations large and small. Indeed, there are signs that monarchy may even be undergoing something of a renaissance. In 1994, the Estonian Royalist Party, holders of almost 10% of the seats in the national parliament, offered to crown Britain's Prince Edward as the king of Estonia, because of their admiration for "him . . . , Britain, its monarchy, democracy and culture" and, presumably, because he had so little else to do.[1] Three years later, the untimely death of the dazzling Diana stirred a lachrymose tidal wave. Then, in 1998, came the once unimaginable spectacle of a Russian leader repentantly sanctioning the interment of the remains of Tsar Nicholas II in the Cathedral of St. Peter and St. Paul.

Avid appreciation of the merits of monarchy lives on in Central and Eastern Europe in particular, and especially in Albania, Romania, Russia, and Serbia. This is not difficult to fathom. The last time some of these nations experienced a sustained period of independence, stability, and prosperity, a monarch sat atop the government. So, while the Estonians' longing to be ruled by a member of the British royal family may conjure up quaint images of the crackpot scheme hatched by the Duchy of Grand Fenwick in *The Mouse That Roared*, the fervor for monarchy in the new democracies is real. Cynics dismiss it as silly, nostalgic romanticism, but could it instead be an altogether rational manifestation of the universal desire to live well and be governed well? Although the royal road has generally been bypassed in the twentieth century, might it be the surest route to societal well-being and good government in the new millennium?

Data and Methods

To find out, we formulated and tested a statistical model based on the data Muller and Seligson (1994) assembled for their analysis of the link between political culture and democratic performance in 27 Western societies. The ultimate dependent variable in our model was a rating of each country's democratic performance during the 1980s.[2]

Posited as immediately prior to democratic performance in the chain of causality were three interrelated dimensions of national political culture: the percentage of the public proclaiming support for revolutionary change, the percentage expressing concern about threats from internal subversion, and the percentage endorsing the idea that most of their fellow citizens were trustworthy. The intuitions underlying this portion of the model were that democracy is not apt to thrive in countries whose citizens clamor for revolution, fear internal subversion, and distrust one another. In turn, we posited as causally prior to these components of political culture three interrelated structural conditions: national wealth (as indicated by per capita gross domestic product), socioeconomic equality (as indicated, inversely, by the income share of the top 20% of the nation's households), and past democratic performance (as indicated by the nation's democratic performance rating during the 1970s). That is, we hypothesized that a culture supportive of democracy would be more likely to flourish in nations that were more prosperous, where wealth was less concentrated, and where democratic institutions had functioned well in the recent past.

To this seven-variable model we added, as the key element, a dummy variable indicating whether the nation was a monarchy (1) or not (0). Of the 27 nations in the analysis, 11 were monarchies; these 11 represent almost 40% of the world's 28 remaining ruling dynasties.[3] We specified monarchy as causally prior to every other variable in the model in order to test its impact on the contemporary structural and cultural requisites of democracy and on democracy itself.

Findings

As shown in the first section of Table 1, several of the variables just described were significant predictors of democratic performance: national democratic performance ratings in the 1980s were significantly higher in nations where the public was less worried about internal subversion and less supportive of revolution, where the top 20% commanded a smaller share of the income, and where national democratic performance ratings in the 1970s had been higher. As its omission from this list implies, monarchy was not among the significant predictors. Indeed, it had essentially no independent effect on democratic performance in the 1980s (t=0.13).

This does not mean, however, that monarchy was inconsequential—far from it. To see why, consider the remaining significant causal links in Table 1, which are shown graphically in Figure 1. These demonstrate the causal impact of monarchy on five of the six intermediate variables in the model. Other factors being equal, in monarchies public support for revolution was significantly less widespread, interpersonal trust was significantly higher, per capita wealth was significantly greater, income was significantly less concentrated, and the political system had been significantly more democratic during the 1970s. Recalling the data shown in the first section of Table 1, three of these factors—public support for revolution, income inequality, and democratic performance in the 1970s—themselves significantly affected democratic performance in the 1980s, and the fourth factor—interpersonal trust—helped sustain a climate of personal and political civility. As a consequence, even though monarchy had no direct effect on democratic performance in the 1980s, it consistently bolstered the conditions that, themselves, promoted democracy and it consistently weakened the conditions that, themselves, undermined democracy.

Discussion

Political scientists, whose learned treatises on the requisites of societal well-being and good government have been responsible for felling millions of trees, have heretofore sacrificed remarkably little wood to advance the study of monarchy or, for that matter, to advance monarchy itself. However, to judge from the results reported above, both monarchy and the study thereof are causes well worth advancing.

Of all the salubrious consequences of monarchy documented here, none will occasion greater consternation among antimonarchists than the observed levelling of incomes. Leftists wedded to the malevolent image of monarchy as "the instrument of the plutocratic establishment . . . which has been successfully deployed to legitimize an unjust and inequitable social structure" (Wilson 1989, 152) obviously have it all wrong, as they would have recognized long ago if they had read their Marx more carefully. Marx argued that during the historical evolution of feudalism

Table 1. Models of the Impact of Monarchy on Societal Well-Being and Democracy

	b	t
Democracy 1981-90 (Adjusted R²=.83)		
Monarchy	-5.57	0.13
Income inequality	-2.06	-3.42*
GDP per capita	-.001	-0.44
Democracy 1972-80	.28	1.51*
Interpersonal trust	.04	0.13
Concern about subversion	-.54	-1.79*
Support for Revolution	-1.04	-1.62*
Constant	181.00	4.21*
Support for Revolution (Adjusted R²=.38)		
Monarchy	-3.73	-1.52*
Income inequality	-.21	-0.84
GDP per capita	.001	1.79
Democracy 1972-80	-.21	-3.43*
Constant	28.40	1.71*
Concern about Subversion (Adjusted R²=.07)		
Monarchy	.64	0.13
Income inequality	.18	0.37
GDP per capita	.001	0.65
Democracy 1972-80	.13	1.09
Constant	-1.92	-0.06
Interpersonal Trust (Adjusted R²=.26)		
Monarchy	15.16	2.73*
Income inequality	.56	1.00
GDP per capita	-.001	-0.54
Democracy 1972-80	.22	1.62*
Constant	-7.01	-0.19
GDP per capita (Adjusted R²=.37)		
Monarchy	$3619.43	3.89*
Constant	$4202.27	7.14*
Income Inequality (Adjusted R²=.47)		
Monarchy	-12.26	-4.68*
Constant	51.94	31.33*
Democracy 1972-80 (Adjusted R²=.24)		
Monarchy	28.28	2.96*
Constant	66.27	10.95*
*t<.10, one-tailed.		

Figure 1. Significant Causal Links

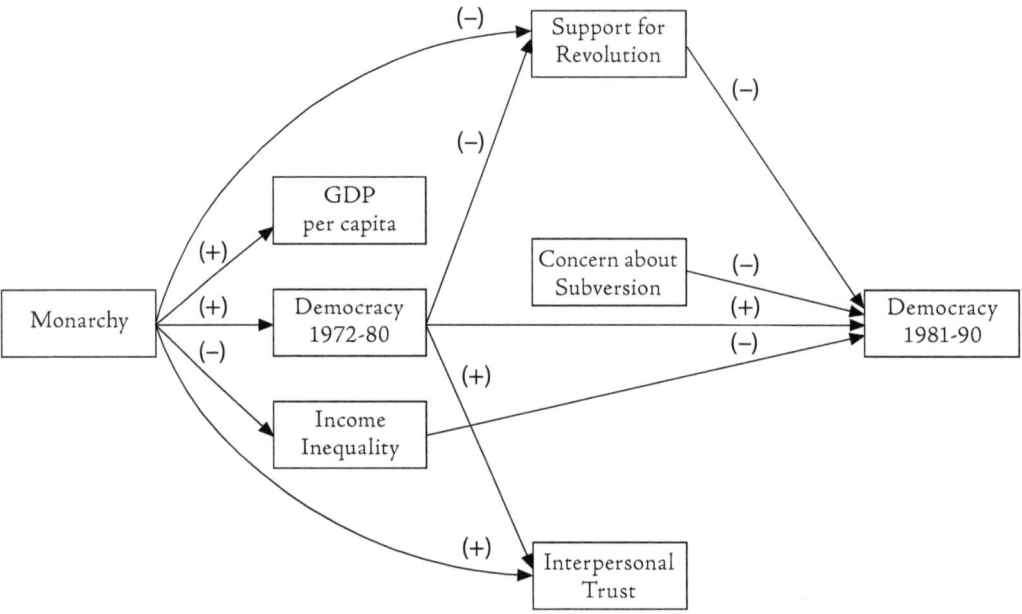

the king acted as a check on, not a tool of, the aristocracy. By the same token, in modern times, the royalty serves as a check on the greed of rapacious capitalist barons by demonstrating that class is a function not merely of wealth but also of selective breeding and upbringing, and by embodying for the lower classes the beneficence of their betters. A strategic implication of our findings, then, is that, in many countries, the forces of progressivism and conservatism should join hands in the fight to restore monarchy, which not only spurs the egalitarian distribution of wealth coveted by the former, but also maintains the sense of traditional order valued by the latter.

The cultured role model of, and the unstinting acts of *noblesse oblige* by, royal families not only help prevent overconcentration of wealth and conspicuous consumption, but also augment the national stock of interpersonal trust. As even one of the British monarchy's most strident critics concedes, the monarchy is of key importance in "binding together the disparate ethnic populations of the UK into a non–ethnically-based British nationality" (Kirby 1998, 37). Belgians Jean, Jan, and Johannes may have little else in common, but under the unifying spell of King Albert II each can trust the others to return his lost wallet, to obey the speed limit, and to give his all—chocolate, waffle iron, or whatever—for the commonweal.

Our findings also expose the illogic of measures currently underway in Britain and elsewhere to slash the royal purse. This pecuniary assault may save a paltry few tens of millions each year, but its penny-wisdom is far outweighed by its pound-foolishness. In the first place, the cost of maintaining the royals in the manner to which they have become accustomed pales in comparison to the intangible benefits of greater interpersonal trust, a more egalitarian income distribution, pan-ethnic unity, and stronger democracy. More concretely, the enrichment of the national treasury is where kings and queens undeniably earn their pelf. According to data collected for Table 1, having a monarch adds $3619.43 per capita each year to a nation's gross domestic product—many times the annual budget for the wages of liveried footmen, the purchase of new polo mallets, the dry cleaning of ermine robes, and the other essentials of the royal lifestyle.

What nation would not want to take advantage of all these royal boons? Of course, some logistical problems remain to be settled before a suitable royal family can be identified for every one of the scores of nations that would benefit therefrom. The Estonian Edwardians and Albanian Zogistas have already made their preferences known, and, fortunately, decades of determined in-breeding among the crowned heads of Europe have produced scores of royal relatives available for consignment, including more double cousins than would be found even in a random sample of Arkansans.

Happily, even those misguided nations that elect not to follow the royal road stand to profit from a rediffusion of monarchy, in the form of a worldwide peace dividend. Political science has convincingly established that democracy leads to peace (Brown, Lynn-Jones, and Miller 1995). As we have demonstrated, monarchy leads to democracy. If every nation crowned just one little monarch, then what a peaceful world this would be!

Notes

1. In a typically arch statement, a spokesman for Buckingham Palace termed this "a charming but unlikely idea" (Hardman 1994).

2. For details concerning this measure and the other measures described in this paragraph, see Muller and Seligson (1994).

3. This classification was based on the Summer 1998 "Special Royals Issue" of *Life* magazine. A valuable methodological lesson for political scientists is that they should remain alert while standing in line at the grocery counter. A definitional issue arose for two countries. Although Elizabeth II is the official head of state of both Australia and Canada and is featured prominently on their currency and postage stamps, we were concerned that royalism might not be as deeply ingrained in these two countries as in other monarchies. Needless to say, our decision to classify both nations as monarchies was made for purely theoretical reasons. The fact that this decision bolstered the strength of our findings was wholly irrelevant.

References

Brown, Michael E., Sean M. Lynn-Jones, and Steven E. Miller. 1995. *Debating the Democratic Peace*. Cambridge, MA: MIT Press.

Came, Barry. 1998. "Downsizing Royalty." *Maclean's* (March 23): 32–34.

Esar, Evan, ed. 1962. *Dictionary of Humorous Quotations*. New York: Paperback Library.

Hardman, Robert. 1994. "Royal Confusion over Estonian Role for Prince." *The Daily Telegraph* (July 11).

Kirby, Mark. 1998. "Death of a Princess." *Capital and Class* 64: 29–41.

Muller, Edward N., and Mitchell A. Seligson. 1994. "Civic Culture and Democracy: The Question of Causal Relationship." *American Political Science Review* 88: 635–652.

Nairn, Thomas. 1994. *The Enchanted Glass: Britain and Its Monarchy*. London: Vintage.

Wilson, Edgar. 1989. *The Myths of British Monarchy*. London: Journeyman Press.

Conspiracy Theories

The RoWoCo and Flea Theory: Truth Behind the Conspiracy

Dr. Dr. Otto I.Q. Besser-Wisser

It is a terrible truth that the round world conspiracy (RoWoCo) has dominated our view of the earth for hundreds of years. The purpose of this short article is to de-mystify and unmask, once and for all, the falsehood of the RoWoCo and to establish, beyond all shadow of doubt, the truth of flat earth theory (Flea Theory). I will do so not in the hysterical and neurotic style of the fake scientists (astronomers, astrophysicists, geophysicists, mathematicians, geologists, oceanographers, geographers and the like) who are employed by the power elite to promote the RoWoCo, but in the calm and measured terms of rational social science.

Let it be clearly understood at the outset that conspiracies are commonplace in the modern world. We live not in the Risk Society or the Postmodern Society, the Deconstructivist or Constructivist era, in a Mediated Society or a Global Village, but in the Conspiracy World. In fact, the greatest meta-conspiracy of them all is the "scientistic" and "empiricist" illusion that conspiracies are ridiculous nonsense, beyond the reach of reason and evidence. A few examples will drive home the point.

1. One has only to read the learned works of that great philosopher and theologian, Dan Brown, to realize how powerful conspiracies are in religious matters.

2. Similarly, the Pastafarians of the Church of the Flying Spaghetti Monster (http://www.venganza.org) have ruthlessly exposed, with incontrovertible evidence and faultless logic, the absurd "theories" about the origins of the universe by so-called scientists from Galileo and Newton to Einstein and Hawking.

3. Our governments have kept from us knowledge of the dreadful dangers of dihydrogen monoxide (DHMO —see http://www.dhmo.org/). DHMO is a powerful and exceedingly dangerous substance. Statistics show that a very high percentage of serial murderers, rapists, and criminals habitually ingest DHMO. We also know for a fact that the increasing quantities of DHMO in the seas causes ice bergs to melt (global warming has nothing to do with it), and that in a solid form DHMO causes unnaturally cold weather, cars to crash, and little old ladies to fall in the streets. DHMO is closely related to the highly addictive

drug known as "cake" about which a question was asked in the Parliament of the LJK, 23 July 1996 (http://www.parliament.the-stationery-office.co.uk/pa/cin199596/cmhansrd/vo960723/text/60723w10.htm) but no satisfactory answer was given.

4. The widely held belief that Wikipedia is a reliable source of information is patently false. In actual fact, Uncyclopedia (http://uncyclopedia.org) is the home of Truth. The word "Wikipedia" is a combination of the words "wicked" and "pedophilia" producing a sound very similar to the Mandarin for "Waiter, there is a fly in my soup." This is enough to give the game away: Wikipedia is a conspiracy of the Chinese government to gradually and slowly insinuate so many lies and untruths into Western civilisation that it will eventually collapse, bringing down capitalism with it. The very fact that the RoWoCo is promoted by Wikipedia (http://en.wikipedia.org/wiki/Flat-Earth-Society) proves the point. Fortunately both Elvis Presley and John Lennon agreed to fake their deaths so that they could work tirelessly together in a remote corner of Greenland to set up Uncyclopedia in order to save civilisation as we know it today.

To return to RoWoCo and Flea Theory: the less cynical and gullible among you may ask "But what evidence do you have for this interesting and wholly plausible idea that the world is flat?" I will not go into the technical details presented so clearly and compellingly by others (see http://www.alaska.net/clund/cdjublonskopf/Flatearthsociety.htm) but will simply observe that it is patently ridiculous to believe that the earth is a large ball of rock flying through space at thousands of miles an hour. Consider this factoid: last year, some 100,000 to 250,000 people went missing in Britain alone. Across the globe millions are reported missing every year. In some cases ordinary and respectable people, who have routinely left for work on the 7:23 train every day for the past 18 years, suddenly go missing. Significantly, the official bodies reporting these figures have no explanation for them. They remain curiously silent on the matter. For Flea Theory it is simple: these poor people have, of course, fallen over the edge of the world while taking a short cut to the library or trying to find a new sandwich bar for lunch.

Anyone who stands on the sea shore and looks into the far distance can see that the world is flat. Ships "disappearing over the horizon" have simply sailed so far away that they can no longer be seen, or, more likely, have sailed over the edge of the world. It is not pure chance that boats sailing close to the coastline can be seen for miles. The pseudo-scientific idea that space craft can photograph the curvature of the world's surface conveniently ignores the irrefutable fact that any camera capable of photographing thousands of miles of horizon must take the photo through a lens that makes straight lines appear curved.

Having demonstrated the ultimate scientific truth of Flea Theory it remains to explain who is behind the RoWoCo and why they perpetuate the lie. The answer is the military-industrial complex. The business element consists of an enormously wealthy and powerful coalition of the tourist trade, travel agents, plane makers, car manufacturers, and oil companies who know full well that no one in their right mind would travel more than half a mile down the road if they thought there was a chance of falling over the edge of the world. But for RoWoCo, huge sections of Western capitalism would implode overnight, leaving the richest and most powerful people in the world shorn of their wealth, power, and prestige.

The second element behind RoWoCo consists of the military and the imperialist politicians who work hand-in-glove with them. They maintain huge armies ready to fight wars in the far corners of the world. But just as Christopher Columbus had to deal with sailors made mutinous by the fear of sailing over the edge of the world, so military campaigns in foreign countries would be impossible if ordinary, fighting soldiers knew the awful dangers of traveling to the Falkland Isles, Iraq, and Afghanistan. The real origins of the tight alliance between the various fractions the military-industrial complex—oil, travel, tourism, manufacturing, the military, and imperialist politicians— is, therefore, the need to maintain the RoWoCo.

Having revealed the Truth about RoWoCo, I will turn in the next issue to the 2+2=4 conspiracy.

Monopoly Is a Capitalist Plot:
A Hegemonic View of Games as Instruments of Economic Indoctrination
A Wuffle

Students of political economy have failed to examine an important element of the socialization process—the games children play. While it may or may not have been true that "Wars were won or lost on the playing fields of Eton," it is clear that the games children play can provide insight into the motivational underpinnings of a society and its economy. We shall focus on one quintessentially American game which has become a part of the American folk heritage—the game of *Monopoly*.[1] Since its invention in 1934 by an unemployed salesman/fix-it man, Americans have bought almost 80 million *Monopoly* sets, and it is a rare American who's never played *Monopoly*.

What does *Monopoly* teach children?

1. In *Monopoly* no one does any work. All profits come as returns to capital or from frivolous amusements like beauty contests. Thus, the capitalist is glorified at the expense of the working man. Indeed, there are no working men (or women) to be found in *Monopoly*. (Buildings, for example, are erected by invisible minions of the bank.) Thus, *Monopoly* hides from view the exploitative face of capitalism.

2. Toddlers are encouraged to think that they can earn money without ever working for it and without the need to expropriate surplus value from the sweating backs of the toiling masses. *Monopoly* encourages the belief that a pitiful annual state dole of only $200 is adequate to relieve social misery and turn anyone into a successful capitalist. *Monopoly* reinforces the myth that America is a land of equal opportunity.

3. *Monopoly* glorifies big business. Innocent youngsters are led to believe that monopolies are the only efficient forms of business enterprise.

4. *Monopoly* glorifies bankers. The Bank in *Monopoly* plays a beneficent role, doling out $200 remittances, declaring bank dividends, bank errors in your favor, and so on. The banker in *Monopoly* is the soul of honesty and integrity, a disinterested

partner to all transactions. *Monopoly* bankers, unlike real bankers, never foreclose on a mortgage. Furthermore, *Monopoly* encourages an identification of the Bank with government. It is the Bank which regulates all transactions, initially owns all property, and pays the $200 dole to those fortunate enough to cross GO.

There is never any bank failure in *Monopoly*—if it runs out of money, the Bank simply prints more. In the context of the bank failures of the 1930s, this feature of the game can be seen as an insidious plot to restore credibility to those discredited bulwarks of the capitalist system. Moreover, *Monopoly* leaves children with the lasting impression that money is what the banks print and that it has no necessary relationship to the real productivity of the laboring masses. In *Monopoly* there is never a problem with inflation or unemployment. The *Monopoly* economy grows steadily at an average rate of $34/player/roll (Ash and Bishop, 1972).

5. *Monopoly* reinforces the capitalist virtues of rapacity, selfishness, and greed. As the noted social critic, Shelly Berman, puts it: "the real attraction of playing *Monopoly* is the thrill you get when you know you've wiped out a friend" (Brady, 1973: 34).

6. Last, but not least, *Monopoly* fosters racism. The *Monopoly* board is chromatically segregated—a thinly disguised reference to racial and ethnic ghettos. (By omitting the colors black, brown, and white, the *Monopoly* board avoids the appearance of racism, while perpetuating the reality.) *Monopoly* encourages its immature players to think that greens stick together and so do blues, and so on. Sticking to your own kind is the only way to be safe. The player who trespasses on territory not his own color is subject to extortion or even extinction. One last point: several generations of *Monopoly* players have grown up thinking that busing was wrong. There are no buses in *Monopoly*—only trains. We do not believe it was coincidence that Atlantic City's Short Line Bus Company was renamed the Short Line Railroad.

Not content with brainwashing American youngsters, the purveyors of *Monopoly* market it in 25 countries. To lull the suspicions of the masses, American place-names are replaced with native ones (e.g., in the British version, Marvin Gardens becomes Picadilly, while in the German edition it becomes elevated to Goethestrasse), but the capitalist message remains the same. The game is, of course, banned in the Soviet Fatherland (Brady 1974: 29).

Notes

1. *Monopoly*® is a registered trademark, copyright by Parker Brothers Game Company, Salem, Massachusetts.

References

Ash, R.B., and R.L. Bishop. 1972. "*Monopoly* as a Markov Process." *Mathematics Magazine* 4: 26–29.

Brady, M. 1973. *The Monopoly Book*. New York: David McKay.

www.ingramcontent.com/pod-product-compliance
Lightning Source LLC
Chambersburg PA
CBHW080731300426
44114CB00019B/2554